The Belt and Road Initiative and the Future of Regional Order in the Indo-Pacific

The Belt and Road Initiative and the Future of Regional Order in the Indo-Pacific

Edited by
Michael Clarke
Matthew Sussex
Nick Bisley

LEXINGTON BOOKS
Lanham • Boulder • New York • London

Published by Lexington Books
An imprint of The Rowman & Littlefield Publishing Group, Inc.
4501 Forbes Boulevard, Suite 200, Lanham, Maryland 20706
www.rowman.com

6 Tinworth Street, London SE11 5AL, United Kingdom

British Library Cataloguing in Publication Information Available

Library of Congress Control Number: 2019955254
ISBN 978-1-4985-8275-9 (cloth)
ISBN 978-1-4985-8277-3 (pbk.)
ISBN 978-1-4985-8276-6 (electronic)

Contents

Acknowledgments

This volume is the result of a small research workshop hosted by the National Security College, Crawford School of Public Policy, ANU, on March 5–6, 2018. The editors in particular would like to acknowledge and thank the Australian Political Studies Association for the award of a research workshop grant of $10,000; and the director of the National Security College, Professor Rory Medcalf, for his support of this project.

Their support provided us with the opportunity to bring together a range of experts on various aspects of China's Belt and Road Initiative (BRI) and the international relations of the Indo-Pacific from around Australia for a day and a half of presentations and discussions. This process was also augmented on the final afternoon of the workshop by a roundtable, hosted by the Department of Foreign Affairs and Trade, with senior policy makers from the Australian government on BRI.

The research workshop and discussion with policy makers provided the contributors with an excellent opportunity to debate, sharpen, and refine their arguments and have contributed to what we believe to be an insightful and policy-relevant volume on one of Chinese president Xi Jinping's signature policy initiatives.

Michael Clarke, Matthew Sussex, and Nick Bisley
June 7, 2019

Chapter 1

Infrastructure, Order, and Contested Asia

How BRI Will Influence Asia's Emerging International Order

Nick Bisley

INTRODUCTION

The remarkable prosperity enjoyed by Asia's many peoples over the past four decades was a direct product of the stable and peaceful regional order established after the Sino-American rapprochement. Yet as has become increasingly clear over recent years, that order is being eroded.[1] Where in the past, the major powers had worked out how to get along with one another, nationalism was a peripheral force and expenditure of defense and security matters was less important than the demands of domestic economic development. Economic power is moving back to Asia, driven primarily by China's remarkable economic reform program, and consequently its ambition and military capacities are growing. Even the most optimistic scholar recognizes that some kinds of changes are required to reflect the tremendous shifts in power, influence, and patterns of geopolitics and geoeconomics that have been brought about over recent decades. No one with any credibility could argue that there should be no adjustments to the regional dispensation when the world's largest country demographically speaking becomes the biggest in economic terms. What is much less clear is how much change will occur and what price has to be paid to achieve a new and stable setting, assuming of course that a new order can be forged that is stable and peaceful.

Where in the past Asia was notable for the acceptance of an order centered around US geopolitical primacy and economic centrality in which most states had an overwhelming policy focus on domestic development the region is becoming increasingly contested.[2] That is meant both in the sense that the contests between states about diverging interests are becoming a more visible part of the region's international affairs while at a higher level there are a growing number of contests about the form and function of the region's international order.

While by no means alone, China is the most significant force in catalyzing the dynamics of an increasingly contested Asia. It is plainly dissatisfied with aspects of the status quo and is beginning to take steps to establish an international environment more conducive to its interests. It is challenging that the region's cartography through its provocative actions in the South China Sea while its creation of the Asian Infrastructure Investment Bank, its leadership of the Shanghai Cooperation Organization, and rejuvenation of Conference on Interaction and Confidence Building in Asia forum reveals an intent to institutionalize its nascent order building project.[3] Since first being announced as a signature initiative of China's paramount leader Xi Jinping the Belt and Road Initiative (BRI) has become the country's most important international policy project. It has been written into the constitution of the Chinese Communist Party at the nineteenth Party Congress in November 2017,[4] cementing its place at the center not only of the country's international policy but at the heart of almost all aspects of Chinese government activity.

BRI is the biggest story in infrastructure and physical connectivity on the planet at present and could end up being among the largest in human history.[5] Some feel that it presents a game-changing endeavor that will fundamentally advantage China in its contest with a declining United States.[6] Others argue that it is a large-scale command economy blunder that will misallocate resources, drive down growth in the country's periphery, and damage the PRC's reputation.[7] Beyond the questions of whether or not BRI's ambitions, such as they are, may be realized there appears to be little reflection on the role that this huge policy program may have on Asia's international order. It is clear that the international environment is in flux and given the scale, character, and ambition of BRI, regardless of its outcome this huge initiative will have a not inconsiderable set of consequences for how Asia's states relate to one another and the broader constellation of rules, norms, and practices that foster orderly relations among regional states.[8] This chapter's purpose is to assess how BRI may influence the emerging international order in Asia and analyze its likely impact on the region's future international environment.

The chapter will be in four parts. The first will provide a brief sketch of the BRI and its core components. It will also define the extant regional order and identify where and to what extent it is experiencing change. The second will identify the main aims Beijing has for its expansive Eurasian gambit, consider how BRI may unfold over time, and elaborate the central risks which must be managed as China's ambitious program is rolled out. Based on this, the chapter will identify the elements of the BRI that are likely to have the most significant impact on the evolving region.

The chapter will conclude that BRI is likely to further accelerate the process of contestation that is already in train in the region. It is also likely to provide a significant set of advantages to China; however, while these will strengthen the PRC's relative position in the region they are not likely to be decisive in the sense that they will not be of a scale or impact that will recreate a Chinese version of American primacy or a neo-tributary system of regional hegemony. There is a strong chance that BRI may "sinify" Asia's order through the exportation of standards and regulations in emerging economies and tie those country's interests more closely to those of China. All of this will mean that the region is likely to shift from its current setting to one which will be China-centered but not be Sino-centric. By this is meant that the region will be organized around a powerful China but one which will neither enjoy primacy nor hegemony and as a consequence great power contests for influence, power, and rules will be the dominant mode of international relations.

BRI AND ASIA'S ORDER: CONCEPTS AND DEFINITIONS

Belt and Road

As the other chapters in this volume have discussed, what is now referred to as the BRI began life in two set-piece speeches given by Xi Jinping early in his tenure as China's paramount leader.[9] As with other aspects of Xi's policy agenda the program began as a set of nebulous pronouncements which sketched out a broad agenda and ambition that government and party officials then spent some fleshing out into more concrete programs.[10] Between 2013 and 2017 BRI moved from being an important initiative signaling China's international ambition and a low-key version of leadership to becoming the centerpiece of the PRC's international engagement. Crucially, it is now a policy that is almost synonymous with party secretary Xi Jinping. In the first instance, China launched the program as a means to display its national confidence and its capacity to address major international challenges—Asia needs vast infrastructure investment to realize its potential and few are in a position to act on this. The move is thus as much about signaling its intent as it is about trying to mold the international environment in ways which hitherto had been the preserve of others, principally Western powers. As has been regularly reported, Asia's demographic scale means that the size of investment necessary to facilitate the population's development is a truly staggering levels of infrastructure investment.[11] In supplying the capital, know-how, and capacity to deliver that infrastructure China could lead and influence its region in ways that were, at least on the face of things, neither especially threatening nor especially disruptive. The idea also conformed to the self-identify of Chinese "win-win" diplomacy in which the PRC behaves only in ways that are mutually advantageous.[12] A large, if somewhat vague, program to better link China and the countries in its periphery, one that harked back to the country's civilizational legacy, and which would not frighten too many fitted Xi's instincts in 2013 perfectly.

At the outset a range of existing infrastructure projects were repackaged and presented as early achievements of the new initiative. The dry port of Khorgos and a number of major highway building projects in Kazakhstan were the most obvious examples of this. Over time, however, BRI began to become more tangible as well as more ambitious and expansive. Beyond repackaging old infrastructure projects, schemes were developed to flesh out the ambitious but vague aims of the early speeches. These varied from maps outlining the modes of connectivity to the development and funding of specific projects, perhaps the most notable significance of these is the China Pakistan Economic Corridor.[13] The project, thought to be worth nearly 50 billion USD, represented the first large-scale program that embodied the multidimensional initiative and which illustrated both the scale and challenges of the BRI program. China was going to finance the construction of road, energy, and railways from the Indian Ocean to the border with China, not only on a vast scale but in some of the most inhospitable terrains on the planet. Linking Kashgar in Xinjiang with the Indian Ocean port city of Gwadar, as well as the major city of Karachi, it is a project that most visibly reflects the multiple facets of the BRI.

By 2017 BRI had progressed significantly. Indeed not only had BRI assembled a vast array of projects and finance capital, it had taken on an explicit political and diplomatic dimension. In that year the first Belt and Road Forum for International Cooperation was held in Beijing. This brought the heads of government and state of twenty-nine countries, as well as ministerial-level representation from more than thirty more, while the IMF, World Bank, UN, EBRD, and Interpol among other intergovernmental organizations were represented at the highest level. BRI had gone global. However, originally BRI was seen as about physically linking China with markets in Europe, the Middle East, and perhaps East Africa. By 2017, countries as far flung as Chile and Trinidad were now involved and crucial BRI now had a significant political dimension as a means of convening leaders from across the globe to help advance Beijing's agenda.

In much of the initial scholarly debate and public discussion of BRI there was a tendency for many to write the whole thing off as a kind of high-end policy thought bubble that was more a gambit to present an ambitious face to audiences domestic and foreign alike than it was about setting out a substantive policy agenda.[14] Others took Beijing's statements seriously, that is, they believed the country was serious about building major infrastructure projects to better connect China to markets in the Indian Ocean littoral, the Middle East, and Europe they just doubted the capacity of the country to deliver in ways that would be either effective or mutually beneficial.[15] That BRI seems to be an ever-growing feast, one that is open to all comers —with perhaps the exception of the United States and Japan according to at least some official Chinese maps—further muddies many attempts to grapple with the initiative and its prospects. The initiative is a singular noun comprised of two large components, a maritime and a continental package of connectivity. Somewhat confusingly the "road" of the title refers to the maritime element and the "belt" the links on land. It involves vast multiplicity of elements across a huge geographic expanse that many find it difficult to work out just what it entails. Moreover, even though the initiative has been developed considerably it remains very much a work in progress. Consequently working out just what "it" is can be somewhat challenging.

As this chapter is intended to assess the ways in which BRI may shape and influence Asia's regional order we need to have a reasonably clear sense as to what BRI entails. To be clear we do not need to pin down exactly what the whole project will finally look like or exactly what will be in or out, rather we need to focus on the core objectives BRI serves and from there determine the extent and likelihood of those objectives being met. While there is temptation to see BRI as overloaded with party-state ambition and goal setting among the many functions the initiative serves one can identify four principal ends which the initiative seeks to achieve. The first relates to physical connectivity; the second is around developmental issues; the third broadly economic ends; and the fourth relates to strategy.

The physical connectivity of BRI is probably its best-known feature. China wants to provide multiple means through which commodities, energy, and goods can flow in and out of China. The aim is to provide a diverse means through which China can access global markets, both inflows and outflows. That means building a wide array of physical infrastructure that will literally carry iron ore, natural gas, oil, consumer goods, and so on in and out of the country. The aim of building this physical network is to provide enhanced opportunities to lower costs, mitigate risks, and drive growth in a country entering into a slower phase of economic development. While infrastructure investment does drive growth directly through employment and related economic activity, its real return is in the market activity that is created or whose costs are greatly reduced and it is this latter dimension that is the main aim of this first goal.

A related second aim of BRI is to provide developmental opportunities to the less well-off countries on China's periphery. As with the World Bank and the IMF the developmental ambitions Beijing has for BRI are not purely altruistic. Rather, China wants to see countries like Pakistan, Myanmar, the Central Asian republics, and others develop economically for a number of other reasons. Most obviously, more economically affluent neighbors increase the number of consumers to whom you can potentially sell Chinese goods. This is a particularly strong motive with Pakistan given its large and young population. China has long been concerned about political instability in its western periphery with a particular concern about militant Islam. Economic development prompted by infrastructure investment, it is hoped, will quell restive populations, promote political stability, and thus make China more secure. Here the aim is almost identical to that of many Western countries' counterterrorism policies which are predicated on the idea that by improving the social conditions in target countries they will snuff out the root cause of the political grievances that give rise to militancy. Equally, the economic development that is prompted by China-centered investment and infrastructure will also help to align the economic interests of the countries part of BRI with those of China.

The economic motivations behind BRI are perhaps their best-known feature. China's economic growth has been remarkable but as the economy enters a more mature phase and seeks to move away from fixed capital investment and low skilled labor as key drivers of growth, the country has a significant amount of spare capacity. The financial system is awash with capital that struggles to find productive places to invest and surplus industrial capacity as well.[16] BRI is in many respects a large-scale and internationalized version of the Chinese Communist Party's approach to development: where the party machinery makes the primary determinations about how capital should be distributed to achieve long-term strategic goals. The party-state needs to find something to do with all that industrial capacity and significant volumes capital and in BRI it has found a means to allocate that in ways which the market alone may not have done.

The other economic motive of BRI is also fairly conventional, that is, to promote growth in China's lesser developed provinces. While Chinese GDP is very high in the aggregate, wealth is extremely unevenly distributed with the highest levels of prosperity experienced in the coastal provinces and in particular in the cities of the eastern seaboard such as Beijing, Shanghai, Tianjin, Xiamen, and Guangzhou. The West and Southern provinces, particularly those on China's borders, are closer to some of the poor societies in Africa's standards of economic development than they are the dynamism of the countries' mega-cities. For example, Gansu has a per capita GDP of around

4,500 USD which puts it akin to Namibia or Iraq, a long way from the levels of the eastern seaboard.[17] The party-state hopes that the massive investment in connectivity will, through Keynesian-style stimulation of demand, drive rapid economic development in these peripheral parts of the country. The party-state also hopes that long-term growth will be sustained through the opportunities afforded by becoming an economic gateway to the world's largest consumer market. In short, BRI is a classic example of targeted programs to drive growth so that the CCP can help Chinese citizens who have hitherto been left behind have the opportunity to catch up to those on the coast.

China's economic growth is heavily focused on its eastern seaboard in part because the coast is the primary means through which the country accesses global markets. The vast quantities of iron ore, coal, crude oil, and other commodities that fuel growth and urbanization arrive in the giant ports of Guangzhou, Xiamen, and Tianjin among others. And in turn the finished goods that the world consumes, the clothing, white goods, electronics, and so on are all shipped to the world from the coast. Reducing the costs of moving goods to market, as well as concentrations of labor, was found on the coast. But this littoral dependence means that China is dependent on those maritime routes remaining open. The maritime approaches are thus extremely vulnerable to predation. Even though the country has grown rapidly, is investing heavily in next-generation war-fighting equipment including aircraft carriers and attack submarines it will be many decades before China might be in a position to reduce its vulnerability at sea. Indeed some think that the gap is so large between the PRC and the US 7th fleet that barring some unimaginable collapse on the part of the United States it is almost impossible for China to be in a position to secure its maritime interests entirely.[18] In particular the huge advantage the United States has in submarine capabilities mean that even if China has the ability to push the US navy back from its coasts and keep its aircraft carriers at arm's length, American submarines can still effectively hem the PLA Navy within its littoral waters due to the key maritime chokepoints in Western Pacific. BRI thus has a vital strategic objective: to reduce the country's maritime vulnerability, particularly for key vital commodity inputs. If enough oil and gas from the Persian Gulf can get to China overland or at least not via the South China Sea then the country can reduce the ability of the United States to coerce it. Over the foreseeable future, the United States will retain the capacity, in extreme circumstances, to choke the Chinese state and economy. The threat of turning off the arteries of economic growth that the US navy represents is an acute source of neuralgia for Chinese strategists. If successful, BRI would help give China a kind of strategic depth which it currently lacks due to its heavy dependence on the maritime approaches on its east.

Regional Order

As the aim of this chapter is to examine the extent to which BRI might change Asia's regional order it is necessary to set out briefly of what the order is constituted. Since the late 1970s, Asia's international environment has been notable for its peace and stability. From being one of the world's most conflict-prone theaters in the Cold War it began from this point onward to experience a period of remarkable peace and economic dynamism. The international arrangements set in place during this time, as well as a set of choices Asia's states made relating to their domestic and international policy, established a remarkably successful order. Not entirely surprising given the scale and nature of the changes brought about over the past forty years, that order is in need of recrafting to reflect the new circumstances.

Although it has become commonplace for liberally inclined states to refer to the region as enjoying a rules-based order, with some even going so far as to include a liberal modifier in that formulation, the most important feature of Asia's old order related to concentrations of conventional military power. Primacy refers to the situation in which a state has a preponderance of military power, which is not challenged by or subject to strategic competition due to the scale of advantage enjoyed by the dominant state.[19] Even though the first ten decades of the forty-year period of stability underwritten by the order included the existence of the USSR during that time it was, at best, a marginal player in Asia. Across East Asia, the United States enjoyed complete command of air and sea domains and in most cases was dominant in land force projection as well. It was able to do this even while not having a significant geographic footprint in the region through its network of alliances and quasi-alliance relationships. While few today tend to reflect on it publically today, the old order was at its heart about a highly uneven distribution of power centered around American dominance of the region.

But just as it is incorrect to think of the old order as purely rules based, its success was also a function of state attitudes both toward primacy, the order, and indeed one another. American military power was accepted by virtually all countries in the region. They may not necessarily have all enjoyed that situation but it was accepted. States also accepted the underlying parameters of the post-1970s geopolitical settlement. The region's states did not arm themselves to contest territorial claims nor was revanchism in the policy kit bag. Equally, they did not need to develop military capacity to protect their interests internationally. Under different circumstances many countries would have had to develop significant militaries to protect their interest keeping sea lanes open and protecting themselves from neighbors they did not trust. This provided a strong incentive for states to focus their efforts on domestic state and nation building. Rather than divert resources into costly military programs and trying to mobilize populations to support military programs or even conflict, Asia's states were able to focus their energy and efforts on development. In short, the geopolitical terms of the regional setting were both beneficial for and accepted by Asia's states.

Third, the striking alignment of the economic and security interests of East Asia's key countries was the order's next key element. If the American position in Asia was geopolitically one of primacy, its economic circumstances were similarly significant. The United States was by far the most important economy for Asia's states. It was the most important source of inbound FDI and was by a significant margin its most important export market. Given how important export-focused industrialization was for so many in the region and the capital hungry nature of so many economies, with the notable exception of Japan, it is not at all surprising that US power was accepted by all. This was not a situation either widely recognized by regional elites or thoroughly welcomed by all. Nonetheless, once the United States and China had reconciled their long-term differences in the 1970s, there was region-wide acceptance of the US role and a willingness to put up with primacy in return for the broader benefits it provided. The geopolitical and geoeconomics setting provided an environment most conducive to the interests and values the United States sought to project internationally. Even in spite of this both the form and function of Asia's old order were accepted by all.

Finally, orders are sustained not just by power and interests but also by norms and institutions. This was the component of the old order that was perhaps least well developed in East Asia. The underlying normative and institutional framework was essentially provided by the core practices of international society as organized by the UN system. But there was little regionally distinctive entrepreneurship of that kind most obviously developed in Europe that meaningfully thickened the normative underpinnings of the order. And while the region did have some distinctive institutional practices and normative frameworks were developed, they were either narrowly focused—ASEAN's membership only expanded from six to all ten Southeast Asian states until the late 1990s—and had a very thin grip on state policy choice. While supporters of the Southeast club's purported normative entrepreneurship claim that the group has been able to shape the practices and interests of nonmembers[20] there is scant evidence to support this in any significant sense during the roughly four-decade period. In the recent rush to develop multilateral mechanisms we have seen ASEAN's normative impact become more visible but ultimately institutional mechanisms continue to have a relatively marginal impact on the overarching pattern of Asia's order.

Notwithstanding much public diplomacy to this effect, Asia's old order was not a purely rules-based order, indeed its most significant feature was the role power played in its organization. It was key not just because brute power kept ambitions in check but because it was accepted and it was aligned with the broadly capitalist global economy. One might go so far as to say it was a power-based order with liberal characteristics. The region's stable power setting allowed for a broadly liberal approach to international economic relations to flourish. But it was an order that had liberal rules sitting atop a robust power-based foundation.

It is worth emphasizing one final aspect of Asia's regional order, that is, its geographic frame of reference. As recent scholarship of regions has shown, regions in world politics reflect not just geographically contiguous zones.[21] Rather they are constituted by dense webs of interaction, economic, political, and military, which bind the fates of states and people together. When combined with geography this creates the perception among elite, both private and public, that the zone is a salient geopolitical and geoeconomic place that warrants a distinctive label. Put more simply, regions must exist in the imagination not just on the ground. The regional order I have described was an order that included the states and peoples of North and Southeast Asia. South and Central Asia were not only physically more separate from the Pacific littoral side of the Asian landmass the configuration of their interests and their interactions were sufficiently separate as to inhabit what were perceived to be effectively different regions. Thus a more accurate rendering of the old dispensation was of an East Asian order. One of the most important developments of recent years, and of which the BRI is an important part, is the expanding geopolitical and geoeconomic conception of Asia's region. The once-discrete theaters of Northeast, Southeast, South, and Central Asia are increasingly being bound into a coherent Asian strategic system.[22] The question this poses for the remainder of this chapter is whether or not the forces creating this larger Asian region are compatible with the arrangements that made East Asia so stable and peaceful.

BELT AND ROAD FUTURES

The extent to which BRI challenges, undermines, or indeed can be incorporated within an order that is broadly in keeping with the past will of course depend on how BRI unfolds. In this section of the chapter I will consider the different ways in which BRI's ambitions may develop so as to assess its impact on regional order. It will examine a spectrum of possibilities from a more maximally successful implementation of BRI's range of ambitions through to a more limited, uneven, and unsuccessful rollout of the PRC's vast international policy program.

A maximalist BRI would entail China achieving significant advances in all four of the core areas noted earlier. That is connectivity between China and global markets would be greatly increased. Rail lines and highways, pipelines and terminals, ports and bridges would be created so as to provide the country with a dense network of options to move commodities, goods, and energy in and out of the country. It would entail its southern and western peripheries being significantly better off than they currently are, perhaps not quite at the level of the big metropolises of Beijing and Shanghai but well over the five-figure GDP per capita mark that would put the entire country well within the middle-income bracket by global standards. The infrastructure forged by BRI would accelerate economic development in its periphery providing much-needed political stability in the Central Asian republics, Pakistan, and elsewhere. And of course these new means through which the country can access global markets would reduce the ability of the United States and its allies to impose costs on China or to coerce it more broadly. A maximalist realization of BRI would significantly enhance the party-state's place in the world and go a long way to support its ambitions to maneuver the country through the challenges of its current phase of economic development.

But the ability to achieve this outcome requires China avoiding some significant challenges. For many outside observers one of the most obvious of these is to include misallocation of capital, that is, when political directives invest capital in ways that are not optimally efficient or indeed downright wasteful. Infrastructure is often regarded as an example of market failure and even in countries with a neoliberal predisposition, strong incentives are required to induce private players to invest in such programs. There is a considerable risk that BRI will lead to significant misallocation of capital, particularly given the extreme politicization of the program and its association with Xi Jinping. It will simply be impossible for holders of capital in China to stay out of BRI. What is less clear is the extent to which market players will be able to shape and influence the kinds of commands they receive. While planners in China are acutely aware of the limitations of top-down initiatives given the Soviet example, the scale of BRI and its importance in the country's policy planning means that rational analysis of risk and opportunity may not be sufficiently optimal. As a result, the surplus capital which BRI is intended to put to productive use risks being invested in ways that either do not produce a decent return or even support what are effectively extravagant "white elephant" programs.

But one must recognize that viewed from a conventional Western investment perspective this seems especially problematic; this is essentially how the PRC has driven its internal economic development during the "reform and opening up" period launched by Deng Xiaoping in the 1970s. Capital has never simply been left to the market to allocate efficiently, directing it by tehnocratic logic with strong political overtones has been the model for Chinese domestic success. BRI aims to internationalize this. What we don't know is whether this will work beyond the party-state's borders.

A second risk that threatens Chinese ambition relates to how the projects will be financed and in particular the consequences of what is called predatory lending practices. The bulk of the infrastructure projects associated with BRI, at least those on the Asian continent, will occur within developing economies. These states will not be well placed to negotiate competitive terms and the temptation for Chinese lenders to impose onerous terms to cover their risk will be significant. The Sri Lankan port of Hambantota is seen by many as indicative of what BRI might entail.[23] Here Chinese firms provided capital to develop a port in Sri Lanka that was not commercially viable. The country already had a functioning commercial port that was not straining against capacity constraints and few could see why shipping would be attracted to a new venture that was further from existing service infrastructure. Somewhat predictably, as the Sri Lankan government failed to meet the loan conditions because they could not generate port usage the asset was subsequently transferred to Chinese firms on a ninety-nine-year lease.

The implications of this are several. First, BRI-style major infrastructure projects risk not just being a drain on capital utility and poor investment choices, they will tie down the country with debt that is difficult or impossible to service, thus leeching money from the economy and prompting declining growth. The specter of either deliberately staged debt traps sprung by China or simply negligence on behalf of either lenders or borrowers will yield the same result is very real. Some even imagine a repeat of the debt crises and decades of lost growth in Latin America in the 1980s.[24] Rather than priming the pump of economic growth in the developing economies on China's peripheries, BRI risks driving growth down and creating cycles of dependence and underdevelopment. The potential for an Asian economic version of the lost decade of growth in the 1980s among many developing economies is real.

A third problem that will have to be managed follows from the growing indebtedness and low growth risk: political resentment within participating countries. China hopes to align the interests and build political capital through what it styles as win-win infrastructure programs. If handled poorly it could produce the opposite effect, reducing Chinese influence and generating significant anti-China sentiment, both among the populace at large and, crucially, among elites. In the early 2000s, Chinese firms expanded their activities in Africa, particularly in extractive industries. The behavior of those companies, particularly in relation to labor practices, badly damaged China's reputation in Africa.[25] A similar experience could transpire in BRI countries. Although Chinese firms have learned from those experiences, they remain not relatively inexperienced in operating abroad in comparison with Japanese, American, and European multinationals. If firm behavior can be one-source resentment, a second problem could flow from Chinese firms cycling investment back to China, thus leaving little "multiplier benefit" in local economies. In parts of Central Asia, Chinese infrastructure investment has employed Chinese workers living in what are effectively Chinese enclaves with little interaction with local communities or economies.[26] In much the same way that Western sourced development aid was criticized in the 1980s for being spent on Western firms, Chinese infrastructure programs risk alienating the recipients by funneling money back to China and limiting the economic spinoffs to the local population. Thus while the PRC aims to improve its political clout, if not carefully managed then the behavior of Chinese companies, the isolation and ghettoization of economic practice, and the failure to localize economic benefits could prove badly counterproductive to Chinese aims.

The final major problem China may create through BRI is what might be called a "bridges to nowhere" problem. That is, China's investment in large-scale infrastructure fails to yield the anticipated benefits because the underlying economic activity fails to transpire. Those who are skeptical of the BRI question the economic utility of many of the projects that have been identified by BRI planners and potential recipients. Road networks across Central Asia and shipping ports in Sri Lanka have already shown that connective tissue does not on its own create markets or demand. They help prime that demand or accelerate it but many believe that the bridges, ports, and roads that China is helping to create will not ultimately have a major economic impact. The train that, with great fanfare, traveled from the United Kingdom to Yiwu in April 2017 is seen as emblematic of this potential problem. While Chinese consumer goods may travel to Europe on a train moving more swiftly, although more expensively, than by sea there is very little that will travel from West to East that would make sense to move by rail and not on a ship. There is a very real risk that after trillions of dollars of investment China may ultimately not be any better connected to global markets in practical terms.

While the physical scale of BRI and the timeframe over which it will develop make forecasting its future extremely difficult, there are three main futures which can be sketched out. The first is a maximally successful BRI in which the mains China has for the initiative are achieved with a high degree of success while managing the challenges and minimizing their deleterious consequences. That is, capital is not more poorly allocated than it has been within China over the past forty years, states are not caught in debt traps to a significant degree, political resentment is avoided through shrewd management of projects and public relations, and connectivity fosters high levels of economic integration with spillover benefits in political and strategic relations. A second scenario entails a much more uneven experience with BRI in which China achieves some of its aims, such as increased strategic depth via hydrocarbon network diversification and improved economic alignment with Chinese interests, but these advances come with costs. For example, resentment toward China is considerable as promised economic welfare fails to materialize. The third scenario involves a minimalist achievement of BRI aims and considerable cost, both economic and political, borne by the PRC. Here, China does improve the access to markets and reduces its current dependence on its eastern seaboard. But this does not stimulate economic growth either in its western provinces or in neighboring countries. The not-especially economically productive new infrastructure creates significant resentment due to the corruption that its construction created and the reversion of many assets back to Chinese hands due to predatory lending practices has severely undermined China's reputation and burnt significant quantities of political capital.

Given that it is relatively early on in the BRI it is virtually impossible to discern with any great confidence which of the paths is most likely. It is perhaps easiest to rule out the most optimistic scenario. So much would have to go China's way on a scale hitherto unheard of in some of the world's most poorly governed states and involving some of the most demanding physical terrain on the planet that it is difficult to envisage those larger goals being largely achieved with a maximal management of costs. While there are risks that BRI ends up as a catastrophic error that will badly damage the PRC I judge this is unlikely to occur due both to the extensive experience in these kinds of projects, the talent of Chines policy makers, the political priority placed on the initiative, and the capacity of PRC to learn from their mistakes. That is not to say that the maximalist vision is likely, rather it is prudent to anticipate that the more likely fate of BRI lies somewhere between the minimalist and uneven scenarios. What implications would such a future have for the emerging regional order?

BRI AND ASIA'S CONTESTED ORDER

For its proponents in Beijing and supporters abroad, BRI is a mutually beneficial program whose benefits come at low cost to others. It is a positive-sum proposition in which benefits accrue to all participants; even if not equally distributed, everyone will be better off. Even if you accept that proposition, and there is good reason to be skeptical about such optimistic claims about such a baroque piece of economic diplomacy, BRI is a contributing factor to an increasingly competitive geopolitical and geoeconomic environment in the world's most dynamic region. On the face of it infrastructure investment, the domain of engineers and technical specialists should not be inherently political. Yet since 2017 infrastructure has become a highly competitive domain in Asia. India and Japan launched their Asia-Africa Growth Corridor in what many perceived to be an attempt to contest China's efforts to dominate development and infrastructure and through these negate Beijing's efforts to gain a geopolitical edge via BRI.[27] More recently the revived quadrilateral security initiative between India, Japan, Australia, and the United States has begun to consider tacking on a development-infrastructure dimension.[28] While both these new plans remain in their infancy, they reflect the concerns felt by those countries that if left uncontested China could gain significant advantage through its BRI efforts. One could equally see in this a kind of proxy for great power competition, although it is perhaps a little early to reach that conclusion.

Asia's old order was notable for a number of reasons but one of the most significant of these was the acceptance of the form and function of the regional order. BRI reflects an ambitious international effort by China to reshape its international environment in ways that are more in line with its interests. Beijing is, in a geopolitically cautious and unthreatening manner, beginning to move away from acceptance and toward contestation about the nature of the region's international arrangements. BRI is, albeit in a sprawling and largely economic program, setting out to change the terms on which it engages with the international environment. And this contestation is one that will remain salient even in the most pessimistic scenario sketched in the chapter.

A second key implication of BRI for Asia's changing order is the way in which it is likely to continue to disrupt the alignment of political and economic interests in Asia. US primacy was both buttressed by and embedded within the politics of key countries in the region because of the economic interests of Asia's key powers. The significance of the US economy meant that there was a strong alignment of economic and strategic interests. As China has become an ever more significant economic partner of most Asian economies this alignment has begun to shift. The PRC is going to continue to strengthen its relative economic position in the region more generally, both in trade and investment terms, and BRI even in this middle road to somewhat successful somewhat costly future will continue to drive that trend. And while it is unlikely that all BRI participants will have their economic interests aligned entirely with Beijing's that will not need to occur to strengthen China's relative position. Even if all China achieves through BRI is a further weakening of the economic and the political foundations of the old order through widening the gap between the political and economic interests of many Asian states it will have strengthened its position. And if, in the more optimistic scenario, China succeeds in not only building connectivity but in so doing exporting its standards and practices, in much the way that the United States did in the postwar period, then it will strongly advantage the PRC.

US primacy in Asia has long been predicated on its supremacy of the maritime security domain. The floating symbols of US power, its aircraft carrier battle groups, ensured unchallenged military might. Even as China has developed various means to reduce the ability of aircraft carriers and the like to operate effectively, the country remains vulnerable to US power and particularly its submarine fleet. For decades the combination of China's focus on domestic development and the massive gap between itself and the United States dissuaded any efforts to contest US power and influence. Now China is testing US capacity to project force and, in the South China Sea, has been surprisingly successful at changing aspects of the underlying status quo. While there are perceptions of US hesitancy that began under President Obama and which have been magnified under President Bush, the reality is that unless China can overcome the constraint imposed by its maritime weakness, it will remain subject to US coercion. And here BRI is likely to strengthen China's hand. By providing ways in which both inputs and outputs can move in and out of China, Beijing loosens Washington's ability to coerce the country. For so long as the PRC is dependent on its eastern seaboard to access energy, commodities, and export markets, the United States will have a decisive advantage in strategic terms. Whether in the form of multiple pipelines or naval basing in the Indian Ocean, BRI provides a strategic depth and reach that it currently does not enjoy. Most importantly, as this side is least prone to market forces and least dependent on external actors, it is the most likely thing to be achieved even in the most pessimistic scenario.

Finally, BRI is a crucial component binding the once-discrete theaters of Northeast, Southeast, South, and Central Asia into a coherent strategic system. As the adoption of the Indo-Pacific strategic framework by Australia, India, and the United States indicates key strategic players in the region are recognizing how increasingly integrated Asia is becoming. Yet the Indo-Pacific frame focuses too heavily on the maritime and underplays the continental. For those who have adopted the label it is unsurprising as their core interests remain largely in the maritime domain. But attention should be paid to both sides and BRI is a key motive force creating that most vexed of international settings, an increasingly economically integrated region that is becoming more contested. BRI in many ways reflects that dualism: it forges ties that bind and is itself a subject of contestation.

CONCLUSION

Hawkish critics of the PRC often present it as a revisionist power set to overturn the prevailing international order in East Asia. This view overstates both China's ambitions and its current trajectory. It does want to recast aspects of the international environment in ways that are more conducive to the country achieving its interests but neither does it want to fundamentally alter the core principles of international politics—it is happy with the state-centric noninterventionist ideas in the UN Charter—nor does it want to pay a high price or take significant risks to challenge US primacy. BRI reflects one of a number of efforts by the PRC to reshape the international environment. It is ambitious, risky, costly, and unlikely to succeed in all the ways PRC leaders would prefer. Yet even in spite of a likely suboptimal realization BRI will put further strain on Asia's old order. As consent is replaced by contestation across the region BRI is likely to accelerate the forces of competition in the region, both as a specific site in which the major powers compete for influence as well as a means through which they play out their contest about the nature of the underlying structures of an emerging regional order. Regardless of its level of success, BRI is likely to continue to increase China's strategic advantage in this regional competition. However, it is unlikely to be something that gives the PRC a decisive edge. Even if it were to be maximally successful it is unlikely to be a platform for the creation of Chinese primacy. BRI is likely to strengthen the prospects of a China-centered but not Sinocentric regional order, one in which contestation among the powerful is the order's defining feature.

NOTES

1. Nick Bisley, "Australia and the Evolving International Order" in Mark Beeson and Shahar Hameri (eds) *Navigating the New International Disorder: Australia in World Affairs*, 2011–15 Oxford: Oxford University Press, 2016, pp. 39–55.

2. Peter Varghese, "A Contested Asia: What Comes after US Strategic Predominance?" 2017 Griffith Asia Lecture 6 September 2017, https://blogs.griffith.edu.au/asiainsights/a-contested-asia-what-comes-after-us-strategic-predominance/.

3. See J. D. Yuan, "Beijing's Institutional Balancing Strategies: Rationales, Implementation, and Efficacy" in *Australian Journal of International Affairs* 72.2, 2018, pp. 110–28.

4. Xinhua, "'Belt and Road' Incorporated into CPC Constitution" in *Xinhua* 24 October 2017, http://www.xinhuanet.com/english/2017-10/24/c_136702025.htm.

5. Nadege Rolland, *China's Eurasian Century? Political and Strategic Implications of the Belt and Road Initiative* Washington, DC: National Bureau of Asian Research, 2017.

6. Anja Manuel, "China Is Quietly Reshaping the World" in *The Atlantic* 17 October 2017, https://www.theatlantic.com/international/archive/2017/10/china-belt-and-road/542667/.

7. Tom Holland, "Why China's 'Belt and Road' is Doomed to Fail" in *South China Morning Post* 6 August 2016.

8. On regional orders see Derrick Frazier and Robert Stewart-Ingersoll, "Regional Powers and Security: A Framework for Understanding Order within Regional

Security Complexes" in *European Journal of International Relations* 16.4, 2010, pp. 731–53.

9. Xi Jinping, "Speech to the Indonesian Parliament" Jakarta 2 October 2013, http://www.asean-china-center.org/english/2013-10/03/c_133062675.htm, and Xi Jinping, "Promote Friendship Between Our People and Work Together to Build a Bright Future" Nazarbayev University, Astana, 7 September Astana speech 2013, http://www.fmprc.gov.cn/mfa_eng/wjdt_665385/zyjh_665391/t1078088.shtml.

10. For an articulation of this fleshing out see National Development and Reform Commission (NDRC), Ministry of Foreign Affairs, and Ministry of Commerce (PRC) "Vision and Actions on Jointly Building Silk Road Economic Belt and 21st-Century Maritime Silk Road," March 28, 2015.

11. Figures cited regularly exceed 15–20 trillion USD. See, for example, ADB, *Meeting Asia's Infrastructure Needs* Manila: ADB, 2017, https://www.adb.org/sites/default/files/publication/227496/special-report-infrastructure.pdf.

12. For an example of this self-identity see Wang Yi, "Toward a New Type of International Relations of Win-Win Cooperation" Speech by Foreign Minister Wang Yi at Luncheon of the China Development Forum, http://www.fmprc.gov.cn/mfa_eng/wjb_663304/wjbz_663308/2461_663310/t1248487.shtml.

13. Daniel S. Markey and James West, "Behind China's Gambit in Pakistan" in *Council on Foreign Relations Expert Brief* 12 May 2016, https://www.cfr.org/expert-brief/behind-chinas-gambit-pakistan.

14. For example, Guy de Jonquieres, "Grand Plans Will Test Xi's Mettle" in *Nikkei Asian Review* 9 December 2015, https://asia.nikkei.com/Economy/Grand-plans-will-test-Xi-s-mettle; Lucio Blanco Pitlo III, "China's 'One Belt, One Road' to where?" in *The Diplomat* 17 February 2015, https://thediplomat.com/2015/02/chinas-one-belt-one-road-to-where/.

15. Rumi Aoyama, "'One Belt, One Road': China's New Strategy" in *Journal of Contemporary East Asian Studies* 5.2, 2016, pp. 3–22.

16. See for example, Zhiyao Lu, "China's Excess Capacity in Steel: A Fresh Look" in *China Economic Watch* Peterson Institute for International Economics, 29 June 2017 https://piie.com/blogs/china-economic-watch/chinas-excess-capacity-steel-fresh-look.

17. Derived from World Bank Dataset, https://data.worldbank.org/indicator/NY.GNP.PCAP.CD?view=chart.

18. Paul Dibb and John Lee, "Why China Will not Become the Dominant Power in Asia" in *Security Challenges* 10.3, 2014, pp. 1–21.

19. On primacy see Robert Jervis, "International Primacy: Is the Game Worth the Candle" in *International Security* 17.4, 1993, pp. 52–67.

20. Alice D. Ba, "Who's Socializing Whom? Complex Engagement in China-ASEAN Relations" in *Pacific Review* 19.2, 2006, pp. 157–79.

21. Barry Buzan and Ole Waever, *Regions and Power: The Structure of International Security* Cambridge: Cambridge University Press, 2009.

22. Nick Bisley, *Integrated Asia: Australia's Dangerous New Strategic Geography* Centre of Gravity Series No. 31, May 2017, http://sdsc.bellschool.anu.edu.au/sites/default/files/publications/attachments/2017-05/cog_integrated_asia-may_2017_0.pdf.

23. Maria Abi-Habib, "How China Got Sri Lanka to Cough Up Its Port" in *New York Times* 25 June 2018, https://www.nytimes.com/2018/06/25/world/asia/china-sri-lanka-port.html.

24. Dipanjan Roy Chaudhry, "Xi Jinping's BRI Risks Debt Trap for 68 Nations: US Experts" in *Economic Times* 14 March 2018, https://economictimes.indiatimes.com/news/international/business/xi-jinpings-bri-raises-risk-of-debt-trap-for-68-nations-us-experts/articleshow/63293814.cms.

25. See Chris Alden, *China in Africa* London: Zed Books, 2007.

26. Connor Dileen, "China's Belt and Road Initiative in Central Asia: Insurmountable Obstacles and Unmanageable Risks?" in *ASPI Strategist* 28 June 2017 https://www.aspistrategist.org.au/chinas-belt-road-initiative-central-asia-insurmountable-obstacles-unmanageable-risks/.

27. Titli Basu, "Japan's Belt and Road Puzzle, Decoded" in *The Diplomat* 28 February 2018, https://thediplomat.com/2018/02/japans-belt-and-road-puzzle-decoded/.

28. Jason Scott, Emi Nobuhiro, and Iain Marlow, "U.S.-Led Group Mulls Asia Infrastructure Effort Amid China Push" in *Bloomberg* 19 February 2018, https://www.bloomberg.com/news/articles/2018-02-18/u-s-led-group-mulls-asia-infrastructure-plan-australia-says.

Section I

GEOPOLITICS, ALLIANCES, AND SECURITY

Chapter 2

Can China's Belt and Road Initiative Build a Peaceful Regional Order?

Acquiescence and Resistance in South Asia

Lai-Ha Chan

The Belt and Road Initiative (BRI), comprising the "Silk Road Economic Belt" and the "twenty-first-century Maritime Silk Road," was first announced in 2013 by China's President Xi Jinping in two separate speeches, made in Kazakhstan and Indonesia respectively. The overall design of this initiative was to foster regional interconnectivity, linking up a total of over sixty countries across Asia and Europe to Africa, and accounting for some 60 percent of the world's population.[1] There are multiple rationales for setting up this infrastructure project, including economic and commercial reasons that incorporate China's need to export its production overcapacity and arrest its domestic economic slowdown.[2] But more importantly it also serves as a soft-balancing response to the US "pivot to Asia," carving out a regional security space in Eurasia to mitigate the threat coming from the east of China in the Asia-Pacific region.[3] Hence international politics has had a role to play in China's decision to establish both the Asian Infrastructure Investment Bank (AIIB) and BRI.

In line with arguments about soft-balancing, this chapter contends that BRI aims to contest or constrain the United States as the incumbent hegemon softly, and to negotiate new rules and norms and provision of (regional) public goods with Eurasian states to encourage them to consent to China's leadership. In other words, the strategic objective of the BRI is regional order (re)building. Via the BRI, China is attempting to redefine shared goals and values across Eurasia and socialize them to regional actors. As a result the success of the BRI depends, to a large extent, on how its target regional audience reacts to the order-building strategy and practices. Do they acquiesce to a China-led regional order or reject it? Which states will be members of that regional order, and which will dissent? What reasons do those states have for either joining BRI or resisting Chinese efforts to co-opt them?

ORDER BUILDING

An international order, according to Hedley Bull, is a stable pattern or disposition of international activity that sustains the elementary, primary, or universal goals of the society of states (or international society). These elementary goals are (1) the preservation of the continued existence of the society of states; (2) the independence or external sovereignty of individual states; (3) international peace understood as the absence of war among states; and (4) limitation of violence, honoring of promises and agreements, and the stability of property possession.[4] Building on Bull's proposition that order is a purposive arrangement, Muttiah Alagappa has defined international order as "a formal or informal arrangement that sustains rule-governed interaction among sovereign states in their pursuit of individual and collective goals." These rule-governed interactions allow not only "a predictable and stable environment in which states can coexist and collaborate in the pursuit of their national, regional and global goals" but also that "differences and disputes can be adjusted in a peaceful manner and change can occur without resort to violence."[5]

Any rules-based interaction is underpinned by an intersubjective consensus on the basic goals of international society, as well as the means of achieving the goals. Bially Mattern refers international order to "a relationship among specific states that produces and reinforces shared understandings of expectations and behaviours with respect to each other."[6] Common to these definitions is the existence of shared understandings of expectations and behaviors. And key to the creation of the shared understandings are contention, conflict, and negotiations between actors of unequal power, including the hegemon, great powers, and other states.[7]

Through the "eye of the beholder,"[8] this chapter adopts an "outside-in" perspective focusing on external perceptions of China's order-(re)building strategy in South Asia. While China is developing a regional order-(re)building strategy through its BRI, I ask a series of questions. First, does Beijing have any obvious followers and/or competitors in its endeavors? Second, will China's infrastructure interconnectivity activities generate acquiescence or resistance among regional states? Third, are states in South Asia concerned about their security and regional stability in the aftermath of the BRI? Finally, does an intersubjective consensus exist between China and regional states? The rest of the chapter is designed to elucidate answers to these questions, before offering some tentative conclusions.

BRI AS A REGIONAL ORDER-BUILDING STRATEGY

The strategic objective of the BRI could be seen as "killing two birds with one stone." In the wake of the Obama's "pivot to Asia," China has created a Eurasian zone of economic influence to its West in order to offset the imminent threat from the United States from the East. Together with the Silk Road Fund and the AIIB, the BRI not only serves as a soft-balancing strategy toward the United States but also reconstitutes the regional order to form and strengthen a Chinese regional sphere of influence. In this context William Callahan has summarized succinctly that the grand strategy of the BRI is "to use economic leverage to build a Sino-centric 'community of shared destiny' in Asia, which in turn will make China a normative power that sets the rules of the game for global governance."[9]

After Obama's Asian pivot, which was widely understood and perceived by China as seeking to contain it, Chinese International Relations experts sought to develop new policy ideas in response. In October 2012, Wang Jisi of Peking University's School of International Studies proposed a "Marching West (西進)" strategy to counteract both the US pivot and the "New Silk Road" initiative unveiled by Hillary Clinton in November 2011.[10] Wang explained the logic behind this Westward policy by pointing out that compared with the countries in Southeast Asia, all the countries west of China (with the exception of India) did not have any significant conflicts with China. This China was well placed to collaborate with them in geoeconomic and geopolitical terms. In addition, as many powers (such as the United States, Russia, India, and Japan) had gradually shifted their economic and security foci to the Central and Eurasian region, Wang argued that China should not regard itself as only an East Asian state. Rather, China should cooperate with those to its west to generate a strategically friendly environment, which would also be conducive to managing the tripartite threats of terrorism, (religious) extremism, and separatism (the "three evil forces") in and around the northwestern region of Xinjiang.[11]

Xue Li of the Chinese Academy of Social Sciences has also contended that the primary strategic objective of the BRI is to resolve the negative effects to China of the US pivot,[12] and allowing the BRI to act as an "enforceable policy" promoting economic and security cooperation in the Eurasian region.[13] Similarly, Zheng Anguang of Nanjing University has claimed that China's strategies in Central Asia should shift from being reactive to proactive, and that the BRI should be seen as Beijing's diplomatic charm offensive to build a new regional order.[14] Under this new geostrategic framework, the AIIB and the Silk Road Fund were set up to strengthen the infrastructure facilities that are still desperately needed in the region. And, as Peter Ferdinand argued, the underlying logic in launching the BRI is a vision that through infrastructure building and connectivity, it "will facilitate foreign policy cooperation and limit the risks of conflict."[15]

In sum, the BRI is designed to serve as an institutional means for China to transform regional order to its liking. Nowhere is this more important than in South Asia, where Chinese geoeconomic goals are meeting its strategic ones with respect to the need to counterbalance India. For this reason, China's infrastructure building activities in three South Asian states (namely Pakistan, the Maldives, and Sri Lanka) are given an in-depth discussion here to illustrate the nature of the BRI's regional order-building project.

THE CHINA-PAKISTAN ECONOMIC CORRIDOR

Since 1949 Pakistan has been one of China's staunchest allies. Yet Beijing's influence over Islamabad waned significantly in the immediate aftermath of the 9/11 attacks on the United States, when the George Bush Jr. administration sought to reinvigorate the relationship so as to meet the active threat of Al Qaeda in Afghanistan and the border areas of Pakistan. But the focus of US counterterrorism policy shifted to Syria and the Middle East following the emergence of ISIS. This, coupled to the withdrawal of US troops from Afghanistan, created a vacuum in terms of US influence over Pakistan that has been filled once more by the PRC. The growing China-Pakistan Economic Corridor (CPEC), a network of rail, road, and energy infrastructure connecting Pakistan's Gwadar Port with China's Xinjiang, is thus regarded as a countervailing measure to the American pivot.

A core infrastructure project of CPEC is to build an 887-kilometer-long highway, N35, to connect the port of Gwadar in southwestern Pakistan with Kashgar in Xinjiang, China. Gwadar, a gateway to oil-exporting Gulf countries, is only 120 kilometers from the Iranian border. This port is of crucial geostrategic importance to China, and also helps to shorten the crude oil shipping time from the Middle East by as much as 85 percent.[16] It is claimed that the port of Gwadar will serve as a hub connecting Russia, Central Asia, West Asia, South Asia, East Africa, and Europe. Indeed, without the port CPEC could only serve as a highway extension connecting Pakistan with Xinjiang.[17] A detailed study of CPEC argues, in particular, that CPEC is principally a geopolitical project that serves a balancing role against India.[18] Although Chinese officials have often downplayed the strategic purpose of Gwadar and stressed that it is a civilian port only, many skeptics (especially from India) see it as a likely future Chinese naval base in the Indian Ocean.[19] From the perspective of New Delhi, one of the controversies about the $63-billion CPEC is that it passes through Gilgit-Baltistan, which is in Pakistan-occupied Kashmir (PoK). Both India and Pakistan claim sovereignty over Kashmir in the northwestern part of the subcontinent, which is now partitioned and ruled by China, India, and Pakistan. China's activities under CPEC and its close relations with Pakistan have further compounded India's anxiety and insecurity about China's intention to undermine India's position in South Asia.

After the United States singled out Pakistan as a "terrorist haven" and suspended its $1.3-billion annual security aid in January 2018, requesting Islamabad to clamp down on groups like the Haqqani network, China-Pakistan ties have further gained traction. The day after Trump's Twitter attack on Pakistan (which stated that Pakistan provided "safe havens to terrorist organisations" and accused Islamabad of "lies and deceit"),[20] Islamabad announced that Pakistan would henceforth adopt the Chinese Yuan in denominating foreign currency transactions.[21] In addition, it was reported that China has been quietly trying to set up an offshore naval military base in Jiwani, Pakistan. This would be China's second foreign offshore military base after Djibouti, established in August 2017. Jiwani, located in the restive province of Baluchistan, is about 80 kilometers to the west of Gwadar Port, which puts it even closer to the Iranian border on the Gulf of Oman. It underwent major upgrades in 2018, allowing it to handle large military aircraft, and with the intention of serving as a joint Chinese naval and air facility.[22]

BRI AND THE MALDIVES

The Maldives has maintained close relations with India for decades, even though the archipelagic state of only 427,000 people was not a priority in China's foreign relations before Washington's Asian pivot. As late as 2011, China did not have an in-residence ambassador to Malé. However, the geostrategic importance of the Maldives lies in its geographic proximity to international sea-lanes, where two-thirds of the world's oil and half of its container shipments pass. In addition, the country is only 700 kilometer from India's Lakshadweep island chain and about 1,200 kilometer from the Indian mainland.[23]

Over the past few years, China's investment in the Maldives has increased notably. In 2012 Abdulla Yameen, who took power from the country's first democratically elected president Mohamed Nasheed, was keen to forge bonds with Beijing at the expense of India-Maldives relations. During Xi Jinping's visit in 2014, the Maldives signed a contract with a Chinese state-owned firm to upgrade its international airport in Malé: the project had been originally contracted to India's GMR Infrastructure during Nasheed's tenure but was terminated in 2012 by his successor Yameen.[24] At the time, India had been strongly critical of the decision, and warned that "to terminate the contract with GMR without due consultation with the company or efforts at arbitration provided for under the agreement sends a very negative signal to foreign investors and the international community."[25]

Since 2014, China has helped the archipelago in various mega-infrastructure projects, such as building a bridge linking Malé to Hulhulé Island; and a 1,000-apartment housing project on reclaimed land on Hulhumalé, which itself is an artificial island.[26] Malé also signed twelve different agreements with China in 2017, including the country's first free trade agreement and a memorandum of understanding to participate in the BRI, during Yameen's visit to Beijing. Even more concerning to New Delhi was Yameen's decision to accept "goodwill visits" by three Chinese naval vessels in August 2017.[27]

In February 2018, the government of the Maldives declared a state of emergency after the Supreme Court overturned criminal convictions against nine of the president's opponents, and ordered the release of political prisoners as well as reinstating disqualified parliamentarians. Instead of obeying the Court's decision, President Yameen arrested two of the judges and sent troops to surround the Court. Mohamed Nasheed, the opposition leader who was in exile in Colombo, called for Indian military intervention, while Yameen sent envoys to China, Saudi Arabia, and Pakistan to seek political support for his government. As described in an opinion article in the *Global Times*, which is strongly allied to the official PRC view, Beijing sided with Yameen and stressed China's opposition to outside interference. It went on to warn that "if India one-sidedly sends troops to the Maldives, China will take action to stop New Delhi."[28]

BRI IN SRI LANKA

The most controversial aspect of BRI as it pertains to Sri Lanka is the Hambantota port in the south of the island state. This is because Hambantota could potentially serve as a vital port for China's energy security, and this alone makes it a strategic node of BRI. Originally the Sri Lankan government had offered the project to India but the latter declined.[29] The US$1.5-billion port started construction in 2008 and the first phase was completed in 2010. Up to 85 percent of the first phase of work was financed by China's Export-Import Bank.[30] At the end of 2017, Sri Lanka's external debt reached $48.3 billion, amounting to 79.6 percent of its GDP, of which US$8 billion was owed to China. It was reported that the annual interest rate of the Chinese debt was as high as 6 percent. The Sri Lankan government handed the port over in 2017 to a Chinese state-owned enterprise, China Merchants Port Holdings, on a ninety-nine-year lease, after Colombo was unable to pay back its loans.

Another major Sri Lankan infrastructure project, Mattala Rajapaksa International Airport, currently being dubbed "the world's emptiest international airport," was also included into a debt-for-equity swap with Beijing. Mattala, located only 20 kilometers from Hambantota port, was built in 2009.

An estimated US$190 million from the US$209 million total construction cost was paid for by the Export-Import Bank of China, through a concessionary loan. As airport's losses began to mount, the Colombo government announced the intention to sell it. India raised concerns that it might become a Chinese air force base and offered to take over the airport in 2017 but was unable to reach a deal with the government in Colombo.[31] Also, much to the dismay of India, Sri Lanka granted docking rights to Chinese submarines in its Colombo port in November 2014. The Sirisena government, which came to power in 2015, did not give a similar permission in 2017.[32]

STATE CAPITALISM: THE ESSENCE OF CHINESE "RULE-GOVERNED INTERACTION"

The BRI embodies a Chinese strategy to advocate its own vision of economic governance, emphasizing the positive role of large-scale project support, and undertaken by state-owned enterprises in the form of tied aid. In other words, the essence of the Chinese lending epitomized by the BRI is state capitalism. Conventional wisdom often has it that China is a strong proponent of nonconditionality.[33] Mikael Mattlin and Matti Nojonen, however, have pointed out that China's lending by state-owned policy banks in fact stipulate numerous conditions. The difference between Western countries and China may simply rest with the fact that they adopt different forms of conditionality: while the former emphasizes certain binding political conditions like good governance and democracy, the latter attaches nonpolitical "conditions" to its development assistance packages.[34] These include requirements such as purchasing Chinese products, using Chinese contracting services, or Chinese labor. Indeed, well before the advent of the BRI, about 70 percent of China's infrastructure development aid to Africa had been used to buy goods or services from Chinese, mostly state-owned, companies. The rest, some 30 percent, was theoretically passed on to local firms, many of which were joint ventures with Chinese companies.[35] This is echoed by another study which points out that almost all of the Chinese aid packages to African countries have stipulated that Chinese workers and machinery be used.[36]

Behind the façade of development aid, China does not promote open market access to its loans and grants. Instead they are embedded in a China-dominated tied aid architecture with goods and services provided by well-connected Chinese state-owned enterprises. The BRI projects in South Asia, as shown in Pakistan, the Maldives, and Sri Lanka, are especially clear examples of this. Several informants in Islamabad have admitted that there was no open bidding for the contracts for the projects financed by Chinese grants.[37] Chinese state-owned companies received the project contracts directly from their government, and produced goods and services for Pakistan in turn. It is therefore often open to speculation as to whether China's state-owned enterprises pursue commercial profits or strategic interests.

COMPETING ORDERS: REGIONAL (DIS)ORDER IN THE MAKING

With the BRI as its regional order-building strategy, China has tried to use its economic influence in the Eurasian region to soft-balance against the United States and to build new rules, exemplified by state capitalism. This section examines how the BRI has been perceived by the existing dominant power in South Asia, India, and how India has reacted to BRI collectively by seeking the support of major liberal democratic powers in the Asia-Pacific, namely Japan and Australia.

THE CHINA-INDIA SECURITY DILEMMA

As argued earlier, China's BRI started as a policy measure to enhance its own security by soft-balancing against the US Pacific threat. However, China's increasing infrastructure investment in South Asia has complicated the balance of power in the region. China's economic power has successfully wooed some of the states in the region, which have shifted their diplomatic relations closer to Beijing than to New Delhi.

To begin with, India has not participated in the BRI, and was conspicuously absent from the high-profile international forum on BRI held by China in mid-May 2017. One day before the BRI international forum in Beijing, India issued a strongly worded statement, explaining India's core concerns about the BRI. The statement reiterated India's concern over its territorial integrity and China's geopolitical influence in the region. It stated that New Delhi would not accept a project that ignored its sovereign integrity and that "[c]onnectivity projects must be pursued in a manner that respects sovereignty and territorial integrity."[38]

India has several reasons for being concerned about the BRI, which is perceived in New Delhi as a Chinese strategic design "to continue establishing the strategic agglomeration over India."[39] A commonly held perception about CPEC in India is that it is China's balancing act "against India with support for Pakistan."[40] Despite India and China having many common interests—both are members of the BRICS and the Shanghai Cooperation Organisation, and the two largest shareholders of the AIIB—they are often at loggerheads over border delineation and national sovereignty, as well as competition for regional leadership. In the 1950s China constructed a road in Aksai Chin, the eastern part of Kashmir, linking Xinjiang with Tibet. The territorial dispute was one of the causes of the Sino-Indian war of 1962, and China has since then retained the occupation of Aksai Chin.[41]

The war with China in 1962 has also had significant impact on India's foreign policy. Despite Nehru's long-cherished foreign policy doctrine of nonalignment during the Cold War era—being "nonaligned" with none of the two superpowers—the border war had subsequently driven India into dependency on the Soviet Union for its weapons supply. In addition, that war also laid the basis for China-Pakistan cooperation in the succeeding years, which was (and still is) perceived as a form of regional containment against India.[42] Because CPEC passes through Gilgit-Baltistan in PoK, India is leery of China's presence and influence in Kashmir through CPEC.[43] During an India-China strategic diplomatic dialogue in Beijing in February 2017, Foreign Secretary of India S. Jaishankar bluntly stated:

> The fact [is] that China Pakistan Economic Corridor . . . violates Indian sovereignty because it runs through Pakistan-occupied Kashmir (PoK) [. . .] the issue for us is a sovereignty issue.[44]

India feels threatened not only by Chinese investment in and use of Gwadar and Jiwani but also by border conflict in the other part of the country. In June 2017 China and India witnessed a military standoff in the Doklam area (also known as Donglang in China), a territory claimed by China and India's ally, Bhutan, and where the Bhutan-China-India borders meet. Around 270 Indian troops were sent to Doklam in an attempt to stop the Chinese from building a road there. Amid the military standoff at Doklam, the most complex weeklong trilateral Malabar naval exercise since its inception, involving the United States, Japan, and India, was held at the Bay of Bengal.[45] Although India made diplomatic efforts to downplay the timing of the exercise and maintained that it had "nothing to do" with the standoff at Doklam,[46] it was the largest naval exercise in the region in more than two decades. Chinese and Western analysts alike perceived this as a balancing response to Beijing's recent assertiveness in the Indian Ocean, and the increasing tensions between India and China.[47]

After a seventy-four-day military standoff at Doklam, both India and China eventually agreed to resolve the crisis through diplomacy, right before the BRICS summit held in China. However, border incursions continue to occur regularly over the Sino-Indian border. For example, in January 2018, months after the Doklam standoff, another territorial conflict occurred over Arunachal Pradesh, when India claimed that a Chinese road-building team with bulldozers had intruded into Indian territory. India's Chief of Army Staff General Bipin Rawat even alleged that China was using "salami tactics," embracing "small, stealth military operations against neighbouring countries which accumulate over time in a large territorial gain."[48]

Table 2.1 China's Foreign Trade with South Asian Countries

Country (Year)	*China's Exports (US$m)*	*China's Imports (US$m)*	*Trade Surplus (US$m)*
Bangladesh (2014)	11,782.27	761.11	11,021.16
Bangladesh (2015)	13,894.71	816.85	13,077.86
Bangladesh (2016)	14,302.23	869.40	13,432.83
India (2014)	54,217.42	16,358.69	37,858.73
India (2015)	58,228.03	13,368.55	44,859.48
India (2016)	58,415.34	11,764.13	46,651.21
Maldives (2014)	103.99	0.38	103.61
Maldives (2015)	172.65	0.18	172.47
Maldives (2016)	320.94	0.24	320.70
Pakistan (2014)	13,244.48	2,753.87	10,490.61
Pakistan (2015)	16,441.89	2,474.76	13,967.13
Pakistan (2016)	17,234.46	1,912.59	15,321.87
Sri Lanka (2014)	3,792.80	248.27	3,544.53
Sri Lanka (2015)	4,304.05	258.52	4,045.53
Sri Lanka (2016)	4,288.43	273.44	4,014.99

Source: *China Statistical Yearbook*, 2016, 2017, http://www.stats.gov.cn/tjsj/ndsj/2016/indexeh.htm, http://www.stats.gov.cn/tjsj/ndsj/2017/indexeh.htm (accessed April 5, 2018).

Apart from territorial integrity, another Indian concern about the BRI is that Beijing might use this initiative to undertake "debt trap diplomacy" to exert influence in its backyard and challenge New Delhi's traditional dominance over the region. Hence the BRI, for India, is little more than a "colonial enterprise."[49] While the BRI is promoting economic interdependence, a significant portion of China-funded infrastructure projects in South Asia are operational or commercial failures, generating little profit to enable South Asian states to repay the loans. India worries that this will provide Beijing "huge leverage" over the Maldives, leaving the country vulnerable to China's demands and pressure. As seen from table 2.1, there is a rapid growth of China's trade surplus with the Maldives, Pakistan, and Sri Lanka in 2014–2016. After the Maldives allowed three Chinese naval ships to stop over Malé in August 2017, New Delhi warned that China might eventually acquire a naval presence in Maldives.[50] In May 2017, New Delhi also warned of "unsustainable debt burden" being created by the BRI.[51] This in fact is one of the major areas of criticism of China's development aid—accusing China of using sovereign debt to bend other states to its will and eventually dominate the Indian Ocean.[52]

COMPETING REGIONAL ORDERS?

As a result, New Delhi has so far not only resisted calls to join the BRI but also sought the opportunity to counter China's regional influence. In response to China's activities in Gwadar, India has invested $85 million to construct infrastructure at Chabahar port in southeastern Iran, adjacent to Gwadar. In May 2016, New Delhi and Tehran signed a MOU to develop a Transit and Transport Corridor involving Iran, India, and Afghanistan. The major purpose of this infrastructure building, including ports, road, and rail networks, was to enhance connectivity to landlocked Afghanistan and with greater Central Asia, with the aim of bypassing Pakistan. The first phase of the Chabahar port was finished at the end of 2017 and India sent its first shipment of 15,000 tons of wheat to Afghanistan through Chabahar. It is anticipated that the port will be fully operational by the end of 2018.[53]

Apart from Chabahar port, India is also actively boosting its naval presence in the Indian Ocean. In 2015, India signed agreements with Mauritius and Seychelles to develop "strategic infrastructure" on two islands—Agalega Island in Mauritius and Assumption in Seychelles.[54] Although the agreement with Seychelles encountered domestic opposition in the island state, India and Seychelles manage to overcome it and revised the agreement in January 2018, which would allow India to build "military infrastructure" in the archipelago.[55] To further counter China's presence in the region, New Delhi also signed an agreement with Oman, allowing the Indian navy access to the Port of Duqm, which sits atop the Indian Ocean and is a crucial waterway to the Persian Gulf.[56]

Beyond South Asia, India has allied with Japan in providing infrastructure projects to developing countries. The Asia-Africa Growth Corridor (AAGC), which aims to link Africa with India, Bangladesh, Myanmar, Cambodia, and Laos together by sea, was proposed by both India and Japan during the annual meeting of the African Development Bank held in Gujarat, India, in May 2017.[57] In addition, India is also quietly seeking the opportunity to collaborate with ASEAN countries in infrastructure building. In addition to a 1,360-kilometer trilateral highway project involving India, Myanmar, and Thailand, New Delhi is also considering boosting its financial assistance for a highway going from India to Vietnam through Cambodia and Laos. During its Republic Day celebrations in January 2018, New Delhi unprecedentedly invited all ten ASEAN leaders to attend.[58]

THE NEW STRATEGIC LEXICON: THE "QUAD" AND THE "INDO-PACIFIC"

This geopolitical backdrop underpins the logic behind the revival of the Quadrilateral Security Dialogue (or "Quad," as it is often termed). The Quad originated after the 2004 Boxing Day tsunami that caused immense damage along the coasts of most landmasses bordering the Indian Ocean. Four democratic powers—Australia, India, Japan, and the United States—proposed an informal network of cooperation over the provision of military hardware and humanitarian relief to the affected areas.[59] This event highlighted the potential for deeper maritime cooperation between the four participants. In 2017, Japan's prime minister Shinzo Abe announced the intention to turn this informal alliance into a more strategic partnership to balance against the rise of China. The four-way dialogue was designed to preserve the common interests among the like-minded regional powers, including a liberal rules-based regional order and the maintenance of stability in Asia.

The United States and Japan were initially the strongest backers of the Quad, while India and Australia were "the two weaker links in the Quad chain."[60] Yet in 2008, not long after the Quad was established, Australia under the Rudd government retreated from it over the fear that the Quad would affect its economic relations with China.[61] However, with a growing concern about China's increasing assertiveness in the region and the relative decline of the America's power, there is a growing nervousness about peace and security in the region. None of the states in Asia can realistically balance China's growing economic and military strength on their own.[62] Based on this, the Quad was revived in 2017 during Donald Trump's November visit to Asia.

An apparently new geostrategic spatial term—the "Indo-Pacific"—also came of age in 2017 when the United States unveiled a new vision of a "free and open Indo-Pacific region," after the term had been gaining currency in Australia for several years beforehand. Since then, the term "Indo-Pacific" has replaced "Asia-Pacific" in the new US strategic lexicon, including in the 2018 US National Security Strategy and its National Defence Strategy.[63] The latter document even labeled China "a strategic competitor" in the Indo-Pacific. In May 2018, the US military also announced that its Pacific Command would be renamed the Indo-Pacific Command.[64] Meanwhile, Australia also renamed its "Asia-Pacific Group" under the Department of Foreign Affairs and Trade the "Indo-Pacific Group."[65] However, India has been behind the promotion of the new notion for several years.[66] As argued by Chengxin Pan, the new concept is neither an innocent nor a neutral description but "a manufactured super-region designed to hedge against a perceived Sino-centric regional order," and the key actors of the new construct are the United States, Australia, Japan, and India.[67]

The revival of the Quad and the use of the term "Indo-Pacific" is a visible response to Chinese expansion in the region and those BRI-related investment activities. A common perception among the four Quad democracies is that China poses a challenge to the stability of their "liberal rules-based" order.[68] India's nervousness might even be greater than the other participants, since China's controversial BRI activities in Pakistan, the Maldives, and Sri Lanka are all challenging New Delhi's dominant position in South Asia.

Hence, New Delhi has become more proactive in seeking to hedge against military threats in the Indian Ocean strategic space.

CONCLUSIONS

The BRI was initially a convenient way to enhance China's security by building an alternative to existing rules, and soft-balancing against the United States. However, China's infrastructure building in South Asia now threatens to upend the balance of power in the region, deepening the security dilemma between China and India in the process. India has numerous reasons for being concerned over the BRI. While the CPEC highway not only passes through the territories sensitive to New Delhi, Chinese management of the Gwadar and Jiwani ports has also made New Delhi anxious about its national security. In addition, China's recent assertiveness in the Indian Ocean and its investment activities in the region are perceived as encircling India via "debt trap diplomacy" in its own backyard, challenging its traditional leadership role in the region.

As a balancing response, India has sought every opportunity to offset China's regional influence. The common thread running through India's counter-BRI policies, from the AAGC, the Quad, the Malabar exercises, and its increasing political and economic bonds with the ASEAN member-states has been an effort to counter China's presence in the region. Behind the façade that China and India have established a bilateral "strategic partnership," they compete openly for political and economic influence. Indeed, the China-India relationship arguably remains "the most competitive relationship between two of the world's mega-states in the twenty-first century."[69] The effectiveness of China's soft-balancing and regional order-(re)building will largely depend on how China manages its relations with its regional archrival, India. This chapter has, however, demonstrated that shared understandings of what regional powers should behave in the establishment of the BRI in South Asia are in fact absent.

NOTES

1. Gerald Chan, "China's new silk roads: A new global financial order?" in Bo Zhiyue (ed), *China-US Relations in Global Perspective* (Wellington: Victoria University of Wellington Press), 2016, p. 66.

2. Hong Yu, "Motivation behind China's 'One Belt, One Road' initiatives and establishment of the Asian Infrastructure Investment Bank," *Journal of Contemporary China*, 26 (105), 2016, pp. 353–368.

3. Lai-Ha Chan, "'Soft balancing against the US 'Pivot to Asia': China's geostrategic rationale for establishing the AIIB," *Australian Journal of International Affairs*, 71 (6), 2017, pp. 568–590.

4. Hedley Bull, *The Anarchical Society: A Study of Order in World Politics* (Basingstoke: Palgrave, 3rd edition), 2002, pp. 8 and 16–19.

5. Muthiah Alagappa, "The study of international order: An analytical framework," in Muthiah Alagappa (ed), *Asian Security Order: Instrumental and Normative Features* (Stanford, CA: Stanford University Press), 2003, pp. 33–69, 39.

6. Janice Bially Mattern, *Ordering International Politics: Identity, Crisis, and Representational Force* (New York: Routledge), 2005, p. 30.

7. Evelyn Goh, *The Struggle for Order: Hegemony, Hierarchy and Transition in Post-Cold War East Asia* (Oxford: Oxford University Press), 2015, pp. 7–13.

8. Antje Wiener, "In the eye of the beholder: A sociology of knowledge perspective on norm transfer," *Journal of European Integration*, 37, 2015, pp. 211–228.

9. William A. Callahan, "China's 'Asia Dream': The Belt and Road Initiative and the new regional order," *Asian Journal of Comparative Politics*, 1 (3), 2016, pp. 226–243, 228.

10. For a study of the "New Silk Road," see Joshu Kucera, "The new Silk Road," *The Diplomat*, 11 November 2011, http://thediplomat.com/2011/11/the-new-silk-road/ (accessed 16 June 2018).

11. Wang Jisi, ""西進"，中國地沿戰略的再平衡 ("Marching westwards": The rebalancing of China's geostrategy," 環球時報 (*Global Times*), 12 October 2012, http://opinion.huanqiu.com/opinion_world/2012-10/3193760.html (accessed 18 March 2017).

12. Xue Li, "中國"一帶一路" 戰略面對的外交風險 (Diplomatic risks facing China's Belt and Road strategy)," 國際經濟評論 (*International Economic Review)*, no. 2, 2015, pp. 68–79, 69.

13. Li Wen and Cai Jianhong, ""一帶一路" 對中國外交新理念的實踐意義 (Practical significance of the Belt and Road on new philosophy of Chinese diplomacy)," 東南亞研究 (*Southeast Asian Studies*), no. 3, 2015, pp. 4–9.

14. Zheng Anguang, "簡析"一帶一路"背景下中國的中亞戰略"新常態" (Explaining the "new normality" of China's Central Asia strategy under the "One Belt, One Road" initiative") 當代世界與社會主義 (*Contemporary World and Socialism*), no. 4, 2015, pp. 26–31.

15. Peter Ferdinand, "Westward ho—the China dream and 'one belt, one road': Chinese foreign policy under Xi Jinping," *International Affairs*, 92 (4), 2016, pp. 941–957, 950.

16. Lai-Ha Chan and Pak K. Lee, "Power, ideas and institutions: China's emergent footprints in global governance of development aid," *CSGR Working Paper No. 281/17*, Centre for the Study of Globalisation and Regionalisation, University of Warwick, 2017, p. 24, www.warwick.ac.uk/csgr/papers/281-17.pdf.

17. Li Xiguang, "從瓜達爾看21世紀新秩序 (To view the new order of the 21st century from Gwardar)," 文化軟實力 (*Cultural Soft Power*), no. 2, 2017, pp. 10–14.

18. Jeremy Garlick, "Deconstructing the China-Pakistan economics corridor: Pipe dreams versus geopolitical realities," *Journal of Contemporary China*, 27 (112), 2018, pp. 519–533.

19. Daniel S. Markey and James West, "Behind China's gambit in Pakistan," *Council on Foreign Relations Expert Brief*, 12 May 2016, https://www.cfr.org/expert-brief/behind-chinas-gambit-pakistan (accessed 16 June 2018).

20. Haroon Janjua, "'Nothing but lies and deceit': Trump launches Twitter attack on Pakistan," *The Guardian*, 2 January 2018, https://www.theguardian.com/world/2018/jan/01/lies-and-deceit-trump-launches-attack-on-pakistan-tweet (accessed 12 February 2018).

21. State Bank of Pakistan, "Use of Chinese Yuan for denominating foreign currency transactions in Pakistan," 2 January 2018, http://www.sbp.org.pk/press/2018/Pr-CYN-02-Jan-18.pdf (accessed 12 February 2018).

22. Bill Gertz, "China building military base in Pakistan," *The Washington Times*, 3 January 2018, https://www.washingtontimes.com/news/2018/jan/3/china-plans-pakistan-military-base-at-jiwani/ (accessed 12 February 2018).

23. Ramachandran Sudha, "The China-Maldives connection," *The Diplomat*, 25 January 2018, https://thediplomat.com/2018/01/the-china-maldives-connection/ (accessed 17 February 2018).

24. Daniel Bosley, "Maldives gives airport contract to Chinese firm during Xi's visit," *Reuters*, 16 September 2014, https://in.reuters.com/article/china-maldives/maldives-gives-airport-contract-to-chinese-firm-during-xis-visit-idINKBN0HA1TS20140915 (accessed 18 June 2018).

25. Indrani Bagchil, "India slams Maldives for cancellation of GMR's airport project," *The Times of India*, 27 November 2012, https://timesofindia.indiatimes.com/india/India-slams-Maldives-for-cancellation-of-GMRs-airport-project/articleshow/17391671.cms (accessed 17 February 2018).

26. Sudha, "The China-Maldives connection."

27. Mohan Malik, "Caught in a tug-of-war," *Asian Affairs*, March 2018, http://www.asianaffairs.in/magazine/caught-in-a-tug-of-war/#.Wsh_h4jwbAI (accessed 16 June 2018).

28. Ai Jun, "Unauthorized military intervention in Male must be stopped," *Global Times*, 12 February 2018, http://www.globaltimes.cn/content/1089435.shtml (accessed 17 February 2018).

29. Darren J. Lim and Rohan Mukherjee, "What money can't buy: The security externalities of Chinese economic statecraft in post-war Sri Lanka," *Asian Security*, 14 (1), 2017, pp. 1–20, 7–8, https://doi.org/10.1080/14799855.2017.1414045.

30. Go Yamada and Stefania Palma, "Is China's Belt and Road working? A progress report from eight countries," *Financial Times*, 1 April 2018, https://www.ft.com/content/6c5435b4-33b0-11e8-ac48-10c6fdc22f03 (accessed 4 April 2018).

31. Yamada and Palma, "Is China's Belt and Road working?"

32. Sachin Parashari, "Chinese submarine docking in Lanka 'inimical' to India's interests: Govt," *Times of India*, 4 November 2014, https://timesofindia.indiatimes.com/india/Chinese-submarine-docking-in-Lanka-inimical-to-Indias-interests-Govt/articleshow/45025487.cms (accessed 7 April 2018); and *South China Morning Post*, "Sri Lanka refuses port for Chinese submarine after Indian leader Modi's visit," 12 May 2017, http://www.scmp.com/news/asia/diplomacy/article/2094093/sri-lanka-refuses-port-call-chinese-submarine-after-indian (accessed 7 April 2018).

33. Mikael Mattlin and Matti Nojonen, "Conditionality and path dependence in Chinese lending," *Journal of Contemporary China*, 24 (94), 2015, pp. 701–720; and Xiaobing Wang, Adam Ozanne and Xin Hao, "The West's aid dilemma and the Chinese solutions?" *Journal of Chinese Economic and Business Studies*, 12 (1), 2015, pp. 47–61.

34. Mattlin and Nojonen, "Conditionality and path dependence in Chinese lending."

35. Jamil Anderlini, "China insists on 'Tied Aid' in Africa," *Financial Times*, 25 June 2007.

36. Tukumbi Lumumba-Kasongo, "China-Africa relations: A neo-imperialism or a neo-colonialism? A reflection" *African and Asian Studies*, 10 (2–3), 2011, pp. 234–266.

37. Interviews in Islamabad, May 2017.

38. Indian Government, "Official spokesperson's response to a query on participation of India in OBOR/BRI Forum," 13 May 2017, http://www.mea.gov.in/media-briefings.htm?dtl/28463/Official_Spokespersons_response_to_a_query_on_participation_of_India_in_OBORBRI_Forum (accessed 7 February 2018).

39. Gautam Sen, *China-One Belt and One Road Initiative: Strategic & Economic Implications* (New Delhi: Vivekananda International Foundation), 2016, p. 2.

40. Jabin T. Jacob, "China's Belt and Road Initiative: Perspectives from India," *China and World Economy*, 25 (5), 2017, pp. 78–100, 82.

41. Owen Bennett Jones, *Pakistan: Eye of the Storm* (New Haven and London: Yale University Press), 2009, p. 92.

42. Baldev Raj Nayar and T.V. Paul, *India in the World Order: Searching for Major-Power Status* (Cambridge: Cambridge University Press), 2003, p. 80.

43. Stratfor, "South Asia: A bump in the Belt and Road," *Stratfor Worldview*, 16 May 2017.

44. K.J.M. Varma, "CPEC violates sovereignty: India tells China," *Press Trust of India*, 22 February 2017, http://www.ptinews.com/news/8435073_CPEC-violates-sovereignty.

45. Malabar exercise has been an annual bilateral event between India and the United States since 1992. In 2007 this naval exercise expanded to include Japan, Australia, and Singapore. Australia and Singapore have since 2014 not participated in the exercise, but Japan re-joined it in 2014 and a year later, became a permanent member of it. See P. Pandey, "Malabar 2017: Trilateral naval exercise concludes amid India-China standoff," *The Diplomat*, 19 July 2017, https://thediplomat.com/2017/07/malabar-2017-trilateral-naval-exercise-concludes-amid-india-china-standoff/ (accessed 5 February 2018).

46. Press Trust of India, "India, Japan, the US hold joint naval exercises," 10 July 2017, http://ptinews.com/news/8874268_India--Japan--the-US-hold-joint-naval-exercises (accessed 5 February 2018).

47. Steve George and Huizhong Wu, "US, India and Japan begin naval exercises, as China looks on," *CNN*, 12 July 2017, https://edition.cnn.com/2017/07/11/asia/india-japan-us-malabar-exercises/index.html (accessed 5 February 2018).

48. Aman Thakker, "Amid Chinese protests over Arunachal Pradesh, India stands firm," *The Diplomat*, 23 January 2018, https://thediplomat.com/2018/01/amid-chinese-protests-over-arunachal-pradesh-india-stands-firm/ (accessed 6 February 2018).

49. Indrani Bagchi, "India slams China's One Belt One Road Initiative, says it violates sovereignty," *Times of India*, 14 May 2017, https://timesofindia.indiatimes.com/india/china-road-initiative-is-like-a-colonial-enterprise-india/articleshow/58664098.cms; and Rajiv Ranjan, "How can China convince India to sign up for "One Belt, One Road'?" *The Diplomat*, 5 May 2017, https://thediplomat.com/2017/05/how-can-china-convince-india-to-sign-up-for-one-belt-one-road/ (both accessed 24 June 2017).

50. Shan Anees, "Three Chinese naval ships arrive in Maldives," *Raajje.mv*, 27 August 2017, https://raajje.mv/en/news/16679 (accessed 17 February 2018).

51. Indian Government, "Official spokesperson's response to a query on participation of India in OBOR/BRI Forum," 13 May 2017, http://www.mea.gov.in/media-briefings.htm?dtl/28463/Official_Spokespersons_response_to_a_query_on_participation_of_India_in_OBORBRI_Forum (accessed 7 February 2018).

52. Nyshka Chandran, "China's using cheap debt to 'bend other countries to its will,' academic says," *CNBC*, 22 December 2017, https://www.cnbc.com/2017/12/22/one-belt-one-road-china-loans-are-debt-bondage-says-brahma-chellaney.html (accessed 6 February 2018).

53. Harsh V. Pant, "Take note: Asia's 'Quad' is back," *The Diplomat*, 10 November 2017, https://thediplomat.com/2017/11/take-note-asias-quad-is-back/ (accessed 7 April 2018).

54. Shubhajit Roy, "India to develop strategic assets in 2 Mauritius, Seychelles islands," *Indian Express*, 12 March 2015, http://indianexpress.com/article/india/india-others/india-seychelles-sign-four-pacts-to-boost-security-cooperation/ (accessed 19 February 2018).

55. *Times of India*, "Access to Omani port to help India check China at Gwadar," 14 February 2018, https://timesofindia.indiatimes.com/india/access-to-omani-port-to-help-india-check-china-at-gwadar/articleshowprint/62908230.cms (accessed 19 February 2018).

56. *Times of India*, "Access to Omani port to help India check China at Gwadar."

57. Avinash Nair, "To counter OBOR, India and Japan propose Asia-Africa sea corridor," *Indian Express*, 31 May 2017, http://indianexpress.com/article/explained/to-counter-obor-india-and-japan-propose-asia-africa-sea-corridor-4681749/ (accessed 7 February 2018).

58. Kiran Sharma, "India's Modi courts ASEAN leaders to counter China's Belt and Road," *Asian Review*, 25 January 2018, https://asia.nikkei.com/Politics-Economy/International-Relations/India-s-Modi-courts-ASEAN-leaders-to-counter-China-s-Belt-and-Road (accessed 9 February 2018).

59. Andrew Shearer, "Quad redux: A new agenda for Asia's maritime democracies," *The Interpreter*, 10 November 2017, https://www.lowyinstitute.org/the-interpreter/quad-redux-new-agenda-asia-maritime-democracies (accessed 11 December 2017).

60. Euan Graham, "The Quad deserves its second chance," *Debating the Quad*, ANU Centre of Gravity Series paper, No. 39, 2018, pp. 4–7, 5, http://sdsc.bellschool.anu.edu.au/sites/default/files/publications/attachments/2018-03/cog_39_web_-_debating_the_quad.pdf (accessed 7 April 2018).

61. Shearer, "Quad redux."

62. Pant, "Take note."

63. See The White House, National Security Strategy of the United States of America (Washington, DC), 2017, https://www.whitehouse.gov/wp-content/uploads/2017/12/NSS-Final-12-18-2017-0905.pdf; and Summary of the 2018 National Defense Strategy of the United States of America: Sharpening the American Military's Competitive Edge, https://www.defense.gov/Portals/1/Documents/pubs/2018-National-Defense-Strategy-Summary.pdf (both accessed 10 June 2018).

64. Idrees Ali, "In symbolic nod to India, U.S. Pacific Command changes name," *Reuters*, 31 May 2018, https://www.reuters.com/article/us-usa-defense-india/in-symbolic-nod-to-india-us-pacific-command-changes-name-idUSKCN1IV2Q2 (accessed 10 June 2018).

65. https://dfat.gov.au/about-us/department/Documents/dfat-org-chart-executive.pdf (accessed 10 June 2018). According to Ian Hall of Griffith University, the Indo-Pacific Group was created after DFAT published its Foreign Policy White Paper in 2017. Personal conversation with Ian Hall in March 2018.

66. C. Raja Mohan, *Sumudra Manthan: Sino-Indian Rivalry in the Indo-Pacific* (Washington, DC: Carnegie Endowment for International Peace), 2012.

67. Chengxin Pan, "The 'Indo-Pacific' and geopolitical anxieties about China's rise in the Asian regional order," *Australian Journal of International Affairs*, 68 (4), 2014, pp. 453–469, 453.

68. Graham, "The Quad deserves its second chance."

69. Quote from Sen, 2016, p. 3.

Chapter 3

Sino-Russian Relations and the Belt and Road Initiative

Navigating Hedging, Accommodation, and Entrapment Dilemmas in Central Asia

Michael Clarke and Matthew Sussex

Since President Xi Jinping's announcement of the "Silk Road Economic Belt" portion of China's "Belt and Road Initiative" (BRI) during an official visit to Kazakhstan in June 2013, Beijing and Moscow have increased their security, economic, and diplomatic relationship. President Xi, during his official state visit to Russia in July 2017, assessed relations to be at their "best time in history" and that China and Russia were each other's "most trustworthy strategic partners."[1] Such rhetorical flourishes have prompted some analysts to raise the possibility that enhanced collaboration between the two may constitute an "axis of authoritarianism" bent on destabilizing the Western-led international order and diminish the capacity for the United States to influence strategic outcomes across Eurasia.[2] Bobo Lo, in contrast, famously framed Sino-Russian ties as an "axis of convenience" wherein the relationship is essentially "tactical and instrumental" and defined by "expediency and opportunism."[3] Here, Moscow and Beijing are happy to leverage their bilateral relationship in the context of their other important regional and global relationships but remain unable to establish a true condominium of interests due to the continued salience of a number of historical, normative, and domestic factors that inhibit the consummation of their "strategic partnership" into a formal alliance.

The two extremes of this debate, while capturing important elements of the relationship, tend to obscure its complexity. The "proto-alliance" side accurately captures both Moscow and Beijing's shared dissatisfaction with aspects of the existing international order, and signals the overlap of their normative preferences. In this manner such perspectives provide accounts of the "thick" underpinnings of the relationship based on shared practices, rules, and identities. The "axis of convenience" side of the debate, meanwhile, accurately captures the "thin" interests-based, functional aspects of the relationship based on complementary strategic and economic objectives.

Since the end of the Cold War Sino-Russian relations in Central Asia have consistently defied predictions of each side of this debate. In the immediate post-Cold War years, a "new Great Game" over spheres of influence in the region was envisaged, while the events of 9/11 and the US invasion of Afghanistan were variously described as a "defeat" for Chinese foreign policy in the region, or the death knell for Russian influence among the Central Asian republics.[4] In practice, however, Russian influence in Central Asia remained while Chinese influence followed a consistently upward trajectory without inducing overt strategic rivalry between the two.

These developments beg a number of important questions. First, has the relative stability of Sino-Russian relations in Central Asia been simply due to the convergence of "thin," interest-based calculus, or to the evolution of a "thick" underpinning to the relationship based on a shared understanding or vision for regional order? Second, what will be the effect of China's ambitious BRI on the bilateral relationship in Central Asia? With respect to the first question, we suggest that the relative stability of Sino-Russian relations in the region has been fostered by the convergence of a number of key structural, regional, and domestic factors. These have remained relatively consistent over time, and demonstrate the interplay between "thick" (normative) and "thin" (interests) variables. Sino-Russian ties in this context are consistent with the concept of an alignment rather than an alliance.

However, the relationship is still prone to the central dilemmas typical of the "alliance game": hedging, accommodation, and entrapment. We suggest that BRI in particular will heighten these dilemmas as China's trans-Eurasian connectivity agenda fundamentally challenges Russian preferences across the strategic, economic, and normative domain of its interests. This in turn suggests a number of possible scenarios for regional order in Central Asia over the course of the next decade: an overt great power contest between China and Russia (and possibly third actors) for influence, with increased "multi-vectoring" by Central Asian states; accommodation of Chinese preferences by both Russia and the Central Asian states; and, finally, a Russia weakened by ongoing sanctions and deterioration of relations with Europe and the United States that is ultimately entrapped into dependency on China.

THE SINO-RUSSIAN "STRATEGIC PARTNERSHIP": ALIGNMENT, ALLIANCE, OR SHARED "FRAME OF MIND"?

Glenn H. Snyder once famously asserted that the "supergame" of international security could be divided into three analytical subgames: the armaments game, the adversary game, and the alliance game.[5] A central engine of each of these "games" is the security dilemma—"the self-defeating aspect of the quest for security in an anarchic system." Snyder focused in particular on the role of the security dilemma in the formation (primary phase) and management of alliances (secondary phase) in multipolar and bipolar systems. In the primary phase, states have two options: to seek allies or to abstain. Snyder maintained that alliances will ultimately form due to the fact that some states may seek to "increase it [i.e. security] substantially by allying," while others "fearing that others will not abstain will ally to avoid isolation or to preclude the partner from allying against them."[6]

This model, as Snyder notes, predicts only that alliances will form, and does not predict "who will align with whom, or how the benefits, risks, and costs of an alliance will be divided." The latter is determined by alliance bargaining in which the potential allies compete in offering each other shares of the alliance's benefit, while seeking to maximize their own share of the benefits. "If these were the only interests at stake," Snyder continued, "the alliance bargaining process would be completely indeterminate—that is, each state would be equally eligible as the ally or adversary of every other state."[7]

Yet that is of course not the case in reality. Other interests predispose states to align with some and against others. Here, we distinguish between "general" and "particular" interests, where the former derive from the anarchical structure of the system and geographic position of the states in question; while the latter derive from specific cultural, ethnic, or ideological values/characteristics that predispose states to conflict or affinity with others. These latter interests establish a "tacit pattern" of conflict or affinity as the backdrop "against which the overt alliance bargaining process takes place."[8] From this point the "alliance game" enters a second phase in which the key question for each state is "how firmly to commit themselves to the proto-partner and how much support to give that partner in specific conflict interactions."[9]

Consideration of these questions gives rise to the "horns" of "abandonment" and "entrapment." Given the anarchical environment and uncertainty of other's intentions, "abandonment," in varying forms (realignment with adversaries, abrogation of alliances, or failure to provide support when it is expected) is "ever present." "Entrapment," conversely, may occur "when one values the preservation of the alliance more than the cost of fighting for the ally's interests."[10] In this instance, the greater dependence on the alliance and/or the greater the commitment to the ally "the higher the risk of entrapment."

Crucially, the risks of either outcome "vary inversely: reducing one tends to increase the other." Thus, strong commitment to an ally reduces fear of abandonment but increases the risks of entrapment by bolstering belief in one's support in the event of conflict. Likewise, weak commitment reduces the risks of entrapment but heightens the fear of abandonment. Additional choices here may also adversely affect bargaining leverage. Conveying a strong commitment to the ally may reduce the credibility of subsequent threats of nonsupport. "An alliance with rigid commitments," Robert Kann thus observed, "leads to an attitude in which each state tries to minimize its own obligations and to maximize those of its partners. Consequently, in most alliances there exists a built-in centrifugal tendency toward weakening the ties."[11] Such considerations generally lead to strategies of "weak or ambiguous commitment" and/or "hedging."[12] "Hedging," as defined by Evelyn Goh, constitutes "a set of strategies aimed at avoiding (or planning for contingencies in) a situation in which states cannot decide upon more straightforward alternatives such as balancing, bandwagoning, or neutrality."[13]

Sino-Russian relations are not formally framed as an alliance—which is understood as "a promise of mutual military assistance between two or more sovereign states"[14]—but rather as a "strategic partnership." Where an alliance is externally oriented toward a third-party adversary or group of adversaries,[15] a "partnership" is internally oriented as its primary function "is to reduce uncertainties from unknown intentions between two states" with a "minimal requirement that they will not threaten each other."[16] Given this distinction some contend that "strategic partnerships" are therefore *not* synonymous with alliances.[17] However, both alliances and partnerships are manifestations of the broader concept of "alignment" in international relations/politics. "Alignment" between two states implies "a set of mutual expectations [. . .] that they will have each other's support in disputes or war with particular other states."[18] Whereas a central value of an alliance is its deterrent value vis-à-vis potential adversaries—usually explicitly codified within the text of a legal treaty—the core value of a partnership ("strategic" or otherwise) lies in a more general (and sometimes ambiguous) expectation or sense of support.[19] Snyder suggests that "alignment" is "defined as expectations of states about whether they will be supported or opposed by other states in future interactions,"[20] while Michael D. Ward posits that "alignment is not signified by formal treaties, but is delineated by a variety of *behavioural actions*" not solely focused on the military or security dimension of international politics.[21]

Thomas Wilkins's analysis of Sino-Russian relations, as well as his broader effort to construct "a conceptual taxonomy of alignment,"[22] builds on Ward's observation of the importance of "behavioral actions" in framing alignments. While noting that there is no "agreed definition" of the term in IR, Wilkins suggested that "strategic partnership" is best described as a "structured collaboration between states to take joint advantage of economic opportunities, or to respond to security challenges more effectively than could be achieved in isolation."[23] Furthermore, Wilkins identified a number of properties that "strategic partnerships" exhibit that demonstrate their differentiation from alliances as a form of alignment in international politics: they are organized around a "system principle" (like desire for a multipolar world); they are often goal rather than threat driven; and they are informal in nature and "entail low commitment costs" which "permits partners to retain a greater degree of autonomy and flexibility, thus mitigating the 'entrapment' dynamic common to orthodox alliances."[24]

Huiyun Feng, in turn, has posited what she terms a "threat-interest model" of "strategic partnership" to map the development of Sino-Russian relations.[25] Here, the Sino-Russian relationship is tracked through the convergence and divergence of each party's external security threats and/or perceptions and economic interests with the two variables providing four types of possible partnership. For Feng, the Sino-Russian partnership has developed through each of these stages. Partnership 1 is a "simple partnership" where both shared neither external threat perception nor economic interests. Partnership 2 reflects a "security partnership" where the two shared external threat perceptions but not economic interests. Partnership 3 suggests divergent external threat perceptions but convergence of economic interests; and partnership 4 indicates convergence of both external threat perceptions and economic interests.[26]

A potential problem for both Beijing and Moscow is that the concept of "strategic partnership" as a form of alignment bears close resemblance to the much older diplomatic concept of an *entente*.[27] The principal prerequisite for an *entente* is that there be a shared set of interests that may constitute the basis for cooperation and/or coordination in the future. Sir Eyre Crowe, describing the most famous entente, the so-called *entente cordiale* between Great Britain and France of 1904 (and 1912), remarked that it was based on "a frame of mind, a view of general policy which is shared by the governments of two countries." Crowe, however, also cautioned that due to this "general policy," "For purposes of ultimate emergencies it may be found to have no substance at all." China's BRI agenda, however, holds the potential to undo the bases of the Sino-Russian shared "frame of mind" in Central Asia. With Xinjiang serving as a central hub, China's initiative seeks to stimulate trans-Eurasian economic and infrastructure connectivity that will link China, Central Asia, Russia, and Europe. This stands in contrast to Russia's regional integration initiative, the Eurasian Economic Union, an effort at protective integration within the post-Soviet space to maintain Russian influence.

THE SINO-RUSSIAN ENTENTE IN CENTRAL ASIA: SECURITY, DEVELOPMENT, AND GEOPOLITICS

The Sino-Russian entente in Central Asia can be demonstrated via the overlap of interests in three core areas across much of the post-Cold War period: shared interests in stability, security, and order; complementarity of economic interests; and shared desire/interest in the development of a "multipolar" international order (in both strategic and normative terms).[28] Throughout the 1990s and 2000s, China and Russia developed a clear coexistence in the region, with each generally recognizing the other's comparative advantages in each core area. Thus Moscow retained the role and status of security provider and China became increasingly predominant economically.

Structurally, both Moscow and Beijing since the end of the Cold War have sought to leverage their bilateral relationship as a means of combating the perceived detrimental effects of US unipolarity at the global and regional level. There has thus been significant overlap in Russian and Chinese elite narratives and preferences for a "multipolar" international order, the creation of alternate normative orders to those authored/led by the West, and the protection/reassertion of state sovereignty. This has been most clearly expressed in Chinese and Russian involvement in Central Asia's major multilateral organization, the Shanghai Cooperation Organization (SCO). Regionally, both Moscow and Beijing have sought influence in what they perceive to be a potentially unstable region, albeit for different reasons. For Moscow, its discrete and "thin" interests in Central Asia—such as maintaining access to hydrocarbons, combating Islamist terrorism, or protecting ethnic Russians—have been framed by the broader goal of maintaining its self-image as a great power. The participation of some 3,200 Chinese troops in Russia's showy September 2018 *Vostok* exercises, which purportedly involved over 300,000 Russian personnel from all services of its armed forces, is a case in point here: Moscow has been keen to portray the Sino-Russian relationship as increasingly in lockstep over primary security challenges.[29] This status-oriented approach has tended to mean that "Russia's actual policies in Central Asia have been a function of its prevailing relationship with other great powers," most notably China and the United States.[30] Beijing, in contrast, instrumentalized its approach to the region in order to first to secure its long-restive province of Xinjiang, and second to leverage that geopolitical position to pursue broader economic and strategic objectives.

SINO-RUSSIAN RELATIONS IN THE IMMEDIATE POST-SOVIET ERA: THE PRIMACY OF DEFENSIVE PRIORITIES

In the immediate wake of the collapse of the Soviet Union and independence of the Central Asian states, Sino-Russian relations were arguably defined by a shared domestically oriented mind-set and largely defensive set of interests vis-à-vis Central Asia. For Russian President Boris Yeltsin, Central Asia in the early 1990s was a low priority due to a combination of major factors. First, Yeltsin's early foreign policy was driven by a "Euro-Atlanticist" agenda that perceived Russia's future security and prosperity as best ensured by alignment with the developed and democratic West. For those such as Yeltsin's foreign minister Andrei Kozyrev, this meant that

> Russia must shed its tradition of distinctiveness and its illusions of serving a "special role" as a "bridge" between Europe and Asia. And it must avoid the temptations of assuming a leading role in the Commonwealth of Independent States (CIS), not only because reintegration of Russia's economy with those of the other former Soviet republics would slow market-oriented reforms and integration with Atlantic and European economic institutions, but also because Russia's assumption of a peacekeeping role in the troubled bordering states would restore the privileged status of the military thereby threaten the tender shoots of democracy in Russia.[31]

Second, the residual effect of historical, military, cultural, and economic ties of the Soviet era predisposed Yeltsin's government to expect continued Central Asian deference to Russian preferences and interests. Finally, Yeltsin sought to end Russia's propping up of the region economically, which in 1992 amounted to direct and indirect subsidies worth approximately US$9 billion.[32] Such factors initially resulted in a Russian benign disregard for Central Asia so long as it did not directly threaten Moscow's immediate security or economic interests.[33] This situation changed by May 1993 with the release of Russia's Foreign Policy concept which jettisoned the "Euro-Atlanticist" agenda in favor of reassertion of Moscow's "rights and responsibilities" in the former USSR. This document was also notable as it identified China as the Asia-Pacific's most important state and prioritized consolidation of bilateral relations.[34]

In Beijing, the Tiananmen Square massacre in June 1989 and the collapse of the Soviet Union in 1991 ensured that regime survival became the core goal of the Chinese Communist Party. For Deng Xiaoping that could only be assured through coupling continued "reform and opening" and the delivery of economic growth/development with firm one-party rule. In order to effectively carry this out China required a stable international environment characterized by a return to "multipolarity" (*duojihua*)—a "return" to a global balance of power among many power centers. However, as this failed to materialize with American primacy underscored by the First Gulf War, China's foreign policy sought to "bide time and build capabilities" (*taoguang yanghui*) through developing multiple regional and global linkages to grow China's economy, resolve long-standing disputes with neighbors, and hedge against the perceived ill-effects of US predominance.[35]

In the Central Asian context, Beijing had three core interests that were a function of its security concerns in Xinjiang: ethnic separatism, border demarcation, and economic ties. Historically, a major dilemma for China in its attempts to attain control over Xinjiang—sharing borders with the contemporary Central Asian republics, Russia, Mongolia, Pakistan, and Afghanistan—stemmed from the region's intimate connection to the geopolitical and cultural zone of Central Eurasia. This zone, dominated by largely pastoral-nomadic Turkic and Mongol peoples, exposed successive Chinese dynasties "to raids or invasions by the steppe nomads of Inner Asia" with the result that the "strategic culture formed by this history and political geography was [. . .] a profoundly continentalist one."[36] Significantly, the ability of China-based polities to project power has been seen by some scholars to have been dependent on their capacity to ensure continental stability.[37] From 1949 to the 1980s Beijing sought such stability via the negation of the region's historical, geographic, and cultural orientation toward Central Asia, especially via Han Chinese settlement.

Externally, the souring of Sino-Soviet ties, including military clashes along their shared frontiers, including in Xinjiang, placed a further premium on seeking continental stability via isolation.[38] The collapse of the Soviet Union in 1991 freed China from the need to guard against such potential state-based continental security threats, thus raising the possibility that it could mitigate strategic challenges along its eastern maritime frontiers through a strategic orientation toward its Eurasian frontiers. China's strategy was to open Xinjiang to Central Asia in order to achieve economic growth and ensure the stability and security of the region. The opening to Central Asia also resulted in Uyghur communities in the now-independent Central Asian republics reestablishing links with the Uyghurs of Xinjiang and, more concerning for Beijing, the emergence of Uyghur advocacy organizations in the Central Asian republics, particularly Kazakhstan and Kyrgyzstan.

All three major Chinese interests—economic ties, separatism, and border demarcation—were explicitly raised by then-Chinese premier Li Peng on his diplomatic tour of Central Asian capitals in April 1994.[39] This was followed by President Jiang Zemin's visit to Moscow in September 1994 where he and President Yeltsin signed a joint statement establishing a "constructive partnership" between their two countries. Practical outcomes of this commitment focused on confidence-building measures such as a declaration that neither party would target the other with nuclear weapons, and force reductions along their shared border.[40] Such defensive concerns were also central to the establishment in 1996 of the multilateral talks among China, Russia, Kazakhstan, Kyrgyzstan, and Tajikistan, thereafter called the "Shanghai Five" (S-5).[41] The April 1996 S-5 "Agreement on Confidence-Building in the Military Sphere in the Border Areas" was wide-reaching and encompassed a package of fourteen agreements on border issues and military confidence-building measures. The text of the agreement also emphasized the need to maintain the multilateral nature of security dialogues in the region, demonstrating China's desire to resolve its long-standing fear of vulnerability along its western frontier.[42]

Alongside the S5 agreement, Presidents Jiang Zemin and Boris Yeltsin also issued a joint Sino-Russian statement announcing the two parties' intention to upgrade bilateral relations to that of a "strategic partnership." Even at this early stage it was clear that the grouping was perceived by China as an important means through which to not only secure its Western frontier but also to further its wider strategic interests. Indeed, a joint Sino-Russian statement regarding the establishment of a Beijing-Moscow "strategic partnership" issued after the summit emphasized the need to counter "hegemonism" (i.e., US primacy) and the importance of achieving "regional and global stability, development and prosperity" on the basis of "the principles of mutual respect for sovereignty and territorial integrity, mutual non-aggression, non-interference in each other's internal affairs, equality and mutual benefit and peaceful coexistence."[43] This was clearly congruent with Beijing and Moscow's goals of developing multiple regional and global relationships to counter what they perceived to be the negative aspects of US primacy in international affairs. On the issue of China's specific interest in the security of Xinjiang, the S-5 summit of 1996 was also used to pressure the leaders of Tajikistan, Kyrgyzstan, and Kazakhstan to declare that they were "opposed to any form of splittist activities"—code for cooperating with Beijing to control the activities of pro-independence Uyghur émigré organizations within these Central Asian states.[44]

The inclusion and ongoing importance of the issue of "separatism" within the multilateral framework of the S-5 reflected solely *Chinese* interests, as none of its partners in these groupings themselves faced serious separatist challenges. From 1996 to 2000, China succeeded through the S-5 process and its increasingly close bilateral relations with Kazakhstan and Kyrgyzstan in effectively neutralizing Uyghur advocacy organizations in Central Asia. Indeed, the 1998 S-5 joint statement, in a clear reference to such organizations, stated that the member states would not "allow their territories to be used for the activities undermining the national sovereignty, security and social order of any of the five countries." Over the course of the next two years, regional developments, including the consolidation of the Taliban in

Afghanistan and the intensification of the insurgency of the Islamic Movement of Uzbekistan in the Ferghana Valley, helped China persuade its S-5 partners to take a stronger stance on what it increasingly termed the "three evils" of "separatism, extremism and terrorism."[45] As one observer put it:

> Agreement on "the three evils" indicated that the member states were ready to move beyond the initial phase of merely removing obstacles to peaceful co-existence and to work instead to develop new areas of co-operation (or, to put it differently, to move from negative to positive security co-operation).[46]

Chinese concerns here dovetailed with those of Russia as its foreign policy continued to veer away from the "Euro-Atlanticism" of the early 1990s and toward a "Eurasianist" one focused on bolstering Russian claims to great power-hood by reconstituting its political, military and economic hegemony in the "near abroad."[47] In Central Asia, Moscow attempted to leverage its economic and military-security levers by ensuring its continued monopoly on major oil and gas infrastructure and attempting to play the role of regional security provider.[48] However, as numerous observers have noted, its ability to effectively pursue this agenda was fundamentally weakened by Yeltsin's autocratic turn after 1993, economic crisis in 1997–1998, and the Central Asian states' (especially Uzbekistan, Kazakhstan, and Kyrgyzstan) own emergent "multi-vector" diplomacy to hedge against such Russian reassertion.[49]

Economically, the Sino-Russian entente in Central Asia was also framed by a mutual perception of complementary interests and capacity. Beijing's objective was to entrench Deng's "reform and opening" agenda in order to drive continued economic growth and development to underpin continued one-party rule. Russia was perceived in Beijing as an important source of advanced military hardware, especially after the imposition of Western post-Tiananmen sanctions, and natural resources.[50] In Central Asia, the economic relationship was conditioned by China's Xinjiang-derived objectives of seeking greater economic integration with the region, including establishing Xinjiang as a "Eurasian continental bridge," and to enhance resource security via diversification of supply. One outcome of this latter interest was the first substantive forays of Chinese state-owned energy companies such as Sinopec and China National Petroleum Corporation into Central Asia, mainly toward the Caspian Sea basin.[51]

FROM 9/11 TO THE "COLOR REVOLUTIONS"

The impact of 9/11 on Sino-Russian relations in Central Asia was contradictory. On the one hand, the "tilt" of the majority of Central Asian republics and Russia toward the United States after the invasion of Afghanistan undermined

China's diplomatic gains in the region in the mid-1990s. In 2001 and 2002 all of the Central Asian states except Turkmenistan, which adhered to an explicit foreign policy of neutrality, signed military-cooperation and base-access agreements with the United States, and received significant economic-aid packages.[52] Unsurprisingly, Putin sought to leverage the US reaction to the events of 9/11 for Russia's own interests: to place US-Russia bilateral ties on a more favorable footing; gain US and/or international support for its campaign in Chechnya (which it framed as antiterrorist); and to eradicate Taliban and Al Qaeda influence in Central Asia.[53] Additionally, cooperation with Washington also contributed to Moscow's long-held desire to "demonstrate its regional importance as a leading power."[54]

While the Central Asians and Russians tilted toward the United States, Beijing sought to reassert its role in the region both bilaterally and multilaterally through the SCO. A key element in this process was its promotion of a normative framework for interstate relations in Central Asia which privileged the maintenance of "stability" and noninterference in the "internal affairs" of member states.[55] This was reflected in the establishment and operation of the SCO's "Regional Anti-Terrorism" center in Tashkent (Uzbekistan), the SCO's joint annual military exercises since 2003, and the organization's response to the Tulip Revolution in Kyrgyzstan and the Andijan Incident in Uzbekistan in March and May 2005, respectively. These developments (the first of which overthrew the long-standing regime of Askar Akayev and the second of which shook Islam Karimov's regime in Tashkent) highlighted the negative effect of US influence on stability, and resulted in the SCO's Astana Declaration at the group's July 2005 summit that called for the immediate withdrawal of the US military presence in the region and cessation of US "interference."[56]

Since 2001, by virtue of bilateral security agreements with key Central Asian states (Kazakhstan and Kyrgyzstan) and police/security cooperation through the SCO, China has successfully extradited a significant number of alleged Uyghur "separatists and terrorists" from Kazakhstan, Kyrgyzstan, and Uzbekistan.[57] In the post-9/11 decade the SCO has developed a number of further initiatives, such as establishing the Regional Anti-Terrorism centers (RATs) in Tashkent in 2004 that have served to stifle Uyghur opposition in Central Asia. RATs, according to a prominent Chinese scholar Zhao Huasheng,

> conducts routine work related to anti-terrorist activities, such as giving advice and proposals on combating the "three forces"; gathering, analyzing, and sharing among member states relevant information; creating a data bank of terrorist organizations and personnel; organizing seminars on the topic of anti-terrorism; providing help in training experts; and maintaining contacts with other international security organizations, among other responsibilities.[58]

In this fashion the SCO from the Chinese perspective seeks to expand "the fight against 'East Turkistan' from China to the SCO itself."[59] Such processes are also emblematic of China's development of a "shared discourse about trans-regional security threats" (the "three evils") that has fostered statist multilateralism among the SCO partners. By framing their responses to such trans-regional security threats by the prioritization of "sovereignty, the protection of state borders and regime security," SCO member states can "cooperate on issues of 'high politics' while safeguarding (and legitimising) their specific political institutions, (state-sponsored) domestic identities and interests."[60]

In summary, the development of the S-5 and the SCO reflects China's endeavor to establish multiple regional and global relationships in order to counter US primacy in the international system—a goal achieved to an extent in 2005 and 2006 when the Central Asian states tilted back toward the SCO and China. Moreover, as the statements from the 2005, 2006, and 2007 SCO summits demonstrate, China increasingly views the SCO as a forum in which to present its foreign policy as a distinct alternative to that of the United States. Of central importance here has been China's commitment to embed within the SCO a normative framework—focused on maintaining "stability" and guided by concepts of noninterference in "internal affairs"—that supports the regional political status quo. Yet it should be noted that China's success in embedding the normative values of "stability" and "noninterference" within the SCO was not an unvarnished good as far as Sino-Russian ties were concerned. At the group's August 2008 summit meeting in Dushanbe, Tajikistan, for instance, Russian president Dmitry Medvedev attempted but ultimately failed to get the SCO's unconditional support for its incursion into Georgia, due to both Chinese and Central Asian misgivings about Moscow's transgression against the principle of "noninterference."[61] For Beijing, such a transgression impinged on its strict Westphalian notions of state sovereignty and its concerns vis-à-vis Xinjiang, Tibet, and Taiwan. In Central Asian capitals, in contrast, the Russo-Georgia war underlined Moscow's heightened predilection to assert its "rights and responsibilities" in its "near abroad."

CRACKS IN THE SINO-RUSSIAN ENTENTE IN CENTRAL ASIA, 2008–2018

Central Asia's apparent receptiveness to China's initiatives was also affected by the region's evolving view of the respective roles of the United States and Russia. The Obama administration's approach to Central Asia as a whole arguably became captive to its dilemmas in Afghanistan. That Washington would view the region through this particular lens was not surprising given

President Obama's "surge" of 30,000 extra US troops into Afghanistan from July 2009 and withdrawal of the bulk of US and NATO forces by 2014. For the Central Asian states that had benefited from the arrival of the United States on the regional stage after 9/11, however, the prospect of declining US attention to the region suggested they would be squeezed between an ascendant Beijing and a weakened yet assertive Russia.

An outgrowth of Washington's Afghan-centric approach was its explicit broadening of the definition of Central Asia to an amorphous "Greater Central Asia" encompassing the five post-Soviet states but also Afghanistan, Pakistan, Iran's Khorasan province, and China's Xinjiang province.[62] For many policy makers and commentators in Washington, much of Central Asia's apparent instability was due to a perceived lack of integration with the liberal global order (understood in both political and economic terms). This became apparent with the administration's launch of its "New Silk Road Initiative" in 2011 that aimed to promote the liberalization of trade, economic cooperation, and "people-to-people" links between Central and South Asia.[63]

This initiative was clearly driven by the Obama administration's desire to set the conditions for the consolidation of an independent and stable Afghanistan after the withdrawal of US troops. Then-undersecretary of state for economic, agricultural and energy affairs, Robert Hormats, noted that the "basis for the 'New Silk Road' vision is that if Afghanistan is firmly embedded in the economic life of the region, it will be better able to attract new investment, benefit from its resource potential, and provide increasing economic opportunity and hope for its people."[64] Key to this vision would be for the United States to assist countries in this region to reorient their key infrastructure (such as highways, railways, telecommunications networks, and so forth) southward and assist in "removing the bureaucratic barriers and other impediments to the free flow of goods and people."[65]

The success of such an initiative would have also ultimately served a wider goal for the United States. The consolidation of a friendly regime in Afghanistan would provide Washington with the capacity to develop north-south linkages between Central and South Asia to compete against the west-east linkages being developed by China and Russia.[66] That would have contributed to an enduring American geopolitical interest: to ensure that no one power or group of powers would dominate Eurasia. Yet the initiative was undermined almost from the start by the administration's shifting priorities, the lack of economic integration among the Central Asian states themselves, and the administration's broader "pivot" or "rebalance" to the Asia-Pacific. The latter, from the perspective of Central Asia's elites, signaled a decline in US attention and commitment to the region from the high point of the early 2000s.[67]

If China's recent initiatives in Central Asia have been based on economic and strategic strength, Russia's have been based on weakness. Indeed, the catalyst for Russia's renewed interest in integration projects in the "post-Soviet space" was the Global Financial Crisis (GFC) of 2008–2009 and its impact on Russia's resource-led economic growth. While Russia's economy had achieved significant levels of growth between 1999 and 2007, with the size of the economy increasing sixfold from US$200 billion to US$1.3 trillion and per capita GDP increasing to US$7,000, it had remained overly reliant on the export of its energy resources particularly to Western Europe.[68] The GFC not only "exposed the limits of this strategy" but the consequent decline in Russia's economic growth prompted Moscow to seek the reinvigoration of integration in the post-Soviet space as a means of weathering the fallout from the crisis.[69] Russian trade with Central Asia had also begun to decline by 2007, with China overtaking Russia as the region's major foreign trade partner.[70] Russia had by the mid-2000s also begun to refocus on its major advantage vis-à-vis Central Asia—its dominant role in the energy sector—as a means of both buttressing its traditional position in the region and its domestic energy demand. Moscow's attempts to maintain control over exports from Central Asia do not stem from a need for extra oil and gas imports "but rather because it wants to re-export petroleum for a profit." Thus, "the Central Asian energy market has in fact sustained the Russian market with low-cost energy while sales to Europe are made at much higher prices."[71] Falling European demand post-GFC however ultimately undermined this strategy.

It is in this context that President Vladimir Putin attempted to reanimate the concept of a "Eurasian Union" (an idea first touted by Kazakhstan's president Nazarbayev in 1994) in a October 2011 op-ed in *Izvestia*, in which he foresaw it as a "supra-national body" that would "coordinate economic and currency policy" as a means of providing a "new post-crisis" development model.[72] Yet Putin's push for the "Eurasian Union" to encompass Russia, Kazakhstan, and Belarus—but also Ukraine—jeopardized the entire project. Ukrainian president Viktor Yanukovych's decision to reject a trade deal with the European Union in favor of joining the Eurasian Union precipitated the domestic upheaval that ultimately toppled him and precipitated Russia's 2014 annexation of Crimea.

The fallout of the Ukrainian crisis for the post-Soviet space has been damaging for Russia's partners in the Eurasian Union. In January 2015, for example, the Kazakh government cut its GDP growth forecast to 1.5 percent from its previous prediction of 4.8 percent, with President Nazarbayev acknowledging the knock-on effects from Western sanctions on Russia and a decline in oil prices.[73] With respect to the former one Kazakh analyst noted that the country's trade with Ukraine prior to the crisis had exceeded its trade with the rest of Central Asia, but bilateral trade subsequently declined by a third from its high of $4 billion per year.[74]

Moscow's partners have also begun to doubt the economic viability of the project with Kazakhstan particularly questioning Moscow's desire to woo states such as Armenia, Kyrgyzstan, and Tajikistan to join. Kazakh analyst Sultan Akimbekov, for instance, has suggested that Moscow is more intent on making a political statement in this instance by making the Eurasian Union into "an 'umbrella' brand to bring together a large number of states in the post-Soviet space" as a means of demonstrating its power and sway over its weaker neighbors rather than forge an effective economic grouping. Additionally, he questions whether the Eurasian Union has in fact brought tangible economic benefits to Kazakhstan since it took effect, noting that while the value of the Kazakhstan's exports to Russia in 2012 was almost exactly the same as four years prior, Kazakhstan has emerged under the Union as "an increasingly important sales market for Russia and Belarus."[75]

Politically, the Ukrainian crisis has also awakened misgivings in both Minsk and Astana as to Putin's ultimate goals. The Russian president's invocation of Moscow's duty to defend ethnic Russians as a justification for annexation of the Crimea has revived concern in Kazakhstan about possible Russian irredentism in the country's northern reaches. Russian rhetoric since has not allayed such concerns either. Putin's statement in August 2014 that not only had the Kazakhs "never had statehood" before the Soviet collapse but that Kazakhstan was part of the *Russki mir* (Russian world), predictably drew the ire of Astana. President Nazarbayev took to state television to assert that "Kazakhstan has a right to withdraw from the Eurasian Economic Union," and that "Kazakhstan will not be part of organizations that pose a threat to our independence."[76] Such Russian posturing also prompted Nazarbayev to announce plans to officially celebrate the founding of Kazakh statehood in 1465 by the Kazakh khans Kerey and Janybek, while the *Astana Times* editorialized on the legitimate history of the statehood of the Kazakh people.[77]

Yet BRI and increasing bilateral economic relationships with Beijing are not unproblematic for much of Central Asia. The former, despite some recent Russian protestations to the contrary, runs counter to Moscow's protectionist agenda within the rubric of its Eurasian Union. This is because Beijing is clearly focused on facilitating freer economic interaction throughout Central Asia. One analyst has remarked in this respect that the real concern for Russia vis-à-vis the SREB is "China's business-is-business approach with others, which differs from both the West's political strings for economic intercourse and Russia's heavy doses of geopolitics."[78] A deeper problem for Beijing, as prominent Chinese international relations scholar Wu Zhengyu notes, is that

> if China increases its economic penetration of Central Asia, that region's countries will likely, in the interest of maintaining political and strategic autonomy, opt to strengthen strategic cooperation with other powers as a means of hedging against political risks caused by economic dependence. . .. Chinese inroads into the Central Asian region may probably create another instance of separation between political relations and economic links.[79]

THE FUTURE OF SINO-RUSSIAN RELATIONS AND BRI: THREE SCENARIOS OF ENTRAPMENT AND ACCOMMODATION

How might the relationship between China and Russia play out in the near future? While much of this chapter has thus far focused on convergent interests and cooperation between the two, here we outline four scenarios that may disrupt the Beijing-Moscow entente. Each has been selected on the basis of their potential to drive one party uncomfortably close to the other, or to exacerbate existing problems in the relationship. This could lead either to entrapment dilemmas for each actor, or prompt weakening of the coincidence of interest that has been influential in shaping their evolving strategic partnership. In brief, these scenarios are heightened by Russia-West animosity; a Russian "opt-out" of BRI, with the attempt to construct its own trade corridors; the spread of significant terrorism in Central Asia; and/or state failure or collapse in that subregion.

Of course, there are many other potential scenarios that could negatively impact upon Sino-Russian relations. But these are instructive in a number of ways. The first risks Russian entrapment in BRI, which would not only compromise Putin's "Euro-Pacific great power" vision,[80] but would effectively turn Russia into a Chinese vassal state, necessary primarily for its ability to serve as a Eurasian trade conduit rather than an "equal partner" in Xi's great power relations model. The second would prompt increased Sino-Russian competition, and potentially fracture the alignment between the two nations. The final two scenarios—linked to transnational security concerns associated with conflict spillover and fragility—would impact on Chinese and Russian domestic and regional concerns. Specifically, they would challenge both China's normative agenda (as reflected in the SCO), as well as its direct security concerns in Xinjiang.

HEIGHTENED RUSSIA-WEST ANIMOSITY

There is a strong likelihood that Russia's attempts to challenge the West—utilizing both traditional and new security instruments—will result in heightened Western pushback, especially from the United States. Already there are signs that this is occurring. In spite of the reticence by the Trump White House to castigate or punish Russia, the United States reacted with a heightened sanctions regime against Moscow after two precipitating events.

The first of these was the poisoning of Sergei and Yulia Skripal in Salisbury during March 2018 with the highly specialized nerve agent Novichok, which prompted a coordinated set of diplomatic expulsions (including sixty by the United States), with the intention of degrading Russia's intelligence-gathering networks in the West.[81] The second was the significant domestic pressure placed on the Trump administration by Congress and the Senate to take a firmer stance on Putin's support for Bashar al-Assad in the Syrian civil war, following the gassing of numerous civilians in the rebel-held town of Douma. The new round of sanctions against oligarchs and companies with ties to Putin—although subsequently curtailed by Trump—prompted an 11 percent drop on the Russian stock market on April 9, 2018. The value of the aluminum company Rusal, controlled by Putin confidante Oleg Deripaska, was halved on the Hong Kong stock exchange, and other leading Russian businesses such as Gazprom also experienced losses.[82] The ruble lost 2.5 percent of its value, which was its largest single-day slide in two years.

Of course, these events tended to overshadow ongoing concerns by senior US and NATO commanders at the deepening of military competition between Russia and the transatlantic West. Whereas Putin had made much in his March 2018 State of the Nation address of a series of new "doomsday" weapons platforms, including a nuclear-powered cruise missile and an unmanned submarine that could carry a nuclear payload to Western ports,[83] Russia has for some time been making both public and private renovations to both its doctrine and force posture with respect to NATO. This included a new nuclear doctrine based on the "escalate to de-escalate" principle,[84] which Western leaders widely viewed as a tacit intention to start conventional wars and then threaten the use of nuclear weapons: a gamble that relied on the assumption that NATO would be too fragmented or lack the political will to wage war in the Baltics or Eastern Europe. Russian attempts to prod NATO have also included the permanent deployment of *Iskander* SRBMs in the Kaliningrad enclave, giving it a significant A2AD capacity that covers the Visegrad states and reaches toward Germany,[85] as well as the deployment of new front-line combat divisions assisted by the Russian military modernization process that has been in progress since 2010.

The risk for Russia is that its increasingly assertive posture toward the West will drive it firmly into the Chinese orbit, an outcome that Kremlin decision makers have been eager to avoid. For its part, Beijing sees no real problem with Moscow adopting the role of chief antagonizer, since this makes Russia take on the increasing burden of security management toward its western flank, and distracts NATO and its allies from Beijing's move into the maritime space in the South China Sea, the Pacific, and the Indian Ocean.

The main problem for Beijing concerns the negative optics of being associated with a bellicose Russian regime. Current indications are that China has decided to wear these costs, as reflected in the very public show of Chinese solidarity with Russia by Wang Yi in April 2018.[86] Yi's expression of a deepened strategic partnership, and hostility toward a unipolar order was in sharp contrast to China's prior irritation at the Russian decision to occupy Crimea in 2013, and its ongoing support for Russian separatists in the Donbas region of Ukraine from 2014 onwards. Beijing had privately reacted angrily to Moscow's moves, believing them to undermine the emphasis both nations had placed on the importance of sovereignty and noninterference in international law.

Viewed in this context, the Chinese pivot on its public support for Russia is a significant development underscoring the strength of the relationship. But as noted earlier, there are few costs from heightened Russia-West animosity for China. The main risks here will be borne by Moscow. The likelihood of a hard US reset on Russia is increasing, and any challenger to Trump in 2020—either Republican or Democrat—will have a strong incentive to run on a "get tough on Russia" foreign policy ticket, either to distance themselves from association with Russian meddling in US elections, or a desire for revenge. If this eventuates, the Kremlin will find itself further starved of access to Western capital, and more reliant on Chinese investment. It will also deepen its reliance on BRI as its main trade corridor to Asia as well as Europe, enmeshing it firmly within a China-centric trading order, and with little prospect of seeking out a viable alternative.

A RUSSIAN "OPT OUT" OF BRI

If increased Russia-West tensions magnify the entrapment risks for Moscow, what of the alternative: a decision by the Kremlin to seek alternatives to BRI? By this we do not mean a Russian pivot back toward Europe and the West, mainly since the political and diplomatic climate is so poisonous as to make this impossible in the short- to medium-term. Instead, we are referring to the various mechanisms the Putin regime has investigated to create its own energy and trade corridors independently of China. And while Beijing has been tolerant of such efforts, publicly stating that the Eurasian Union and BRI are complementary parallel tracks for trade regionalism, it would be concerning to China should Russia be even partially successful in creating trade route independence from Beijing.[87] Here, three of these Russian attempts are worthy of particular note: Russia's keenness to develop a rail network through the Korean peninsula; its desire to develop a pipeline network to India; and ongoing development of an Arctic trade route.

The idea of a Russia-Korea rail corridor, commencing on Russian territory and transiting via the narrow border to the DPRK before terminating at the South Korean port of Pusan, has been proposed several times. Most recently it was linked to a decision in 2013 by then-South Korean president Park Geun-Hye to accelerate the pace of Eurasian cooperation, which resulted in the signing of seventeen cooperation agreements between Russia and South Korea at the St. Petersburg G20 meeting.[88] They incorporated visa exemptions, technology transfers, shipbuilding contracts, and South Korean cooperation in the Russia–North Korea rail and port project linking Khasan and Rajin, with the aim of potentially opening a transport corridor from East Asia to Europe.[89] This would give Russia the potential to pipe gas from the "power of Sibera" network into Asia. An upgrade of Pusan's cargo handling capacity would also permit LNG to be shipped to the region from the main Russian gas development projects on Sakhalin Island. Yet Russia's position here is tenuous. Even ignoring tensions on the Korean peninsula, Russia continually risks being squeezed out between Chinese and US lobbying of Seoul for infrastructure development projects. Second, many of the development efforts on Sakhalin—launched in order to diversify away from pipelines as part of Putin's own "pivot to Asia" launched in 2013—have stalled due to lack of Russian access to capital, and pipeline infrastructure development is heavily reliant on Chinese investment, which provides Beijing with significant leverage on priority areas for the Russian energy sector.

A further attempt by Russia to circumvent BRI can be found in its negotiations with India to deepen cooperation in energy and arms sales. Moscow has frequently invited India to become a full member of the SCO, in an echo of the Russia–India–China "strategic triangle" proposal launched (with little success) by former Russian foreign minister Yevgeny Primakov during the late 1990s. Russia and India have strong military ties dating back to the Cold War era. Around 70 percent of Indian military hardware is Russian, and Russia and India have been participating in the Indra biannual military exercises since 2003.[90] In addition to exercises there have been joint construction projects, such as the (albeit slow and fraught) development of the Sukhoi/HAL Fifth Generation Fighter Aircraft, and a Russian-led initiative to construct about twenty nuclear reactors in India at a cost of US$43 billion.[91] Perhaps the most noteworthy of Russia's efforts here have been proposals for the construction of an oil pipeline and a gas pipeline, which have been mooted since around 2014. However, the routing of the pipeline has run up against Indian strategic concerns, given that Pakistan or Afghanistan (as well as China itself) would be the main transit zones for Russian energy.[92] The proposals have also been outpaced by BRI and activist Chinese trade diplomacy, which by 2018 had effectively captured Pakistan within its network of Beijing's chief economic partners.

The final component of Russian efforts to outflank BRI concerns the development of an Arctic trade route. These have been ongoing for at least a decade, and a variety of attempts to engage Russia in multilateral fora to constrain it—such as by the Nordic Council, for instance—have thus far led to failure. In August 2017, a Russian tanker sailed through the Arctic without an icebreaker for the first time, signifying that the Northern Sea Route (NSR) may well be a viable commercial proposition.[93] In theory, when calculated between Yokohama and Hamburg, the distance between the two is only 7,200 nautical miles, or some 37 percent less than the conventional route via the Suez Canal. Considering also that the US Geological Survey estimates identify the Arctic region as the likely home for over 70 percent of the world's undiscovered natural gas,[94] it is not surprising that Russia has been attempting to exert not only sovereignty claims over much of the region but also proceeding with its own development projects without waiting for the political questions to be resolved. Yet despite a freer hand in development, which is constrained by political factors beyond Moscow's control in the cases of North Korean rail and Indian energy proposals, the costs involved to make the NSR viable remain immense. Infrastructure is either weak or nonexistent, with the exception of Russian military bases. The route will require a large icebreaker fleet for the foreseeable future. And the low cost of oil—with prices almost halving since 2013—means that fuel costs now matter much less than during their height around the time of the Iraq War.

In sum, then, the prospects for a Russian "opt out" of BRI appear on current evidence to be either largely constrained or unworkable. The situation on the Korean peninsula is trending further toward conflict than accommodation, making Russian proposals for trade cooperation involving both the ROK and DPRK seem fantastical. The idea of an energy conduit to India, while consistent with past Kremlin desires for strategic triangles in Eurasia, is reliant on significant Sino-Indian rapprochement that has not transpired. And even in the most promising endeavor of the NSR, Russia faces external challenges that it has little ability to impact, as well as a massive development cost to bring it to fruition. On this basis, it is reasonable to conclude that Chinese trade preferences will continue to shape the agenda for Russia, leaving it in the unenviable position of entrapment in the BRI.

TERRORISM AND/OR STATE FAILURE OR COLLAPSE IN CENTRAL ASIA

A potentially game-changing development for Beijing vis-à-vis BRI and China's diplomacy in Central Asia may stem from either the advent of a major, mass-casualty terrorist attack targeting either Xinjiang or Chinese interests or personnel in Central Asia (including Afghanistan) or a further "colour revolution" or regime collapse in one of the Central Asian capitals. Either of these developments would pose major challenges to Beijing's approach to the region and BRI by forcing it to choose to abide by its normative constructs of "nonintervention" and the "Shanghai Spirit" or pursue means of more directly protecting its core security and economic interests.[95]

After 9/11 Beijing consistently blamed two externally based militant groups—the East Turkistan Islamic Movement (ETIM) and Turkistan Islamic Party (TIP)—for this. ETIM had established a marginal presence in Taliban-controlled Afghanistan but was dealt a major blow when its leader was killed by the Pakistani military in Waziristan in October 2003. TIP emerged as a successor organization in 2005 closely aligned with Al Qaeda. ETIM and TIP both however appear to have had limited capacity to mount operations beyond the "Af-Pak" frontier in this period.

Within Xinjiang itself, Beijing has intensified its use of a variety of repressive and surveillance instruments of an emergent "security state"—including a militarized police presence, the use of facial recognition scanners, regular scanning of electronic devices and social media for "suspect" content, and the detention of thousands of Uyghurs in reeducation camps.[96] Such tactics have reinforced long-standing perceptions of marginalization among Uyghurs in Xinjiang and prompted significant numbers of Uyghurs to migrate abroad, often via insecure and illicit channels. This has created not only a flow of unregulated migration with adverse consequences for the migrants themselves but also security challenges for both China and transit countries as migrants become targets of people smugglers and/or jihadi recruitment efforts.[97]

Despite these efforts the threat posed by Uyghur terrorism has arguably increased. It is clear that TIP now has a significant presence in Syria where it fights alongside Al Qaeda's affiliates Jabhat al Nusra and Jabhat Fateh al-Sham.[98] The group has also enhanced its capabilities to mount operations beyond this geographic base, and was implicated in the suicide attack on the Chinese embassy in Bishkek, Kyrgyzstan, on August 30, 2016, and the 2016 New Year's Eve Istanbul nightclub attack. Additionally, Uyghur militants have also been recruited by the terrorist organization known as the Islamic State in Iraq and Syria (ISIS).[99]

There is thus a self-fulfilling prophecy between Beijing's instrumentalization of the threat of terrorism within its domestic governance of Xinjiang and its foreign policy, which has correlated with an increase in terrorist attacks in Xinjiang itself, and the threat posed by groups such as TIP. Indeed, it is possible that the pervasiveness of the "security state" in Xinjiang and the dynamics of the Syrian crisis have converged to provide the necessary conditions for the consolidation of such transnational links between Uyghur militants and like-minded groups beyond Xinjiang.[100]

This should give pause to Beijing on a number of fronts. The instruments of the "security state" have arguably reinforced long-standing perceptions of marginalization among Uyghurs in Xinjiang, increasing the potential for the radicalization that Beijing has long feared. Meanwhile, BRI's focus on enhancing trans-Eurasian connectivity promises to make China's foreign policy interests truly global in scope. It will do so by enmeshing it in regions and security dilemmas—such as those in the Middle East and South Asia—in which it has historically had both a limited role and a limited capability to influence events.

Regime change or another "colour revolution" in Central Asia would also challenge China's approach. Beijing's response to the overthrow of the Akayev government in Kyrgyzstan and Andijan Incident in Uzbekistan in 2005 was instructive of its status quo-oriented preferences vis-à-vis the forms of government throughout the region. This position has remained firm throughout more recent crises. China, we have also noted, refused to provide either its or the SCO's imprimatur to Russia's military interventions in Georgia in 2008 or Ukraine and the Crimea in 2013–2014. Yet each of these incidents of regime change or Russian intervention has not impinged directly on either China's economic or strategic interests in Central Asia nor its Xinjiang-focused security concerns.

A potential scenario that could alter this would be regime transition and/or failure with the end of President Nursultan Nazarbayev regime in Kazakhstan. Much of the stability engendered in Kazakhstan has been largely down to Nazarbayev's leadership. But in 2018 he celebrated his seventy-eighth birthday, and his continued leadership cannot be relied upon in the long term. Whereas both Putin and Xi doubtless prefer stability over change in Kazakhstan, how to achieve this is a reminder of their divergent preferences. Russia has long mooted the possibility of a move into the north of the country to protect ethnic Russians and secure its interests in ensuring that Kazakhstan remains closely tied to the Eurasian Union in economic terms, and to the CSTO in security affairs. For China, on the other hand, the goal has been to ensure that economic growth—underwritten in the energy and infrastructure sectors by Beijing—will give China not only significant leverage over Kazakhstan but also act as a stabilizing factor on its society.

CONCLUSIONS

While China and Russia both confront potential challenges to their own discrete interests in Central Asia in the short to medium term, it appears that Russia faces the most pressing choices in the context of Sino-Russian relations. Despite official claims of complementarity, Chinese and Russian interests across the security/strategic, economic, and normative domains are pregnant with latent tensions. The most pressing of these concerns each party's competing integration efforts, the EEU and BRI. Moscow's effort in this regard is of minimal attractiveness to many of the post-Soviet states, based as it is on clear and familiar geopolitical gambit to ensure Russian preeminence in its "near abroad."

In this regard, Moscow has already "more or less accepted the defection of the Baltic states" to the Western orbit but is challenged by BRI elsewhere along its Eurasian periphery.[101] BRI, in contrast to Russia's "protective integration," offers a trans-Eurasian or even transcontinental vision of economic and infrastructure connectivity, without an overt geopolitical agenda. Arguably, thus far, Russia has accommodated itself to China's BRI agenda. Yet, the question remains as to whether this is sustainable for Russia in the medium to long term, given the trends of its economic decline and conflictual relations with the United States and much of Europe. In this context, then, continued accommodation of China in Central Asia risks sliding inevitably into entrapment.

NOTES

1. Cheang Ming, "'Best Time in History' for China-Russia Relationship: Xi and Putin Boost Ties," *CNBC*, 4 July 2017, https://www.cnbc.com/2017/07/04/china-russia-ties-reaffirmed-after-xi-jinping-and-vladimir-putin-meet.html. The Sino-Russian "strategic partnership" was established in 1996.
2. Scott W. Harold and Lowell Schwartz, "A Russia-China Alliance Brewing?" *The Diplomat*, 12 April 2013, http://thediplomat.com/2013/04/a-russia-china-alliance-brewing/; Michael J. Green, "Should America Fear a New Sino-Russian Alliance?" *Foreign Policy*, 13 August 2014, http://foreignpolicy.com/2014/08/13/should-america-fear-a-new-sino-russian-alliance/.
3. Bobo Lo, *Axis of Convenience: Moscow, Beijing, and the New Geopolitics*, (Washington, DC: Brookings Institution Press, 2008), p. 5.
4. For example Rajan Menon, "The New Great Game in Central Asia," *Survival*, 45 (2) (2003), pp. 187–204.
5. Glenn H. Snyder, "The Security Dilemma in Alliance Politics," *World Politics*, 36 (4) (1984), p. 461.
6. Ibid., p. 462.
7. Ibid., p. 463.
8. Ibid., pp. 464–465.
9. Ibid., p. 466.
10. Ibid., pp. 466–467.
11. Robert A. Kann, "Alliances versus Ententes," *World Politics*, 28 (4) (1976), p. 612.
12. Ibid., p. 467.

13. Evelyn Goh, "Meeting the China Challenge: The US in Southeast Asian Regional Security Strategies," *Policy Studies*, 16 (Washington DC: East–West Center, 2005), pp. viii and 2–3. See also Evan Medeiros, "Strategic Hedging and the Future of Asia-Pacific Stability," *Washington Quarterly*, 29 (1) (2005), pp. 145–167.

14. Arnold Wolfers, "Alliances," in David L. Sills (ed), *International Encyclopedia of the Social Sciences* (New York: Macmillan, 1968), p. 268.

15. Stephen Walt, *The Origins of Alliances* (Ithaca, NY: Cornell University Press, 1987).

16. Huiyun Feng, *The New Geostrategic Game: Will China and Russia Form an Alliance against the United States?* (Copenhagen: Danish Institute for International Studies, 2015), p. 12.

17. Thomas Wilkins, "Russo-Chinese Strategic Partnership: A New Form of Security Cooperation?" *Contemporary Security Policy*, 29 (2) (2008), pp. 358–383.

18. Glenn H. Snyder, "Alliance Theory: A Neorealist First Cut," *Journal of International Affairs*, 44 (1) (1990), p. 105.

19. Kann, "Alliances versus Ententes."

20. Glenn H. Snyder, *Alliance Politics* (Ithaca: Cornell University Press, 1997), p. 6.

21. Michal D. Ward, *Research Gaps in Alliance Dynamics* (Denver: University of Denver, 1982), p. 7. Emphasis added.

22. Thomas Wilkins, "'Alignment,' not 'Alliance'—the Shifting Paradigm of International Security Cooperation: Toward a Conceptual Taxonomy of Alignment," *Review of International Studies*, 38 (2012), pp. 53–76.

23. Wilkins, "Russo-Chinese Strategic Partnership," p. 363.

24. Wilkins, "'Alignment,' not 'Alliance,'" p. 68.

25. Feng, *The New Geostrategic Game*.

26. Ibid., pp. 14–15.

27. See Matthew Sussex, "The Sino-Russian Entente," *Lowy Interpreter*, 14 September 2018, https://www.lowyinstitute.org/the-interpreter/sino-russian-entente.

28. Enrico Fels, "The Geopolitical Significance of Sino-Russian Cooperation in Central Asia for the Belt and Road Initiative," in Maximillian Mayer (ed), *Rethinking the Silk Road: China's Belt and Road Initiative and Emerging Eurasian Relations* (London: Palgrave, 2018), p. 249.

29. "Analysts: Russia's Vostok-18 Troop Numbers, 'China Alliance' Claims Questionable," *VOA News*, 11 September 2018, https://www.voanews.com/a/russia-china-war-games/4566448.html.

30. Alexander Cooley, *Great Games, Local Rules: The New Great Power Contest in Central Asia* (Oxford: Oxford University Press, 2012), p. 51.

31. Robert A. Donaldson, "Boris Yeltsin's Foreign Policy Legacy," *Tulsa Journal of Comparative and International Law*, 7 (2) (2000), pp. 290–291.

32. Kirill Nourzhanov, "Central Asia's Domestic Stability in Official Russian Security Thinking under Yeltsin and Putin: From Hegemony to Multilateral Pragmatism," in Michael Clarke and Colin Mackerras (eds), *China, Xinjiang and Central Asia: History, Transition and Crossborder Interaction into the 21st Century* (London: Routledge, 2009), pp. 151–152.

33. Diana Digol, "Russia's Foreign Policy in Central Asia: From Yeltsin to Medvedev," in Maria Raquel Friere and Roger Kanet (eds), *Russia and Its Near Neighbours: Identity, Interests and Foreign Policy* (London: Palgrave, 2012), pp. 177–178.

34. *Russia's National Interest and Threats to its Security*, 26 May 1993, cited in Donaldson, "Yeltsin's Foreign Policy Legacy."

35. See for instance Bates Gill, *Rising Star: China's New Security Diplomacy* (Washington DC: Brookings Institution Press, 2010), pp. 22–25.

36. Carnes Lord, Andrew Erickson and Lyle Goldstein, "China Sets Sail," *The American Interest*, 5 (5) (2010), https://www.the-american-interest.com/2010/05/01/china-sets-sail/.

37. Jakub Grygiel has argued, for instance, that the Ming dynasty's ambitious naval missions under Admiral Zheng He between 1405 and 1433, which projected Ming influence throughout South East Asia, the Indian Ocean, and into the Persian Gulf, coincided with the stabilization of its northern frontiers. See Jakub Grygiel, *Great Powers and Geopolitical Change* (Baltimore: Johns Hopkins University Press, 2006), pp. 123–162.

38. On the Sino-Soviet military clashes in the late 1960s see for example, Yang Kuisong, "The Sino-Soviet Border Clash of 1969: From Zhenbao Island to Sino-American Rapprochement," *Cold War History*, 1 (1) (2000), pp. 21–52; and Lyle J. Goldstein, "Return to Zhenbao Island: Who Started Shooting and Why it Matters," *The China Quarterly*, 168 (2001), pp. 985–997.

39. See Michael Clarke, *Xinjiang and China's Rise in Central Asia: A History* (London: Routledge, 2011), pp. 111–112.

40. Feng, *The New Geostrategic Game*, p. 20.

41. For the evolution of the S5 process see Clarke, *Xinjiang and China's Rise in Central Asia*, pp. 127–130.

42. Marc Lanteigne, "*In Media Res*: The Development of the Shanghai Cooperation Organization as a Security Community," *Pacific Affairs*, 79 (4) (2005/06), p. 608.

43. See "PRC: 5-Nation Military Agreement Signed in Shanghai," *Beijing Xinhua*, 26 April in China Daily Report, FBIS-CHI-96-082, 26 April 1996, p. 22; and "Jiang Zemin Meets Kazakh. Kyrgyz, Tajik Presidents," *Beijing Xinhua*, 26 April 1996, in China Daily Report, FBIS-CHI-96-083, 29 April 1996, pp. 15–16.

44. Clarke, *Xinjiang and China's Rise in Central Asia*, p. 129.

45. "'Shanghai Five' Nations Sign Joint Statement," *People's Daily*, 6 July 2000, http://en.people.cn/200007/06/eng20000706_44803.html. On the rise of radical Islamism in Central Asia, see Ahmed Rashid, *Jihad: The Rise of Militant Islam in Central Asia* (Yale University Press, 2002).

46. Flemming Splidsboel Hansen, "The Shanghai Cooperation Organization," *Asian Affairs*, 39 (2) (2008), p. 220.

47. For this trajectory see for instance, David Kerr, "The New Eurasianism: The Rise of Geopolitics in Russia's Foreign Policy," *Europe-Asia Studies*, 47 (6) (1995), pp. 977–988; Graham Smith, "The Masks of Proteus: Russia, Geopolitical Shift and the New Eurasianism," *Transactions of the Institute of British Geographers*, 24(4) (1999), pp. 481–494; and Derek Averre, "Russian Foreign Policy and the Global Political Environment," *Problems of Post-Communism*, 55 (5) (2008), pp. 28–39.

48. Stephen Blank, "Energy, Economics and Security in Central Asia: Russia and its Rivals," *Central Asian Survey*, 14 (3) (1995), pp. 373–406.

49. See for example, Sally N. Cummings, "Happier Bedfellows? Russia and Central Asia under Putin," *Asian Affairs*, 32 (2) (2001), pp. 145–147; and Nourzhanov, "Central Asia's Domestic Stability," pp. 154–155.

50. For Russian arms trade with China in the 1990s see Alexander A. Sergounin and Sergey V. Subbotin, "Russia's Arms Transfers to East Asia in the 1990s," *SIPRI Research Report*, No. 15 (1999), pp. 69–73.

51. See for instance, Martha Brill Olcott, "Pipelines and Pipedreams: Energy Development and Caspian Society," *Journal of International Affairs*, 53 (1) (1999), pp. 305–324; and P. Andrews-Speed, X. Liao and R. Dannruther, *The Strategic Implications of China's Energy Needs* (Oxford: Oxford University Press, 2002), pp. 58–59.

52. Boris Rumer, "The Powers in Central Asia," *Survival*, 44 (3) (2002), pp. 59–60.

53. Nourzhanov, "Central Asia's Domestic Stability," pp. 155.

54. Cooley, *Great Games, Local Rules*, p. 53.

55. Thomas Ambrosio, "Catching the 'Shanghai Spirit': How the Shanghai Cooperation Organization Promotes Authoritarian Norms in Central Asia," *Europe-Asia Studies*, 60 (8) (2008), pp. 1321–1344.

56. Cooley, *Great Games, Local Rules*, p. 82.

57. See Michael Clarke, "Widening the Net: China's Anti-Terror Laws and Human Rights in the Xinjiang Uyghur Autonomous Region," *International Journal of Human Rights*, 14 (4) (2010), pp. 542–558.

58. Zhao Huasheng, "China's Views of and Expectations from the Shanghai Cooperation Organization," *Asian Survey*, 53 (3) (2014), p. 440.

59. Ibid., p. 441.

60. Nicole J. Jackson, "Trans-Regional Security Organisations and Statist Multilateralism in Eurasia," *Europe-Asia Studies*, 66 (2) (2014), p. 185.

61. S. Farizova, "Allies Let Him Down," *Kommersant*, 29 August 2008; and Stephen Blank, "The Shanghai Cooperation Organization and the Georgian Crisis," *China Brief*, 8 (17) (2008), https://jamestown.org/program/the-shanghai-cooperation-organization-and-the-georgian-crisis/.

62. S. Frederick Starr, "A Partnership for Central Asia," *Foreign Affairs*, 84 (4) (2005), pp. 164–178.

63. Joshua Kucera, "The New Silk Road?" *The Diplomat*, 11 November 2011, http://thediplomat.com/2011/11/the-new-silk-road/?allpages=yes.

64. Robert Hormats, "The United States' 'New Silk Road' Strategy: What is it? Where is it Headed?" Address to the SAIS Central Asia-Caucasus Institute and CSIS Forum Washington, DC, 29 September 2011, http://www.state.gov/e/rls/rmk/2011/174800.htm.

65. Ibid.

66. Fatema Sumar, "The New Silk Road in Action," *Foreign Policy*, 29 April 2014, http://foreignpolicy.com/2014/04/29/the-new-silk-road-initiative-in-action/.

67. Joshua Kucera, "Clintons Dubious Plan to Save Afghanistan with a New Silk Road," *The Atlantic*, 2 November 2011, http://www.theatlantic.com/international/archive/2011/11/clintons-dubious-plan-to-save-afghanistan-with-a-new-silk-road/247760/.

68. Andrei Tsygankov, "Russia's Power and Alliances in the 21st Century," *Politics*, 30 (4) (2010), p. 45.

69. Andrej Krickovic, "Imperial Nostalgia or Prudent Geopolitics? Russia's Efforts to Reintegrate the Post-Soviet Space in Geopolitical Perspective," *Post-Soviet Affairs*, 30 (6) (2014), pp. 509–510.

70. Niklas Swanstrom, *China and Greater Central Asia: A New Frontier?* (Central Asia-Caucasus Institute, Silk Road Paper, December 2011), pp. 48–49.

71. Niklas Swantsrom, "Central Asia and Russian Relations: Breaking Out of the Russian Orbit?" *Brown Journal of World Affairs*, 19 (1) (2012), p. 108.

72. Gleb Bryanski, "Russia's Putin says Wants to Build 'Eurasian Union,'" *Reuters*, 3 October 2011, http://www.reuters.com/article/2011/10/03/us-russia-putin-eurasian-idUSTRE7926ZD20111003.

73. Joanna Lillis, "Kazakhstan: Astana Faces Up to Economic Doom and Gloom," *Eurasianet*, 19 January 2015, http://www.eurasianet.org/node/71671. For the government's 2014 economic forecast, see "Negative Impacts from Urkaine Related Sanctions," Embassy of the Republic of Kazakhstan, September 19, 2014, http://www.kazakhembassy.in/index.php/Latest-NEWS/negative-impacts-from-ukraine-related-sanctions.html.

74. Cited in Maksyn Bugriy, "Nursultan Nazarbayev's Ukraine Diplomacy," *Eurasia Daily Monitor*, 12 (8), 14 January 2015, http://www.jamestown.org/regions/centralasia/single/?tx_ttnews[tt_news]=43400&tx_ttnews[backPid]=53&cHash=25c95d26d026275f740b4c869597462b#.VPeMeVO5-X0.

75. Sultan Akimbekov, "Needless Rush: Another Look at Eurasian Integration," *Russia in Global Affairs*, 21 March 2014, http://eng.globalaffairs.ru/Needless-Rush-16499. A similar critique has been offered by other Kazakh observers, see Alibek Konkanov and Bakhytzhan Kurnanov, "No Reason to Rush into a Eurasian Economic Union," *East Asia Forum*, 24 May 2014, http://www.eastasiaforum.org/2014/05/24/no-reason-to-rush-into-a-eurasian-economic-union.

76. Anna Dolgov, "Kazakhs Worried after Putin Questions History of Country's Independence," *The Moscow Times*, 1 September 2014, http://www.themoscowtimes.com/news/article/kazakhs-worried-after-putin-questions-history-of-country-s-independence/506178.html; and Erica Marat, "How Russki Mir Enters Central Asian Politics," *Central Asia-Caucasus Analyst*, 22 January 2015, http://new.cacianalyst.org/publications/analytical-articles/item/13130-how-russkii-mir-enters-central-asian-politics.html.

77. "Kazakh Statehood is 550 Years Old: Nazarbayev," Embassy of the Republic of Kazakhstan, 23 October 2014, http://www.kazakhembassy.in/index.php/Latest-NEWS/kazakh-statehood-is-550-years-old-nazarbayev.html; and "Why Celebrate 550 Years of Kazakh Statehood?" *The Astana Times*, 28 January 2015, http://www.astanatimes.com/2015/01/celebrate-550-years-kazakh-statehood/.

78. Yu Bin, "China-Russia Relations: Putin's Glory and Xi's Dream," *Comparative Connections* (January 2014), p. 6.

79. Wu Zhengyu, "Toward 'Land' or Toward 'Sea'? The High-Speed Railway and China's Grand Strategy," *Naval War College Review*, 66 (3) (2013), p. 61.

80. For Putin's speech on this topic, delivered at the plenary session of the St Petersburg International Economic Forum in 2013, see Vladimir Putin, "Speech at

the St Petersburg Forum Plenary Session," 21 June 2013, http://en.kremlin.ru/events/president/news/18383. See also Fiona Hill and Bobo Lo, "Putin's Pivot: Why Russia is looking East," *Brookings Institution*, 31 July 2013, http://www.brookings.edu/research/opinions/2013/07/31-russia-china-pacific-pivot-hill.

81. Emily Tankin, "Russia Promises Retaliation after Western Expulsions," *Foreign Policy*, 26 March 2018, http://foreignpolicy.com/2018/03/26/russia-promises-retaliation-after-western-expulsions/.

82. Ben Chapman and Oliver Carrol, "Russia Stock Market Crashes 11% after US Imposes Sanctions on Oligarchs Linked to Kremlin," *The Independent*, 9 April 2018, https://www.independent.co.uk/news/business/news/russia-stock-market-latest-updates-us-sanctions-oligarchs-kremlin-putin-deripaska-a8296536.html.

83. Jeffrey Lewis, "Putin's Nuclear-Powered Cruise Missile is Bigger than Trump's," *Foreign Policy*, 1 March 2018, http://foreignpolicy.com/2018/03/01/putins-nuclear-powered-cruise-missile-is-bigger-than-trumps/.

84. Bruno Tertrais, "Russia's Nuclear Policy: Worrying for the Wrong Reasons," *Survival*, 20 March 2018, https://www.tandfonline.com/doi/full/10.1080/00396338.2018.1448560.

85. Bruce Jones, "Russian Duma Confirms Islander-M Kaliningrad Deployment," *Janes Defense Weekly*, 8 February 2018, http://www.janes.com/article/77745/russian-duma-confirms-iskander-m-kaliningrad-deployment.

86. "Wang Yi Holds Talks with Foreign Minister Sergei Lavrov of Russia," press release, Embassy of the PRC in Finland, 5 April 2018, http://www.chinaembassy-fi.org/eng/zxxx/t1548987.htm.

87. See for example, Jeanne Wilson, "The Eurasian Economic Union and China's Silk Road: Implications for Russian-Chinese Relations," *European Politics and Society*, 17 (1) (2016), pp. 120–122.

88. Matthew Sussex, "Russia's Asian Rebalance," *Lowy Institute for International Policy*, 2016, p. 13, https://www.lowyinstitute.org/publications/russia-s-asian-rebalance.

89. Ibid.

90. Ibid., p. 5.

91. "Going Nuclear: Russia and India Agree to Build 12 Power Reactors by 2035," *Russia Today*, 11 December 2014, http://www.rt.com/business/213411-going-nuclear-russia-india/.

92. Nicholas Trickett, "Can Russia Piggyback on China's 'String of Pearls'?" *The Diplomat*, 9 November 2017, https://thediplomat.com/2017/11/can-russia-piggyback-on-chinas-string-of-pearls/.

93. Patrick Barkham, "Russian Tanker Sails through Arctic without Icebreaker for First Time," *Guardian*, 24 August 2017, https://www.theguardian.com/environment/2017/aug/24/russian-tanker-sails-arctic-without-icebreaker-first-time.

94. Kathrin Hille, "Russia's Arctic Obsession," *Financial Times*, 21 October 2016, https://ig.ft.com/russian-arctic/.

95. That this type of scenario has been actively considered was affirmed by senior Chinese academics and think tank experts focused on Sino-Central Asian in discussions with the author in Shanghai, 25 March 2016.

96. For detailed accounts of the "security state" in Xinjiang, see Julia Famularo, "How Xinjiang Has Transformed China's Counterterrorism Policies," *The National Interest*, 26 August 2015, http://nationalinterest.org/feature/how-xinjiang-has-transformed-china% E2%80%99s-counterterrorism-13699; and Josh Chin and Clément Bürge, "12 Days in Xinjiang: How China's Surveillance State Overwhelms Daily Life," *The Wall Street Journal*, 17 December 2017, https://www.wsj.com/articles/twelve-days-in-xinjiang-how-chinas-surveillance-state-overwhelms-daily-life-1513700355.

97. See Raffaello Pantucci, "Uyghur Terrorism in the Fractured Middle East," in Michael Clarke (ed), *Terrorism and Counter-Terrorism in China: Domestic and Foreign Policy Dimensions* (London: Hurst/Oxford University Press, forthcoming August 2018).

98. For analysis of the Syria connection see Ibid.; and Michael Clarke, "Uyghur Militants in Syria: The Turkish Connection," *Terrorism Monitor*, 14 (3) (4 February 2016), https://jamestown.org/program/uyghur-militants-in-syria-the-turkish-connection/#.VrRpdLIrKUk.

99. Michael Clarke, "China's Terrorism Problem Goes Global," *The Diplomat*, 7 September 2016, https://thediplomat.com/2016/09/chinas-terrorist-problem-goes-global/.

100. See Michael Clarke, "Xinjiang and the Transnationalization of Uyghur Terrorism: Cracks in the New Silk Road?" *The ASAN Forum*, 10 February 2017, http://www.theasanforum.org/xinjiang-and-the-trans-nationalization-of-uyghur-terrorism-cracks-in-the-new-silk-road/.

101. Wilson, "The Eurasian Economic Union and China's Silk Road," p. 123.

Chapter 4

Combating the Three Evil Forces on the Silk Road

Uyghur Terrorism and Chinese Security Diplomacy

Stefanie Kam Li Yee

This chapter demonstrates that China's Belt and Road Initiative (BRI) has presented China with economic opportunities, as well as security challenges, including terrorism risks. A number of countries along the BRI suffer from long-standing problems of militancy and terrorist attacks. For instance, insurgent violence in the Afghanistan-Pakistan border has made Chinese critical infrastructure vulnerable to attacks. To manage these security challenges, Beijing has sought to contain the Uyghurs and pursued unilateral, bilateral, and multilateral diplomatic security approaches in the Middle East, and Southeast Asia, and in the direct peripheries of Central Asia and South Asia, where it is concerned about the spread of the three evils (terrorism, separatism, and extremism).

Counterterrorism cooperation has emerged as one such important tool for safeguarding the security there and for disrupting the infiltration of militants into Xinjiang. To prevent the rise of Uyghur ethno-nationalist sentiments, Beijing has also tried to insulate the Uyghurs from Central Asia. Beijing has also invested in stabilizing missions and counterterrorism cooperation in regions farther afield. This chapter unravels the entanglements between domestic security challenges and international developments in the BRI and the diplomatic management strategy China has adopted in dealing with security threats in each region.

The chapter begins by first exploring the terrorism threat posed by the Uyghurs in Xinjiang, followed by the rising importance of counterterrorism to China's security and foreign policy. This will be followed by a discussion on the role of Chinese security diplomacy as a management strategy to deal with these threats, serving the purpose of blocking new and existing forms of Uyghur transnational linkages from being cultivated to pursue what China sees as the "three evils." At the same time, I show how Beijing has managed to exercise its security diplomacy in the Middle East and Southeast Asian regions, both of which also feature in the BRI, so as to enhance its economic and political leverage pertinent to its BRI.

CHINA AND THE TERRORISM THREAT

The security challenges China faces today are distinct from the security issues of the past. This is particularly so since the end of the Cold War in 1991 and the dissolution of the Soviet Union. The newly independent Central Asian republics also saw a rising sense of national fervor, which spread to Xinjiang. Along with that, decades of liberalization policies of the post-Mao era, since 1978, have also led to an increase in cross-border commerce and mobility of people. This created more opportunities for transnational bonds and foreign support for Uyghurs to be cultivated. The nexus between what is considered internal and external threats has concomitantly become increasingly blurred, and the emergence of transnational bonds has become a force multiplier on the international stage, particularly given how China is situated amid a "terrain of hazards."[1] In this iteration, security challenges occurring in the international system can be conceived along the lines of four rings of "threat," namely threats to political stability and territorial integrity from internal and external threats (including disaffected minority groups), second, threats derived from its neighbors with whom China shares borders (Central Asia and South Asia), third, threats from China's connection geographically with its geopolitical regions (Middle East, Southeast Asia), and fourth, threats from the world beyond China's immediate neighborhood. While the first two arise from the domestic-regional nexus, the second two arise out of the regional-global nexus. From this perspective, it can be argued that the BRI has the potential to reconstruct the range of threats such that threats embedded within the domestic-regional nexus and regional-global nexus have the potential to overlap and affect one another.

The Internal-external Security Nexus

The internal-external security nexus can be defined as the relationship between internal and external security that have a transboundary dimension.[2] In the case of Xinjiang's Uyghurs, the ethnic and religious linkages with Central Asians in the former, and Muslims in South Asia, have served as a mobilizing force animating their territorial claims for an independent

East Turkestan. Hence, the issue of Uyghur terrorism is tied to the external security of its regional neighborhood. At the heart of this internal-external security nexus lies Xinjiang, home to the Uyghur Muslim ethnic minority, and a region with a history of territorial and cultural separation. China sees Xinjiang as a "core interest" and the Uyghurs as an important source of this security challenge. On the one hand, following the opening up of China's borders in 1978, and since the late 1990s, as a result of China's efforts to develop the west, cross-border mobility and trade ties with its Central Asian and South Asian neighbors have increased. On the other hand, in the 1990s, the fall of the Soviet Union led to a rise in nationalism in the neighboring Central Asian republics and a growth of political movements by Uyghurs in Xinjiang.[3]

The increased nationalism also coincided with religious fervor, a transnational development which saw "an increased pressure of religious sectarianism in Central Asia and the transfer of Middle Eastern style political/religious dilemmas direct to China's borders."[4] This development in particular was political Islam. In 1990, a major riot occurred in Baren Township, Akto County, in which the perpetrators attacked the local police establishments under the banner of Islam. The riots were believed to have been instigated by Soviet-trained Uyghurs who fought during the Soviet-Afghan war.[5] The 1990s were characterized by a number of major incidents of unrest, including the 1997 Yining riots. Official reports put the death toll at nine, while dissident reports estimated the number killed at more than 100 and even as many as 167. In recent years, terrorist attacks in Xinjiang have persisted. These include a knife attack at Kunming railway station in March 2014, in which twenty-nine people were killed and over a hundred injured, and six bomb and knife attack at the Urumqi South Railway Station in Xinjiang in April 2014, which left at least three dead and injured seventy-nine people. In May 2014, thirty-one people were killed when five people in two cars drove into a crowd at a busy market in Urumqi. On July 28, nearly 100 people were reportedly killed in an attack by knife-wielding Uighurs on government offices and a police station in Elixku. On September 21, 2014, fifty people were killed in a series of attacks, including at least six people who were killed in series of bomb blasts in Luntai County, Southwest of the regional capital, Urumqi. In spite of heightened security measures in the region, the violence continued into 2015. In September 2015, knife-wielding assailants carried out an attack at the Sogan colliery in Aksu, Xinjiang, killing at least fifty people, including five policemen.

Following the 9/11 attacks in the United States, China's National Defense White Paper in 2002 devoted an entire section to the terror threat. The report identified terrorism as a top-ranking security issue, specifically pointing to the restive Western Xinjiang region, where separatists want to create an independent "East Turkistan." In portraying China too, as a victim of terrorism, the White Paper said that "The 'East Turkistan' terrorist forces are a serious threat to the security of the lives and property of the people of all China's ethnic groups." The report disclosed that various terrorist activities have been underway in Xinjiang since the 1950s and lists 200 "terrorist" incidents carried out by Uyghur separatists since 1990.[6] Movements like the Falungong and the Tibetan separatists as well as the Uyghur lobbyists in Germany, Japan, and the United States have featured in international media and this has enhanced their visibility to the outside world.[7] Owing to the Chinese government's intermittent control over Xinjiang in the past as well, the proximity to regions with problems of militancy and terrorism, China is keenly aware of the combined challenges of ethno-nationalist fervor, religious extremism, in particular political Islam, and militancy in its neighboring Central Asian and South Asian countries in challenging the homogeneity and territorial integrity of the state.

THE SECURITY-ECONOMIC NEXUS

Since the BRI was announced in 2013, China has pushed forward in its plans to enhance trade and investment interconnectivity between China and Europe, Central Asia, the Middle East, Africa, and South Asia. The Silk Road Economic Belt component of the project focuses on connecting China to Europe through Central Asia and Russia, the Persian Gulf through Central Asia and Southeast Asia, South Asia, and the Indian Ocean. The Maritime Silk Road focuses on utilizing sea routes and Chinese coastal ports to link China with Europe via the South China Sea and Indian Ocean, and the South Pacific Ocean through the South China Sea. Official discourse points to development plans along the trade route aimed at improving connectivity in the areas of "policy, infrastructure, trade, currency and people."[8] The document further states, "In advancing the Belt and Road initiative, China will fully leverage the comparative advantage of its various regions, adopt a proactive strategy of further opening up, strengthen interaction and cooperation among the eastern and western and central regions, and comprehensively improve the openness of the Chinese economy." Apart from these goals, China hopes to facilitate trade and investment, develop infrastructure, strengthen people-to-people relations, and enhance financial integration.

Despite an official BRI plan in place, many have pointed out the open-ended nature of the project, which lacks a clear or fixed geographical scope. Six land corridors are identified in the 2015 National Development and Reform Commission report, while the Maritime Silk Road is said to encompass two routes, one through the South China Sea and the Indian Ocean to ports in the Mediterranean, and another through the South China Sea to the South Pacific. Given the high stakes in these Chinese investment projects, which include the Sino-Pakistan corridor (estimated at US$46 billion); the Ogaden Basin Gas Pipeline in Ethiopia (estimated at US$5 billion); and the Mes Aynak copper mine in Afghanistan (estimated at US$3 billion), there is a need for China to become more invested in the security landscape along these critical regions. To overcome these challenges, China has also engaged nonstate security actors in the form of private security companies to manage security threats. An example is Frontier Services Group, a company that announced in mid-March 2017 that the firm was planning to build two operation bases in Xinjiang and Southwest China's Yunnan Province.[9] The increasing presence of Chinese companies abroad, compounded by the fact that Chinese security service companies lack advanced management theories, has made it imperative for China to look to their more well-trained Western counterparts in the arena of security to manage risks in areas where Chinese firms operate. During the 2000s, a number of incidents involving Chinese nationals killed by terrorists abroad placed Chinese authorities on alert. Chinese nationals have also been killed in a number of terrorist attacks linked to Al Qaeda and the Islamic State (ISIS) terrorist group. The following are a list of terrorist attacks in Pakistan, Afghanistan, Jordan, South Sudan, and Kyrgyzstan where Chinese citizens, businesses, peacekeepers, and government facilities have been killed during the years 2004 to 2016.

On May 3, 2004, a car bomb attack in southwest Pakistan killed three Chinese engineers who were working on a project to develop port facilities in the city of Gwadar[10]; on June 10, 2004, eleven Chinese construction workers were shot dead in Afghanistan. The Chinese nationals were working for the China Raiway Shisju group and were working to help build the Kunduz-Baghlan road; on October 9, 2003, two Chinese engineers, Wang Peng and Wang Ende, were taken hostage by a group of terrorists led by a former Guantanamo Bay detainee Abdullah Mehsud, a member of the Pakistani Taliban. Following days of failed negotiations, a military intervention by the Pakistani military resulted in one release and one death; on November 9, 2005, members of Al Qaeda in Iraq carried out a series of coordinated bomb attacks on three luxury hotels in Amman, Jordan. Among the sixty others who were killed, three were academics from China's National Defence University[11]; in February 2006, three Chinese engineers were killed by gunmen in Pakistan's troubled southwestern province of Balochistan. The attacks were condemned by the Pakistani government as an "act of terrorism" and unconfirmed reports say the Baloch Liberation Army claimed responsibility for the attacks[12]; on July 8, 2007, unidentified gunmen killed three Chinese workers and wounded another near Peshawar in what Pakistani officials said was a terrorist attack in retaliation for the bloody siege at the Red Mosque in Islamabad[13]; on July 11, 2016, two Chinese UN peacekeepers were killed in Juba (South Sudan); on August 30, 2016, a suicide bomb attack at the Chinese Embassy in the Kyrgyz capital of Bishkek killed the bomber himself and wounded three others;

on May 30, 2016, an IED attack by the Sindhudesh Revolutionary Army severely injured a Chinese engineer in Karachi (Pakistan); on November 20, 2015, three Chinese executives were killed in Bamako (Mali) after an attack by the Islamist militant groups Al Mourabitoun and Al Qaeda in the Islamic Maghreb at the Radisson Blu hotel.

THE AL QAEDA AND ISIS THREAT

Although the threat from transnational terrorist groups like Al Qaeda and ISIS is, in comparison to the threat in Western countries like the United States and the United Kingdom, less severe in China, China is particularly concerned about the ties between Uyghurs and Al Qaeda. In recent years, China has also expressed concerns about the threat of Chinese fighter returnees that have fought on the battlefields in Syria and Iraq alongside ISIS.[14]

In recent years, China has also been featured in ISIS propaganda. In September 2015, in the eleventh issue of its English magazine *Dabiq*, ISIS identified Chinese and Norwegian hostages and gave a Telegram number for individuals to pay their ransoms. In November 2015, The Turkistan Islamic Party (TIP) released the eighteenth issue of its magazine *Islamic Turkistan*, through the Global Islamic Media Front. In February 2016, Al-Bayan Radio of the Islamic State (IS) began issuing its daily news bulletins in Uyghur, with the IS adding yet again to the languages in which it makes its propaganda available. In July 2016, Al Qaeda leader Ayman al-Zawahiri addressed Muslims in the Xinjiang Uyghur Autonomous Region of northwestern China in the ninth episode of his "Islamic Spring" series, promoting their cause and urging them to have patience amid the "long battle" with the "atheist Chinese occupiers." On August 30, 2016, a suicide bombing attack occurred at the Chinese embassy in Bishkek, Kyrgyzstan, killing the perpetrator and wounding six others—three of whom were Kyrgyrz nationals working at the embassy and the other three Chinese nationals working at the embassy. Although no group stepped forward to claim responsibility for the attack, on September 6, 2016, the Kyrgyz government revealed that the attack was a joint operation between the TIP-L and Kateebat at Tawhid wal Jihad (KTJ/"Battalion for Monotheism and Jihad"). Authorities identified the suicide bomber as an ethnic Uyghur of Tajik nationality by the name of Zoir Khalilov. The attacks raised concerns about the probable presence of Uyghur militant elements in the country. In December 2016, Fursan al-Sham, a jihadi media outlet operated by foreign fighters in Syria, published a story tracing the journey of Uyghur fighters from China to Syria.

Throughout 2015 to 2016, TIP continued to release a steady stream of videos containing footage of its fighters' participation in battles in Syria, including in Aleppo, Lattakia, and Hama. In January 2016, TIP also released a visual chant honoring its dead fighters and promoting martyrdom in battle. In July 2016, TIP released a few propaganda videos in Russian, calling on Muslims across the world to join the jihad in Khurasan, Syria, and Chechnya to "protect fenceless Muslims in these lands from the aggression of the infidels." Statements released by TIP highlight the sense of moral outrage felt by perceived injustices experienced by members of their community and are frequently portrayed as a war waged on aggressors in defense of Islam. Such propaganda statements released by TIP reflect the growing alignment with radical Islamist rhetoric by hardline Uyghur separatists. On February 27, 2017, ISIS' media office in Al-Furat Province released a video featuring dozens of Uyghur fighters vowing to conquer the United States, China, and Russia. The video, which was posted on Nasher News, a pro-ISIS Telegram channel, also featured Uyghur children receiving military training, witnessing the execution of and themselves executing prisoners accused of spying, and warning the Jews that the army of Muhammad will return. In a March 2017 video, ISIS also pledged to "shed blood like rivers" in attacks against Chinese targets.

CHINA'S INTERNATIONAL SECURITY DIPLOMACY

Over the last decade, China has advanced a more comprehensive and broader security framework to deal with a range of traditional and nontraditional security threats, while firmly adhering to the principles of state sovereignty, noninterference, and nonuse of force. Apart from protecting Xinjiang from the threat of the three evils as part of its core interests, in its 2015 military strategy white paper, China stated that it would prioritize the role of Chinese "overseas interests" (海外利益) as one of the People's Liberation Army (PLA)'s strategic tasks.[15] This was reinforced at the time of the 2011 Arab Springs uprising, with China's evacuation of thousands of Chinese citizens in Libya and Egypt.[16] In April 2015, China sent a frigate and evacuated several hundred Chinese nationals and foreign nationals from war-torn Yemen.[17] The focus on overseas interests and particularly in evacuation missions indicates China's cognizance of the need to secure Chinese nationals abroad from the transnational threat of terrorism, particularly in unstable regions.

Although China enacted its antiterrorism law in December 2015 which permits the Chinese PLA to be deployed overseas for counterterrorism purposes, over the last decade, China has not held back from participating in global security missions in countries with which it has vested economic and strategic interests, with the added benefit of portraying itself as a "responsible stakeholder" in international affairs.[18] In December 2008, China sent its naval task forces to the Gulf of Aden for the first time to protect its ships against piracy. Since then, it has played an active role in antipiracy missions in the Gulf of Aden. The announcement to build military supporting facilities in Djibouti came in May 2015 and in February 2016 construction commenced. The base is touted as China's first overseas military base meant to support antipiracy efforts in the region. The base is strategically located, with its position opposite the oil-rich Gulf states and a large number of state-owned Chinese enterprise in the region.

CHINA'S SECURITY DIPLOMACY

The earlier section reflected on the role of terrorism on China's internal security, and articulated China's global security diplomacy in response to increasingly transnational challenges which have emerged at the intersection of economic and security interests. It also offered a conceptual definition of the internal-external nexus to reinforce this empirical point of the nature and scope of the terrorism threat on China's security, whether in the form of attacks to Chinese nationals abroad, in the form of transnational ethnic alliances between Uyghur separatists and militants overseas, or regional militants conspiring to carry out attacks on the Mainland and in Xinjiang. As a consequence of this, China has taken action not just at home but also on the international front. Within regional security organizations, China has worked to establish and develop the security and antiterrorism components of the Shanghai Cooperation Organization (SCO), a loose alliance comprising China, Russia, and four other Central Asian States. Born in 1996 as the "Shanghai Group," a body to stabilize and demilitarize shared borders, the SCO, as the organization has called itself since 2001, has progressively been tasked with a larger agenda starting with the promotion of regional trade. While China played a critical role in developing the SCO's contents and structure, it could be argued that this has been done to make the SCO more active in standing against threats emanating from "terrorism, separatism and extremism," and to ensure that China's continued political leverage in neighboring Central Asia and South Asia is seen as wholly constructive. China's growing role in peacekeeping missions in Africa and antipiracy missions in the Gulf of Aden, as well as its recent construction of military supporting facilities in Djibouti reflects the increasing use of security diplomacy in addressing the evolving threat landscape.

China's Role in UN-led Counterterrorism Initiatives

China's active participation in UN-led platforms to combat global terrorism sends a signal that China recognizes the UN as a legitimate platform for advancing international counterterrorism cooperation. The position paper of the PRC at the seventy-first session of the UN General Assembly affirms the stance China takes in standing "for a holistic approach in combating terrorism which addresses both the symptoms and root causes" and the importance of the UN and its Security Council in playing a "lead role in international counter-terrorism cooperation and [pushing] for the establishment of the broadest counter-terrorism front, enhance[ing] coordination and build[ing] consenses, and forg[ing] greater synergy for international counter-terrorism efforts . . . in accordance with the purposes and principles of the UN Charter, and fully implement relevant Security Council resolutions and the UN Global Counter-Terrorism Strategy."[19] Recognizing the importance of the UN as a platform also provided China with the opportunity to take its domestic security concerns to a more global level. Ostensibly, this has benefitted China in its efforts to strengthen its image as a credible partner in counterterrorism engagements, balancing the influences of US-led forces in the war on terrorism and in the past has also leveraged the UN as a platform for legitimizing China's domestic crackdown on Uyghurs in Xinjiang under the framework of counterterrorism. This next section will proceed to explain the approach China has taken toward its Central Asian region and South Asian region with respect to its security diplomacy.

Central Asian Security Diplomacy

Today, a continuing source of regional concern for Beijing is the existence of pan-Turkic nationalism and support for the Xinjiang separatist movement by the Turkic-speaking Uyghur diaspora living in Central Asia. A significant Uyghur community resides in Central Asia, with the largest Uyghur population in Kazakhstan and the smallest in Tajikistan. The first wave of Uyghur migration dates back to 1918 during the Bolshevik Revolution, and in the late 1920s and 1930s Uyghur and Kazakh families emigrated from USSR to China to escape the Stalinist regime "against the kulaks or prosperous peasants along with many other Turkic peoples across Central Asia." In the 1930s the rise in Soviet influence in Xinjiang saw many Uyghurs and Kazaks moving into Xinjiang. The largest-scale migration of Uyghurs to Central Asia was during the 1950s to early 1960s a period in which ties between China and Soviet Union deteriorated. There is a significant Uyghur presence in Kazakhstan, Kyrgyzstan, Uzbekistan, and Turkmenistan and a small Uyghur community in the capital city of Dushanbe. As China seeks to increase economic and political ties with Central Asia, the stability in Xinjiang is key to cementing China-Central Asian ties.[20]

A particular source of economic interdependency between China and Central Asia is the Kazakhstan-China energy pipeline, which connects the

Caspian region to Xinjiang, and is a source of energy transport to China that is crucially linked to its national security.[21] This reliance on strategic infrastructure such as pipelines from Central Asia however has also exposed Chinese critical infrastructures to attacks. As the suicide bombing attack on August 2016 on the Chinese Embassy in Bishkek, believed to have been perpetrated by Uyghurs, demonstrated, Chinese assets and personnel in Central Asia are potential targets of politically motivated attacks.[22] Therefore, Beijing has a vested interest in the stabilization of the Central Asian regimes.

At the domestic level, China has attempted to cut off Uyghur ties to Central Asia through close cooperation with its neighbors, both bilaterally and multilaterally through the SCO, to monitor Uyghur advocate groups and organizations in Central Asia.[23] At the international level, China has attempted to shape the Central Asian government's perceptions of the threat and to ensure that they have zero tolerance for Uyghur mobilization. China's active presence in Central Asia, primarily through the framework of the SCO can also be said to be an exercise of China's "Empty Fortress" strategy, based on the understanding that the country's westernmost regions have poor defense against external threats and are equally as vulnerable to internal dissent and external threats.[24]

SCO

The SCO has allowed China to accrue further diplomatic capital through increasing its economic and security cooperation with the Central Asian republics.[25] The history of the SCO dates back to April 1996, when China, Russia, Kazakhstan, Kyrgyzstan, and Tajikistan signed the Treaty on Deepening Military Trust in Border Regions. This agreement and a similar 1997 treaty reduced military forces and activities along mutual borders, against the backdrop of Sino-Soviet competition.[26] With increasing multi-polarization and economic and information globalization, such practical cooperation transitioned into more expansive goals, culminating in the 2001 Declaration of the Shanghai Organization, which formally established the SCO and added Uzbekistan as a member. The creation of the SCO in 2001 reflects the growing strategic importance of Xinjiang and Central Asia to China in light of overlapping diplomatic, economic, and security interests. The SCO has consistently advocated the need for respect for sovereignty and territorial integrity, as well as noninterference, three of China's core political principles.[27] The SCO's overall mandate is to counter what China deems the three evils—terrorism, religious fundamentalism, and separatism and to serve as a regional security cooperation mechanism for China to cooperate with the member states across Central Asia on a range of security issues.

China's Regional Anti-Terrorism Structure

The Regional Anti-Terrorism Structure (RATS) was created in 2001 as a security organ of the SCO. Since its institution in 2004, the primary purpose of RATS is to coordinate the counterterrorism efforts of SCO members. A regional security pact designed to facilitate cross-border policies combating transnational threats, the RATS is an extension of Chinese interests in Central Asia.[28] The fact that it is based on the policy of noninterference and disavowal of military alliances reflects the role RATS plays in furthering Chinese diplomacy inasmuch as it serves a platform to enhance its security interests.[29] Since the SCO came into existence in 2001, there have been a number of specific terrorism-focused SCO documents which form the legal basis for RATS. These include the Agreement Between the Member States of the SCO on the Regional Anti-Terrorist Structure (signed on June 7, 2002), the Agreement on the Database of the Regional Anti-Terrorist Structure of the SCO (June 28, 2004), the Concept of Cooperation Between Member States in Combating Terrorism, Extremism, and Separatism (June 5, 2005), the Protocol on Amendments to the Agreement Between Member States of the SCO on the Regional Anti-Terrorist Structure (August 28, 2008), and the Convention on Counter-Terrorism of the SCO (June 16, 2009).

South Asian Security Diplomacy

Unlike Central Asia, where the threat for Beijing lies in the existence of pan-Turkic nationalism and support for the Xinjiang separatist movement by the Turkic-speaking Uyghur diaspora living there, South Asian countries, notably Pakistan and Afghanistan, do not have any significant indigenous Turkic Muslims. However political Islam is seen as an important social and political force. Notably, Pakistan, with whom the Xinjiang region shares a 520-kilometer border, has been a hotbed for militant activity during the 2000s, most notably the Tehriki-Taliban Pakistan. The construction of the Karakoram Highway in the 1970s also provided a route through which trade could pass through from the Punjab province of Pakistan to the Khunjerab Pass, into China's Xinjiang Uyghur Autonomous Region.[30] The increased commerce between Pakistan and China was followed by an increase in transnational mobility between Xinjiang's Uyghurs to Pakistan and Pakistanis to Xinjiang. There were rising concerns that some Uyghurs had traveled to Pakistan for religious schooling and in military training camps, and returned to Xinjiang to further the separatist struggle. Beijing began insulating Xinjiang from the unwanted religious and cultural influences of Pakistani Muslims on their Uyghur coreligionists. The events of 9/11 led China to close its borders with Pakistan and increase security measures along the Karakoram Highway.

These, along with increased security measures along the border, were aided in large part by the global mobilization against terrorism. In January 2017, China tightened security at the Khunjerab Pass in an attempt to prevent militants from entering Chinese territory.[31]

In April 2015, China and Pakistan formally launched the China-Pakistan Economic Corridor (CPEC), a series of energy and infrastructure projects aimed at connecting Pakistan's Balochistan with China's northwestern Xinjiang region. The main idea behind the CPEC, from Beijing's perspective, is to integrate the Chinese region with the Eurasian and Indian Ocean region, to foster economic growth in western regions of China and to reduce its dependence on the Straits of Malacca as a transit route for energy and trade.[32] The regional insurgencies and outbreaks of violence in Pakistan, however, raise questions about the vulnerabilities of critical infrastructure to attacks.

The key terrorist groups operate in the border between Pakistan and Afghanistan, and take the form of the Taliban and Al Qaeda where it has found safe havens in the Federally Administered Tribal Areas.[33] Although the threat from Al Qaeda has weakened, Afghanistan remains the key battleground in the global war on terrorism. The illicit product and transaction of narcotics in Afghanistan have also provided terrorist groups in Central Asia with a source of funding. Weak governance and rampant corruption are major internal factors aggravating the current security landscape in Afghanistan.[34] Aware of these sources of instability, China is also a member of the Quadrilateral Coordination Group which comprises representatives from Afghanistan, Pakistan, the United States, and China, and aims to promote efforts toward the peace process in Afghanistan. Aware of the similar security challenges facing countries in South and Central Asia, China has worked multilaterally with counterparts from both regions on counterterrorism. In August 2016, China launched the Quadrilateral Cooperation and Coordination Mechanism in Counter Terrorism with Tajikistan, Afghanistan, and Pakistan and agreed to cooperate in a range of areas, including intelligence sharing, antiterrorist capability building, joint antiterrorist training, and personnel training.[35]

In recent years, and particularly with increased economic investments with Pakistan and Afghanistan through the BRI, Chinese leaders have been determined to ensure that its South Asian neighbors adopt a more stringent line toward Uyghur separatists there. In December 2017, Chinese ministers met with official counterparts from Afghanistan and Pakistan, where they agreed to work together on counterterrorism efforts tied to Uyghur terrorism in Xinjiang.[36]

Middle East Security Diplomacy

China's security diplomacy with Middle Eastern countries is visibly directed in the interests of its economic ties with the country. More than 50 percent of Chinese oil imports come from the Middle East and North Africa region.[37] Given the high stakes of Chinese oil investments in the Middle East, China's main security concern toward the Middle East relates to the potential for terrorism to disrupt its continued access to oil from the Middle East. Beijing's diplomatic security engagements with the Middle East reflects its adherence to its policy of nonintervention in the region. In line with this, China has used its veto power in the UN Security Council, along with Russia, to block resolutions designed to pressure Damascus on the situation in Syria.[38] Beijing has also abstained from interfering in Iran's nuclear program, and remains inactive in the conflicts in Iraq and Yemen.[39] Since joining the UN Peacekeeping Forces in 1990, Beijing has deployed its personnel in UN forces, and is now the second-largest contributor to the UN Peacekeeping budget. Beijing has contributed manpower in UN Peacekeeping Forces in the Middle East and in Africa, including Congo, Darfur, South Sudan, Mali, and Lebanon, countries which suffer from an active terrorism or insurgent threat.

Southeast Asian Security Diplomacy

In the political-economic context of China's BRI in Southeast Asian countries, there are currently companies within the textile and light industry spheres operating in Cambodia's Special Economic Zone, railway and manufacturing investment projects in Thailand, as well as electricity and transportation projects in Myanmar. Indonesia, Myanmar, and Laos are also export destinations for Chinese overproduction of cement. Myanmar, Laos, and Vietnam are situated close to China's Yunnan border, and South Asian countries like India and Bangladesh are also home to active insurgent threats. Geographically advantageous, Yunnan is seen as an international gateway or connector for China, Southeast Asia, and South Asia, and a key littoral or gateway for China's BRI's strategy.[40] Oil and natural gas pipelines that run from Myanmar to Yunnan also carry crude oil imports. In early 2017, violence between Buddhists and the minority Muslim Rohingya group in the state of Rakhine erupted, posing safety concerns about the threat of a terrorist attack to Chinese operations on the Kyaukpyu port and the pipeline, and threatened to put Chinese operations in the area to a halt.[41] Furthermore, amid reports of its expansive development of infrastructure and tourism, as well as oil and gas, in the South China Sea, Southeast Asia's maritime piracy and terrorism risks could also potentially pose risks for Chinese commercial interests there.[42] So far, China has engaged in unilateral means such as deploying paramilitary forces and coast guards to protect its interests from piracy and terrorism. Since 2002, Southeast Asian countries and China have established mechanisms to combat transnational crime, including terrorism, through the existing frameworks under ASEAN.[43] It remains to be seen whether such measures are sufficient in the long-term. Of concern for China is also the infiltration by China's Xinjiang Uyghurs into Southeast Asia by overland and maritime routes in recent years, and their participation in militancy. This concern was reinforced on August 17, 2015, when a bomb attack took place at Erawan Shrine, in the Thai capital of Bangkok, killing 20 people and injuring 125 people.[44] The attacks were reportedly in revenge for the Thai government's deportation of Uyghurs. China has also used economic and diplomatic pressure on Southeast Asian countries, Cambodia, Malaysia, Vietnam, Myanmar, and Laos in the repatriation of Uyghur refugees back to China.[45]

CONCLUSION

With the BRI, China's economic ambitions have increasingly become entangled with regional security challenges. Pertinent to this, three developments have shaped the internal-external security agenda for China. The first is the transnational linkages between the Uyghurs in Xinjiang and their Central Asian ethnic kin, as well as, to some extent, their Muslim kin in Pakistan. Ethnicity, as well as religion in the latter case, provides a salient force for political mobilization. When combined, both ethnicity as a unifying force and political Islam as a transnational ideology can function to exacerbate the Uyghur ethno-nationalist separatist claims for an independent East Turkestan republic. Thus, Beijing's concern lies in containing unwanted religious infiltration contributing to the radicalization of Uyghurs internally, while facilitating economic changes in Xinjiang. The second development in the internal-external security agenda for China concerns the rise in Chinese nationals abroad, particularly in regions which are unstable, with active insurgencies, and which China has vested economic and strategic interests in, such as in the Middle East. This has increased the scope of Beijing's concerns as it has had to ensure the safety and security of their own nationals abroad. In parallel to this, stabilizing missions, as in the case of China's antipiracy missions in the Gulf of Aden and its hiring of private security contractors in countries like Pakistan, have also become viable and attractive security diplomatic engagements China has forged.

Finally, transnational nonstate militant actors like ISIS have also factored into Beijing's strategic concerns about domestic security. Reports of Uyghurs who have joined the ranks of the terrorist group have also served to justify Beijing's continued repressive and authoritarian measures toward the Uyghurs. To manage these security challenges arising from the internal-external nexus, especially in view of the BRI, Beijing is likely to continue to resort to a combination of domestic approaches, such as public security measures, unilateral and bilateral approaches, as with Pakistan and in the

Middle East, and multilateral, as in the SCO. The internal-external nexus model roughly sketched in this chapter will provide a framework for understanding how Beijing has managed and will likely to continue managing its security challenges pertinent to Xinjiang's Uyghurs and in respect to dealing with transnational nontraditional security issues on the BRI, such as terrorism.

NOTES

1. Nathan, AJ & Scobell, A 2012, "How China Sees America: The Sum of Beijing's Fears," *Foreign Affairs*, vol. 91, p. 32.

2. For an overview of this conceptual framework, see Eriksson, J & Rhinard, M 2009, "The Internal—External Security Nexus: Notes on an Emerging Research Agenda," in J Eriksson & M Rhinard (eds), *Cooperation and Conflict*, vol. 44, no. 3, pp. 243–267; see also Jorg Friedrich's theoretical model of the internal-external security nexus in the form of the intermestic security challenge, which I adopt in this chapter loosely: Friedrichs, J 2018, "Intermestic Security Challenges: Managing Transnational Bonds," *European Journal of International Security*, vol. 3, no. 2, pp. 162–186.

3. Dillon, M 2004, *Xinjiang: China's Muslim Far Northwest*, Durham East Asia series, RoutledgeCurzon, London; New York, pp. 59.

4. Harris, LC 1993, "Xinjiang, Central Asia and the Implications for China's Policy in the Islamic World," *The China Quarterly*, vol. 133, p. 111; Christoffersen, G 1993, "Xinjiang and the Great Islamic Circle: The Impact of Transnational Forces on Chinese Regional Economic Planning," *The China Quarterly*, vol. 133, p. 134.

5. Gunaratna, R 2002, *Inside Al Qaeda: Global Network of Terror*, Columbia University Press, New York, pp. 173; Wayne, MI 2009, "Inside China's War On Terrorism," *Journal of Contemporary China*, vol. 18, no. 59, pp. 252.

6. "2002," n.d., viewed 23 August 2018, http://eng.mod.gov.cn/Database/WhitePapers/2002.htm.

7. Blum, SD & Jensen, LM (eds) 2002, *China Off Center: Mapping the Margins of the Middle Kingdom*, University of Hawai'i Press, Honolulu.

8. "Full Text: List of Deliverables of Belt and Road Forum," *Xinhua English.news.cn* n.d., viewed 22 August 2018, http://www.xinhuanet.com/english/2017-05/15/c_136286376.htm.

9. "Blackwater Founder to Open Bases in Xinjiang," *People's Daily Online* n.d., viewed 22 August 2018, http://en.people.cn/n3/2017/0322/c90000-9193291.html.

10. 2004, "Pakistan Car Bomb Kills Chinese," 3 May, viewed 22 August 2018, http://news.bbc.co.uk/2/hi/south_asia/3679533.stm.

11. "Hotel Blasts Kill Dozens in Jordan – Nov 9, 2005," *CNN.com* n.d., viewed 22 August 2018, http://edition.cnn.com/2005/WORLD/meast/11/09/jordan.blasts/index.html.

12. 2006, "China Workers Killed in Pakistan," 15 February, viewed 22 August 2018, http://news.bbc.co.uk/2/hi/south_asia/4716820.stm.

13. "Three Chinese Dead in Pakistan Terrorist Attack," *Reuters* n.d., viewed 22 August 2018, https://www.reuters.com/article/us-pakistan-china-idUSISL27353120070708.

14. Page, J 2016, "Over 100 Chinese Fighters Have Joined Islamic State in Syria," *Wall Street Journal*, 25 July, viewed 22 August 2018, https://www.wsj.com/articles/china-terror-claims-bolstered-by-new-evidence-1469435872.

15. "Terror Overseas: Understanding China's Evolving Counter-Terror Strategy," *European Council on Foreign Relations* n.d., viewed 22 August 2018, https://www.ecfr.eu/publications/summary/terror_overseas_understanding_chinas_evolving_counter_terror_strategy7160.

16. "Backgrounder: China's Major Overseas Evacuations in Recent Years," *China – Chinadaily.com.cn* n.d., viewed 22 August 2018, http://www.chinadaily.com.cn/china/2015-03/30/content_19954649.htm.

17. "Yemen Crisis: China Evacuates Citizens and Foreigners from Aden," *BBC News* n.d., viewed 22 August 2018, https://www.bbc.com/news/world-middle-east-32173811.

18. "China: A Responsible Stakeholder?" *The National Interest* n.d., viewed 22 August 2018, https://nationalinterest.org/blog/the-buzz/china-responsible-stakeholder-16131.

19. "Position Paper of the People's Republic of China at the 71st Session of the United Nations General Assembly," n.d., viewed 22 August 2018, http://www.china-un.org/eng/hyyfy/t1396325.htm.

20. Clarke, ME 2011, *Xinjiang and China's Rise in Central Asia: A History*, Routledge Contemporary China Series, Routledge, London; Hao, Y & Liu, W 2012, "Xinjiang: Increasing Pain in the Heart of China's Borderland," *Journal of Contemporary China*, vol. 21, no. 74, pp. 205–225; Li, M 2016, "From Look-West to Act-West: Xinjiang's Role in China–Central Asian Relations," *Journal of Contemporary China*, vol. 25, no. 100, pp. 515–528.

21. Ji, Y 2007, "Dealing with the Malacca Dilemma: China's Effort to Protect its Energy Supply," *Strategic Analysis*, vol. 31, no. 3, pp. 467–489.

22. "Suicide Bomber Attacks Chinese Embassy in Kyrgyzstan World News," *The Guardian* n.d., viewed 22 August 2018, https://www.theguardian.com/world/2016/aug/30/bomb-attack-chinese-embassy-kyrgyzstan-bishkek.

23. Cunningham, CP 2012, "Counterterrorism in Xinjiang: The ETIM, China, and the Uyghurs," *International Journal on World Peace*, vol. 29, no. 3, pp. 34.

24. Scobell, A, Ratner, E & Beckley, M 2014, *China's Strategy Toward South and Central Asia: An Empty Fortress*, Research report, RAND Corporation, Santa Monica, Calif.

25. Kavalski, Emilian 2010, "Shanghaied into Cooperation: Framing China's Socialization of Central Asia," *Journal of Asian and African Studies*, vol. 45, no. 2.

26. Huasheng, Zhao, "China and Central Asia," in Eugene Runner, Dmitri Trenin, & Zhao Huasheng (eds), *Central Asia: Views from Washington, Moscow, and Beijing* (Armonk, NY: M.E. Sharpe, 2007), pp. 139–142.

27. "Backgrounder: Five Principles of Peaceful Coexistence," *Xinhua*, viewed 14 June 2004; "SCO Summit Issues Declaration, Clarifies Stand on Key Issues," *Xinhua*, viewed 13 September 2013.

28. Wallace, Thomas 2014, "China and the Regional Counter-Terrorism Structure," *Asian Security*, vol. 10, no. 3, pp. 199–220.

29. Huasheng, Zhao 2013, "China's View of and Expectations from the Shanghai Cooperation Organization," *Asian Survey*, vol. 53, no. 3, May/June, pp. 436–460. DOI: 10.1525/as.2013.53.3.436.

30. Elleman, B, Kotkin, S & Schofield, C 2014, *Beijing's Power and China's Borders: Twenty Neighbors in Asia*, M.E. Sharpe, Inc., Armonk, United Kingdom, viewed 19 August 2018, http://ebookcentral.proquest.com/lib/anu/detail.action?docID=1035003.

31. "China and Pakistan: China to Seal Border with Pakistan to Curb Terror," *Times of India* n.d., viewed 22 August 2018, https://timesofindia.indiatimes.com/world/china/china-to-seal-border-with-pakistan-to-curb-terror/articleshow/56468455.cms.

32. Erickson, AS & Collins, GB 2010, *China's Oil Security Pipe Dream: The Reality, and Strategic Consequences, of Seaborne Imports*, Naval War Coll, Newport, RI.

33. Gunaratna, R & Nielsen, A 2008, "Al Qaeda in the Tribal Areas of Pakistan and Beyond," *Studies in Conflict & Terrorism*, vol. 31, no. 9, pp. 775–807.

34. Rubin, BR 2006, "Peace Building and State-building in Afghanistan: Constructing Sovereignty for Whose Security?" *Third World Quarterly*, vol. 27, no. 1, pp. 175–185.

35. "Afghanistan, China, Pakistan, Tajikistan Issue Joint Statement on Anti-terrorism," n.d., viewed 22 August 2018, http://eng.mod.gov.cn/DefenseNews/2016-08/04/content_4707451.htm.

36. "Terrorist Attacks Show Pakistan's Need to Reassure China On Security," *Nikkei Asian Review* n.d., viewed 22 August 2018, https://asia.nikkei.com/Spotlight/Belt-and-Road/Terrorist-attacks-show-Pakistan-s-need-to-reassure-China-on-security.

37. "China's Power in the Middle East is Rising," *The Washington Post* n.d., viewed 22 August 2018, https://www.washingtonpost.com/news/monkey-cage/wp/2018/08/09/chinas-rise-in-the-middle-east/?noredirect=on&utm_term=.c516c9e6afe1.

38. "Russia and China Veto UN Move to Refer Syria to ICC," *BBC News* n.d., viewed 22 August 2018, https://www.bbc.com/news/world-middle-east-27514256.

39. Elleman, B, Kotkin, S & Schofield, C 2014, *Beijing's Power and China's Borders: Twenty Neighbors in Asia*, M.E. Sharpe, Inc., Armonk, United Kingdom, viewed 22 August 2018, http://ebookcentral.proquest.com/lib/anu/detail.action?docID=1035003.

40. Yu, H 2017, "Motivation behind China's 'One Belt, One Road' Initiatives and Establishment of the Asian Infrastructure Investment Bank," *Journal of Contemporary China*, vol. 26, no. 105, pp. 353–368.

41. Garlick, J 2018, "Deconstructing the China–Pakistan Economic Corridor: Pipe Dreams Versus Geopolitical Realities," *Journal of Contemporary China*, vol. 27, no. 112, pp. 528; See also, "China, India Could Help Stabilize Myanmar's Conflict-ridden Rakhine State," *Global Times* n.d., viewed 23 August 2018, http://www.globaltimes.cn/content/1032014.shtml.

42. "China's State Firms Cementing Lucrative Role in South China Sea, New Research Shows," *Reuters* n.d., viewed 23 August 2018, https://www.reuters.com/article/us-southchinasea-china/chinas-state-firms-cementing-lucrative-role-in-south-china-sea-new-research-shows-idUSKBN1KU0MJ.

43. Chow, JT 2005, "ASEAN Counterterrorism Cooperation Since 9/11," *Asian Survey*, vol. 45, no. 2, pp. 302–321.

44. "Bangkok Bombing Spotlights Uyghur Woes in Southeast Asia," *The Diplomat* n.d., viewed 22 August 2018, https://thediplomat.com/2015/08/bangkok-bombing-spotlights-uyghur-woes-in-southeast-asia/.

45. "Uighur Refugees in Southeast Asia Stoke Chinese Worries," n.d., viewed 22 August 2018, https://www.lowyinstitute.org/the-interpreter/uighur-refugees-southeast-asia-stoke-chinese-worries.

Section II

THE POLITICAL ECONOMY OF BRI

Chapter 5

The Geoeconomics of the Belt and Road Initiative

Jane Golley and Michael Wesley

After four decades of rapid growth and development China has become the only serious rival for primacy that the United States has faced in over seventy years.[1] An economy that contributed less than 5 percent of global production in 1975 had become by 2006 the world's largest importer of minerals and energy; by 2007 the world's largest exporter; by 2008 the world's largest manufacturer; by 2012 Asia's largest economy; and by 2014 the world's largest economy in purchasing power parity terms.[2] Barring a major economic crisis, China's ascent to the world's largest economy in nominal terms is likely only a matter of years away, not decades.[3]

But the more successful China has become, the more its relationships with the world's most powerful country, the global economic architecture, and its neighbors have grown antagonistic. Despite deep economic interdependence, Washington increasingly views Beijing in competitive terms. This was evident in former president Obama's "pivot" toward Asia and the Pacific, a key facet of which was the Trans-Pacific Partnership trade agreement (TPP), an ambitious trade liberalization initiative among twelve economies in the region that notably excluded China. But President Donald Trump has taken this competitiveness to a new level. His administration's 2017 National Security Strategy stated clearly that China is making the world's economies "less free and less fair," while the 2018 National Defense Strategy boldly states that "Inter-state strategic competition, not terrorism, is now the primary concern in US national security. China is a strategic competitor using predatory economics to coerce neighboring countries to reorder the Indo-Pacific region to their advantage."[4]

Neither is China becoming any more comfortable with the institutions and norms governing the global economy. On the one hand, as Edward Steinfeld has argued, it was by opening itself up to the influx of market competition, technology, and managerial expertise that China achieved such rapid institutional change and economic growth in such a short period of time—effectively learning to "play our [liberal] game."[5] On the other hand, the dominance of international economic institutions by the United States and its allies is a source of much frustration.[6] For close to two decades, Beijing has been battling against what it sees as a moral hierarchy in the US-led rules-based liberal international order, whereby liberal developed economies are assumed to be at the apex, and all other economies are judged by the degree they deviate from that ideal. China's leaders have been at pains to reiterate that there is no best model for organizing an economy, and that any given country should be able to legitimately choose the economic model that best suits its own circumstances.[7] Hence the Chinese Communist Party (CCP) under President Xi Jinping remains committed to its "long-term goal [since the Cold War] of shifting the international order from material and social structures still characterized by substantial US unipolarity to a multi-polar world (*duojihua shijie*) in which several great powers, including China, play leading roles."[8]

Third, despite its deep integration with other Asian economies its role as one of the only sources of dynamism and growth in the post-Global Financial Crisis era, China has experienced increasingly fractious relations with many of its neighbors. Its relationship with Japan has fluctuated between open hostility and cold formality; it has been engaged in bitter territorial disputes with India, Japan, and the states of Southeast Asia; its ally, North Korea continues to defy Beijing's wishes; Taiwan has elected an independence-minded government; and Sri Lanka, Myanmar, and Malaysia have seen frustrating cancellations and delays in major projects, contributing to a broader deterioration in their respective bilateral relationships with China.

China's new activism in geoeconomics—the use of economic tools to advance geopolitical objectives—is aimed at mitigating these antagonisms. The Belt and Road Initiative (BRI) is the centerpiece of this activism, and offers a uniquely Chinese approach to blunting American hostility while growing past it, shaping "a more enabling international environment,"[9] and encouraging greater deference from, or friendship with, other states on the Eurasian landmass as well as maritime Asia. There are (at least) three elements of the BRI that are uniquely Chinese: its connection to China's internal regional development strategies in the past; its reliance on a complex party-state apparatus; and its modes of development finance. This combination is shaped by the CCP's interpretation of its past successes in unifying China, suppressing antagonisms within its borders, and building a strong and wealthy state. By placing BRI in this context, we argue that it is a form of "geoeconomics with Chinese characteristics," which is quite different from that defined by American scholars.

We then review a sample of responses to the BRI from countries, including Australia, India, Japan, and Russia, all of which reveal a new era of geoeconomics that we believe will dominate international affairs in the decade ahead. While the initiative has been endorsed by many of China's neighbors as well as those further away, it becomes clear that it has not yet caused an appreciative reduction in the three forms of antagonism that complicate China's rise. The reasons for this are instructive for thinking about what the future holds, which address in our conclusions.

GEOECONOMICS WITH "CHINESE CHARACTERISTICS"

The term "geoeconomics" was coined in the aftermath of the Cold War by Edward Luttwak to describe an age of post-ideological rivalry, in which "the logic of conflict [would be pursued] with the methods of commerce."[10] For Western scholars, geoeconomics is a consequence of the paradox that sits at the heart of the emerging world order of the twenty-first century. Increasing economic interdependence, traditionally thought of as the most reliable force for peace and stability internationally, coexists with deepening strategic rivalry between established and rising great powers. This is particularly the case in Asia, where economic interdependence is advancing further and faster than anywhere else on the planet, at the same time as weapons purchases are outpacing every other region of the world.[11] In the age of nuclear deterrence and deep interdependence, a war to resolve this rivalry, as has so often occurred in the past, appears far too costly and ultimately self-defeating for all involved. And so rivalry over primacy, and over the shape of the international order, is displaced into nonmilitary spheres.[12]

In their book *War by Other Means*: *Geoeconomics and Statecraft*, Robert Blackwill and Jennifer Harris lament the demise of America's geoeconomic capabilities in recent decades, arguing that "the global geoeconomic playing field is now sharply tilting against the United States, and unless this is corrected, the price in blood and treasure for the United States will only grow."[13] They see that field tilting decisively in China's favor, emphasizing its growing use of geoeconomic tools to "punish" countries—including Japan, the Philippines, and Taiwan—that act against its foreign policy interests. Among the most recent examples of such behavior followed South Korea's decision to deploy the US-supplied THAAD missile defense system in March 2017, when China's state media actively encouraged the boycotting of South Korean goods, culture, and tourism, inflicting high costs on the South Korean economy until the "thawing" of relations in late 2017.

There has been a marked tendency among American scholars recently to interpret China's geopolitical intentions according to the frameworks that motivate US foreign policy. A prominent example is the tendency of Realist scholars, such as Stephen Walt and John Mearsheimer, to argue that China is seeking to create a version of the "Monroe Doctrine" in Asia.[14] There are strong indications that such "mirror imaging" tendencies may be at work in American scholars' and officials' understandings (or misunderstandings) of the central thrust of Beijing's new geoeconomic strategy—the BRI. While China has used economic leverage to coerce other states in the past, the BRI is officially portrayed in benevolent, "win-win" terms—with no explicit sense of punishment. In May 2017, at the opening ceremony of the Belt and Road Forum for International Cooperation, President Xi Jinping presented the BRI as a China's plan for global "common prosperity," which would boost mutual respect, mutual learning, mutual understanding, and mutual trust.[15] In his keynote speech at the Bo'ao Forum in April 2018, Xi stressed China's lead role in defending globalization and multilateralism, declaring a "new phase of opening up" involving broadened market access, eased restrictions on foreign firms, lower import tariffs, and a more attractive investment environment. The BRI will also "contribute significantly to a more fair, peaceful and prosperous world," according to Xi.[16]

The new form of geoeconomics—and hence of geopolitics—characterized by the BRI is shaped by China's own interpretation of its internal journey since the beginning of the reform and opening era. Here, China's understanding of its own history, as well as the trajectory of global politics, is heavily shaped by Marxist frameworks of historical materialism. According to Marxist orthodoxy, economic growth creates "contradictions" between the basic underlying material structure of human affairs and the inertia of social and political "superstructures."[17] By resolving these contradictions using a scientific understanding of history, the party-state creates progress in human affairs. Seen in these terms, the three levels of antagonism China is experiencing as its wealth and power have grown are entirely understandable as "contradictions" between China's own economic dynamism and the inertia of international alignments and institutions. In this context, BRI represents China's "scientific" program to resolve these contradictions in its favor.

First announced as the One-Belt-One-Road Initiative in 2013, the renamed BRI began with two separate proposals for a Silk Road Economic Belt and a twenty-first-century Maritime Silk Road, connecting the underdeveloped border provinces with China's developing regional partners. It has since expanded to include sixty-four countries that cover the entire Eurasian zone, involving a diverse range of projects with a projected value exceeding $1 trillion. The Initiative calls for a multidimensional infrastructure network, which will include a number of economic corridors (including the China Pakistan

Economic Corridor, China Mongolia Russia Economic Corridor, and the New Eurasian Continental Bridge), combining land, sea, and air transportation routes with major railway, port, and pipeline projects. The Initiative will also create mechanisms for policy dialogue, infrastructure connectivity, tariff reductions, financial support, and people-to-people exchange across the participating BRI countries—the so-called Five Connectivities 五通.

Domestically, the primary motivation of the BRI is to sustain China's economic development. Since 2012, GDP growth has decreased steadily from 7.7 percent to 6.9 percent in 2017. While no single factor is responsible for the slowdown, there is broad acceptance that China's past growth model of exporting labor-intensive manufacturing goods has run its course. Two clear signals of this are the excess capacity in a number of China's industries, including coal, steel, and cement, along with excessive foreign exchange reserves (peaking at over US$4 trillion in 2014). The BRI is seen as a promising solution to all of these domestic problems: cultivating new export markets for Chinese goods (including plenty of coal, steel, and cement), new destinations for Chinese investment, and hence new sources of Chinese growth.

The BRI is also expected to bring both growth and stability to China's less-developed western regions, particularly Xinjiang and Tibet. The proposed Silk Road Economic Belt will reinvigorate investment, transforming Xinjiang into an energy corridor for Eurasia and creating new opportunities to exploit its untapped resources. For Tibet, the Himalayan Economic Rim Project aims to connect the BRI with the Bangladesh-China-India-Myanmar Economic Corridor (BCIM), developing border trade with Nepal, India, and Bhutan with a focus on tourism, Tibetan medicine, and animal husbandry.[18] This development, it is also hoped, will reduce the ethnic tensions and sporadic violence that have plagued the region in the past.

This set of domestic objectives made it easy in the past for most Chinese officials and scholars to focus on the economic benefits of BRI, describing it as China's "greatest international economic ambition"[19] and stressing that it was not a tool of geopolitics—and therefore not a geoeconomic strategy at all. Instead, it was presented as a "non-threatening and non-revisionist power, dissimilar to others in the past," a "concrete implementation of the concept of the 'peaceful rise'"[20] and a "useful complement to the existing global institutions" because China should not (and did not) "expect to replace the established international trading system."[21]

Some interpretations of BRI, however, have made no effort to disguise its geopolitical intent. Huo Jianguo, director of the Chinese Academy of International Trade and Economic Cooperation (a subsidiary of the Ministry of Commerce), for example, described the BRI as a "strategic measure" to extend Chinese influence during a "period of great strategic opportunity." He went on to call it

> [a] grand strategy for foreign affairs in surrounding countries based on a new security concept, [which] expresses innovative developments in concepts and strategic thinking on managing the new style of international affairs of the new central government.

Huo was even more explicit in his description of the BRI as "a grand strategic design to break through [the] pressure created by the United States' TPP negotiations, which are intended to control the rules of international trade going forward in ways that undoubtedly challenge and threaten China."[22]

Such pronouncements from Chinese government officials would not have been possible had they contradicted the party line. Indeed, since 2015, the strategic imperatives underpinning BRI became increasingly evident in official documents and Xi Jinping's major speeches. The 2015 BRI Vision and Actions Plan 2015 released by National Development Reform Commission (NDRC) with the Ministry of Commerce and the Ministry of Foreign Affairs (MFA) stated that "the initiative aims to jointly build the Belt and Road, embracing the trend towards a multipolar world."[23] In his World Economic Forum speech in January 2017, Xi Jinping argued that "inadequate global economic governance makes it difficult to adapt to new developments in the global economy."[24] His speech to the National Party Congress (NPC) in October 2017 went even further, claiming that through the BRI and the Asian Infrastructure Investment Bank (AIIB):

> [W]e have made all-round efforts in the pursuit of major country diplomacy with Chinese characteristics. [. . .] With this we have seen a further rise in China's international influence, ability to inspire, and power to shape; and China has made great new contributions to global peace and development.[25]

The BRI is premised on the conviction that infrastructure links are the best way to harness the attractive power of China's surging economy to resolve the contradictions of outdated strategic perceptions and alignments in China's favor. Two case studies are instructive here. The China Pakistan Economic Corridor (CPEC) is the flagship project of the BRI, valued at US$60 billion, and aimed at connecting the 2,000 kilometers between Kashgar in northwestern China to Pakistan's Gwadar Port, through roads, railways, and pipelines in addition to other specific infrastructure and agricultural projects. The project will provide China secure access to Central Asian energy sources and an entry point in the Arabian Gulf, bypassing the Strait of Malacca and dramatically shortening the time it takes for Chinese goods to reach Africa and the Middle East. In addition to serving as a commercial hub, Gwadar will be transformed into a safe harbor for the Chinese navy, allowing it to project power deep into the Gulf and Indian Ocean. For its part, Pakistan expects to receive some much-needed infrastructure as well as a reliable energy supply to alleviate its persistent power shortfalls. According to Andrew Small, and consistent with this depiction, CPEC embodies a number of strategic goals—including boosting Pakistan's economic capabilities as a solution to growing extremism in the country (connected to China's own concerns about its Uyghur population in Xinjiang) and signaling to the rest of the world that "being a friend of China has clear economic benefits."[26]

Kazakhstan, where President Xi first announced China's Silk Road Economic Belt, has been among the most enthusiastic recipients of the BRI. In March 2018, the Kazakh government reported that fifty-one BRI projects, worth US$27 billion (primarily in energy, mining and infrastructure), would be undertaken by Chinese investors between 2016 and 2022.[27] This builds on strong bilateral cooperation in the past, including substantial investments connecting the two countries' gas pipelines and railways. But as Nargis Kassenova puts it:

> The government's embrace of China goes beyond the simple considerations of benefits from trade and investment. The big eastern neighbour is increasingly seen as successful and growing in power, and that triggers the desire among the leadership to emulate and learn from it. China has become one of the role models for Kazakhstan: a state with a dynamic economy that is comfortable with globalisation trends and open to the world, while in full control of its domestic politics.[28]

The strategic intent behind the BRI is that increasing numbers of China's partners will follow the examples of Pakistan and Kazakhstan, tying a greater proportion of the world's economy to China's economic success, and thereby reducing the relevance of Western-controlled international economic institutions. And while this intent is understandable from China's perspective, it is exactly the kind of geoeconomic influence that many external observers fear the most, with at least some good reason.

THE BRI IN PRACTICE: GLOBAL DEVELOPMENT WITH CHINESE CHARACTERISTICS

Our central point is that the key to understanding China's geoeconomic strategy is to place it in context of the political economy of China's domestic state building. Forty years ago, Deng Xioaping realized that the mitigation of risks to internal unity and external isolation lay in the transformative power of the Chinese economy. While popular perceptions of his subsequent reform and opening up policies are that they were essentially liberalizing, in reality they involved the use of state authority to direct development into sectors and regions regarded as crucial to the prosperity and unity of society. The intention was to develop a system of "Socialism with Chinese characteristics," a term coined by Deng himself in the 1980s. Three intertwining features of this transformation are relevant to understanding the BRI: China's past regional development strategies based on infrastructure, its methods of state-led development, and uniquely Chinese modes of development finance.

REGIONAL DEVELOPMENT BASED ON INFRASTRUCTURE

According to Chinese economist Hu Angang, the BRI is the latest installment in a chain of Chinese regional development strategies that, mostly through their emphasis on infrastructure construction, have been responsible for delivering the economic transformation that comes with the integration of markets, or what Hu calls an "economic terrain revolution."[29] A series of internal regional development strategies have provided the basis for delivering these revolutions within China in the past: the Coastal Development Strategy, the Western Development Strategy, the Revitalization of the Old Industries of the Northwest, the Promotion of the Rise of the Central Regions, and, most recently, the Beijing-Tianjin-Hebei Cooperative Development and the Yangtze Economic Development Belt. Adding BRI to this mix, Hu claims that these make up a "4+3" new regional development strategy that will drive the "recreation of the Chinese economic terrain while expanding outwards to recreate the global economic terrain." He therefore sees BRI as both a Chinese economic development strategy and a plan to reorganize economic development on a global scale.

While the various development strategies outlined by Hu have differed in their modes of delivery, all of them have had distinctive Chinese characteristics, and many of them have been distinctly illiberal. The Coastal Development Strategy, formalized by Deng Xiaoping in 1988—and building on his first decade of "opening up"—certainly introduced a greater role for market forces and facilitated rapid growth of private enterprises along China's coastline. However, it also relied on increased state investment, special economic zone experiments in opening up selected cities to foreign investment, and preferential tax and other policies to promote development where the state saw fit.[30]

Acknowledging that this strategy would obviously create regional income disparities, Deng made it clear that the policy focus would need to turn West toward the end of the twentieth century. President Jiang Zemin duly took this up, with the formal release of the Western Development Strategy in

March 2000. An ambitious suite of policies committing the government to supporting improvements in infrastructure, agriculture, industry upgrading, and education were aimed squarely at narrowing the gap between east and west. Implementation of the strategy relied heavily on state investment, both directly and through policy financing institutions, much of which was channeled into the region's large state-owned enterprises (SOEs) responsible for road building and infrastructure.[31]

While debates within China about the effectiveness of the Western Development Strategy are ongoing,[32] there is no question that an array of smaller economies joined to a larger, more dynamic Chinese economy via infrastructure and distributed supply chains will potentially place Beijing in an extremely powerful position, and indeed are beginning to do so already. Such a network of trade and financial integration could effectively convert many regional economies into satellites of the Chinese economy, highly dependent on that core economy's health and rhythms for their own economic wellbeing. As economic historians have shown, infrastructure-led integration with dominant economies was crucial to British and then American dominance in many regions of the world through an "imperialism of free trade," where the reorientation of an economy toward a core economy then leads to the rise of powerful economic and political elites. These elites in turn further align the satellite's policies toward the preferences of the core state.[33] Albert Hirschman demonstrated this point clearly in his classic study of trade and power, in that the greater the economic dependence of a smaller upon a larger economy, the greater the influence the larger country will have over the policies of the smaller.[34] And given the projections for China's economic growth in the decades ahead, it is difficult to see how its geopolitical influence will do anything other than expand unless the BRI is derailed altogether.

THE ROLE OF THE STATE

The most prominent point of divergence of the BRI from liberal principles involves the multifaceted role of the multilayered Chinese state in turning its high-level national plan into practical action. The main organizing principle of China's regional development strategies is that the central government articulates goals that act as an invitation to Chinese industry, financial institutions, lower-level governments, and other bodies to make proposals within their remit that uphold the stated overall goals of the strategy. The central government then supports, through various means, proposals that it deems acceptable. This interaction allows for the strategy to be enunciated in greater detail as proposals are accepted and carried out, with the objectives being adjusted to reconcile original aspirations and the reality on the ground.

The development of BRI can be understood in this context, as a dynamic interaction between the central state, which defines its objectives, and the institutions and enterprises that will play the main role in actually building it. Even if, as Lee Jones, Jinghan Zeng, and Shahar Hameiri claim, the process does not amount to a "coherent geopolitical plan" being coordinated toward a "singular strategic goal,"[35] it is nonetheless reasonable that the Chinese party-state will have considerable influence on where and how individual BRI projects are implemented, and hence on how those collective projects transform the regional economic landscape over time.

To build on this point, the BRI began to take formal shape in March 2015, with the release of the "Vision and Actions on Jointly Building Silk Road Economic Belt and 21st-Century Maritime Silk Road," a joint report coordinated by the Leading Group for Finance and Economics within the NDRC, and also involving the MFA and the Ministry of Commerce.[36] Regional offices of the NDRC exist in all provinces and, along with various other provincial party-state bodies, play a crucial role in disseminating and acting on policy announcements from the central government. Even prior to the Vision and Actions Plan, the Xinjiang Development and Reform Commission had set to work with the Party Committee to coordinate and develop a "Plan for the Promotion of Xinjiang's Openness and Economic Development under the Framework of the Silk Road Economic Belt," which stressed Xinjiang's role as an energy and transportation corridor, including the development of natural energy routes from Gwadar port to Kashgar, in western Xinjiang.[37] This point was reiterated in the 2017 release of the Xinjiang Autonomous Regional Government's "Xinjiang's Construction Plan for Development of a Transport Center on the Silk Road Economic Belt from 2016 to 2030."[38]

Following the release of the Vision and Actions Plan, many of China's largest industrial and financial enterprises, including most of the central government-owned SOEs (as well as the larger privately owned conglomerates such as Huawei[39] and the Sany Group)[40] also released BRI plans, which typically integrated their existing projects and future planning with BRI's objectives. Huawei executives, for instance, have described their ongoing business of upgrading and developing information and communications technology in Xinjiang as critical to the integration of China's Far West into the BRI project. Similarly, the China Communications Construction Company, one of China's largest SOEs, with over thirty years of experience in building bridges, ports, and railways in BRI countries from Malaysia to Pakistan, has characterized its current railway construction work in Kenya as the embodiment of BRI's mission to extend Chinese cutting-edge technology to parts of the developing world that sorely need it.[41]

SOEs will clearly play a prominent role in the foreseeable future of the BRI, given their current dominance in China's overseas presence. According to SASAC data, at the end of 2014, 107 centrally owned SOEs had established 8,515 branches in over 150 countries, and were responsible for 70 percent of Chinese nonfinancial foreign direct investment. They been particularly successful in securing engineering contracts and providing equipment for electric power, rail, and construction: the very foundations on which BRI will be built.[42]

And this is just as it should be, according to Hu Angang, who has called for SOEs to be the "vanguard" of the BRI, "diligently implementing" each requirement of the state's Vision and Actions, "meticulously formulating plans" that clarify strategic goals, selecting key fields, countries, and regions; and using innovative methods of "collectively going overseas" (抱团出海)—involving cooperation up and down the chain of production, in international capacity, in equipment manufacturing, international construction contracts, and trade in services.[43] If adhered to, Hu concludes that these efforts will make "Chinese techniques" "global techniques," "Chinese standards" "global standards," and "Chinese manufacturing" "global manufacturing."

To be clear, there is ongoing debate as to just how tightly the central government in Beijing can control the overseas activities of SOEs in order to achieve its own strategic goals.[44] Lee Jones and Yizheng Zou, for example, have argued that decentralization, fragmentation, and internationalization have substantially increased SOE autonomy, to the point where some SOEs blatantly defy dictates from the central government in terms of their overseas operations.[45] However, they still identify a long list of means that China's regulatory state has to exert control over these enterprises, from exchange rates, taxes, regulations, licenses, permits, subsidies, and credit to the *nomenklatura* system and CCP's Cadre Responsibility System. This vast list of control mechanisms gives Beijing considerable power to direct financial resources toward those Chinese firms that adhere to its own strategic goals.

CHINESE DEVELOPMENT FINANCE

The Chinese concept of development finance (开发性金融) provides a set of principles that are highly informative about how the BRI will be implemented in practical terms. Chen Yuan, the first chairman of the China Development Bank (CDB) (and, incidentally, the son of one of the "Eight Immortals" of the CCP, Chen Yun), was the first to articulate a Chinese concept of development finance in the late 1990s. Building on the tenets of development finance established by Western powers following the Second World War to fund reconstruction, as embodied in the institutions of the World Bank and the International Monetary Fund, Chen saw a role for state institutions and multilateral finance organizations to finance capital-intensive infrastructure in parts of the world where commercial banks would not lend because of excessive time frames and low yields.[46] But he took this one step further in establishing the principle that Chinese development finance would support development decided by *national strategic interests*. This, he claimed, should be administered by a functionally independent institution (the CDB) with the right to choose the projects it funded. This dual aim, of advancing national strategic interests and remaining independently viable, fostered distinct lending practices that included the Local Government Financing Vehicles that allowed provincial and city governments within China to leverage the rising value of land to fund infrastructure.[47]

In contrast, the multilateral Bretton Woods institutions have been guided by principles that, if ideologically inflected, are presented as supporting the interests of developing countries and the global community in general. It might be argued that institutions like the World Bank have in practice been co-opted by their major donors to pursue their own narrow national interests.

Yet there remains a basic difference in principle. This was made clear by CDB official Wang Wensong, who confirmed that "the CDB serves the nation's economic foreign policy strategy, supporting Chinese enterprise's 'going out' international expansion strategy." Wang provides numerous examples of how the CDB has responded to "fully serve the implementation of the BRI strategy," making progress in all of the Initiative's "five connectivities" (listed earlier). These included not only billions pledged for BRI projects in communications, energy, and resources but also promoting bank and government collaboration to strengthen policy linkages (with seventy "planning collaboration agreements" in sixty countries signed by 2015); and cooperating with lower-level government within China to "effectively transfer national BRI plans" and "carry out region-specific project planning."[48]

There is considerable divergence between these purported goals of the CDB and those of the AIIB. As Ikenberry and Lim argue for the latter, its "decision-making and operations cannot stray too far from western member state preferences," because of the broad base of member states that play a key role in "ensuring that the AIIB embodies the best standards in accountability, transparency and governance."[49] This leads them to conclude that "the operation of these mechanisms does not pose a substantial threat to the liberal international order because they essentially feature China working within the system and respecting its rules to enhance its position and authority."[50]

The same cannot be said for the CDB, nor China's other policy and commercial banks, however. Hameiri and Jones, mirroring their work on the BRI, describe China's international development finance as "crowded, fragmented and poorly coordinated" with competition among policy and commercial banks, functional ministries, provincial governments, and SOEs often resulting in investment activities abroad that are incompatible with western governance norms, including environmental standards that fall short of World Bank requirements. This leads them to conclude that "it is contestation among these agencies that will determine China's *real* challenge to the global governance of development, and that challenge will often be more chaotic and less strategic than is conventionally assumed."[51]

The focus on CDB is warranted here, because it is emerging as the largest financer of BRI projects. Having committed US$890 billion to the BRI from the outset, the CDB and China's other major policy bank, the Export-Import (Exim) Bank, had provided BRI-related lending to the value of US$200 billion by mid-2017, dwarfing the AIIB's contribution of just US$1.03 billion.[52] If, as the plan for BRI anticipates, China continues to ramp up its overseas lending to the point that it is responsible for a large proportion of international development finance—with the CDB dominating this lending and the AIIB continuing to play a minimal role—the impact on the norms of international development finance will be considerable, whether those impacts are clearly directed from Beijing or not.

REGIONAL RESPONSES

The record of BRI in mitigating antagonisms attending China's economic rise has been mixed during its first five years. Part of the problem is that analysts and governments have interpreted Beijing's grand strategy according to a Western, confrontational frame of reference. A prime example was a *New York Times* article's interpretation of the BRI following the inaugural Belt and Road Forum in May 2017:

> Mr. Xi is aiming to use China's wealth and industrial know-how to create a new kind of globalization that will dispense with the rules of the aging Western-dominated institutions. The goal is to refashion the global economic order, drawing countries and companies more tightly into China's orbit.[53]

More recently, Western newspapers have been dominated, with articles expressing fear that BRI-recipient countries will become saddled with rising and unsustainable levels of debt, which will enable China to extend its political influence and power in undesirable ways. An article in the *Sydney Morning Herald* in June 2018 takes this point to the extreme, stating that "The Chinese Communist Party has a history of using infrastructure as a Trojan Horse for domination" in reference to how Beijing plans to use BRI-related infrastructure as a "friendly forerunner to political power."[54]

The Australian government's shifting attitude toward China has reflected all of these concerns since 2017—a year in which the Chinese *Global Times* newspaper ranked Australia as "the least friendly country toward China."[55] In March 2017, the Turnbull government rejected China's request for Australia to "formally align" with the BRI, a position it has maintained since then. In language that was clearly directed at China, its Foreign Policy White Paper released in November that year restressed the need for a "secure, open and prosperous Indo-Pacific" during a period in which "powerful drivers of change are converging in a way that is re-shaping the international order and challenging Australian interests."[56] The White Paper supported Australia's engagement with regional infrastructure initiatives, "including the Belt and Road" but also made it clear that it would "favour infrastructure that has robust social and environmental safeguards and avoids unsustainable debt burdens on the economies of the region." Chinese officials were displeased with the White Paper, giving rise to fears that the deteriorating bilateral relationship with Australia's most important economic partner is already proving costly for its economy.[57] Yet this did not prevent Foreign Minister Julie Bishop from announcing what may be Australia's first geoeconomic move against China, declaring in June 2018 that Australia would compete with China's infrastructure projects in "our sphere of influence"—the Pacific—to offset China's "greater political and strategic influence in the region."[58]

Closer to China's borders, and of greater significance for understanding how the BRI will unfold in the years ahead, are the (continually evolving) responses of the major regional powers: India, Japan, and Russia. India has been the most wary of the security implications of BRI from the outset, with CPEC being "proof positive for the Indian government of China's unilateral pursuit of self-serving political gains."[59] India's reticence to China's growing prominence in the region has increased since 2014, when Prime Minister Modi introduced an "Act East" policy, aiming to "strengthen strategic and economic ties with Southeast Asian countries that would possibly act as a counterweight to the influence of China in the region."[60] In 2017, Modi committed to the International North South Transportation Corridor, involving 7,200 kilometers of ship, rail, and road routes connecting the Indian Ocean and the Persian Gulf to the Caspian Sea, via Iran to Russia and North Europe. Despite joining (along with Pakistan) the China- and Russia-led Shanghai Cooperation Organisation (SCO) in June 2017, India has continued to decline China's invitation to join the BRI, primarily because CPEC passes through Pakistan-administered Kashmir, which India considers its own.[61]

Like India, Japan has responded competitively to the BRI, announcing in 2015 its own US$110 billion infrastructure fund, targeting East-West economic integration between Southeast Asia and the global economy as a deliberate counter to China's North-South infrastructure projects that seek to integrate Southeast Asia with the Chinese economy.[62] In September 2017, following Japanese prime minister Abe's visit to New Delhi, Japan and India released a Joint Statement detailing the many ways in which they would cooperate to promote a "free, open and prosperous Indo-Pacific," including an "open skies" deal for their airlines and a new "Act East Forum" aimed at giving Japan a more prominent role in the sensitive North Eastern states of India on China's border.[63] However, a significant shift in Sino-Japanese relations appears to be underway, with the release in June 2018 of a Japanese government policy on infrastructure exports, which referenced cooperation with China for the first time. This followed a meeting between Abe and Chinese Premier Li Keqiang, at which they agreed to establish a joint committee to coordinate economic cooperation in third countries—a remarkable shift given the tensions that have dominated this bilateral relationship in the past.[64]

Russia's initial response to the BRI was also a competitive one, with the announcement in May 2014 of the Eurasian Economic Union (EEU), in force since January 2015 and aimed at creating a customs union of former Soviet states centered on Moscow.[65] Somewhat like Japan, Sebastien Peyrouse explained Russia's shift from competition and caution to (admittedly suspicious) cooperation with China on the BRI as the intention to preserve its own regional influence while avoiding conflict with China. President Vladimir Putin's declaration of a "great Eurasian partnership" aimed at synchronizing the EEU and BRI in May 2015 attests to this point.[66] Just prior to the eighteenth summit of the SCO on June 9 and 10, 2018, Xi Jinping took this a step further in awarding Putin China's first ever "Friendship medal" to a foreigner, describing Putin as his "best friend" and "confidant."[67] This coincided with Putin's emphasis on India, China, and Russia as the "major players" in the eight-member bloc, which clearly pleased Modi, who declared on Twitter that "the friendship between India and Russia has stood the test of time. Our ties will continue to newer heights in the coming years."[68] If these friendships remain intact, we can be quite certain that a new era of geoeconomics lies ahead of us.

These are just some of the opening moves in this new era, in which the world's largest economies are competing for the allegiance of the smaller economies in their orbits. Despite the economic benefits that infrastructure-based competition will bring with it, many of the region's smaller economies still view their engagements with China in defensive terms, fearing that its economic power will translate into unwanted political influence. Myanmar's sudden transition from military dictatorship to democracy was viewed by many as the junta's response to a perception that international isolation was pushing the country into an unhealthy dependence on China. Soon after announcing the country's transition to democracy, the generals paused several infrastructure projects that were central to Beijing's development plans.[69] Likewise, the shock defeat of Sri Lanka's long-term leader Mahinda Rajapaksa at the 2015 presidential election was partially attributed to his opponent Maithripala Sirisena's pledge to block a major Chinese port development near the capital Colombo.[70] A more recent example was the 2018 election loss of former Malaysian prime minister Najib Razak (and his subsequent arrest on corruption charges), at least in part because of accusations that he was "selling out the country" to China. Newly elected prime minister Mahatir Mohammad has pledged to review all Chinese projects and renegotiate any "unequal treaties."[71]

CONCLUSIONS

This chapter has depicted the BRI not as "grand strategy" with a singular objective but rather as a multifaceted geoeconomic strategy aimed at solving the "contradictions" China faces as a rising—or now risen—global power: that of growing rivalry with the United States, its number one trading partner; growing frustrations with the global economic architecture; and increasingly fractious relations with its neighbors, many of whom are nervous about China's rising economic power and what it might do with it.

Our argument is that BRI is at the center of China's response to these contradictions, a point that becomes apparent when we leave behind western definitions of geoeconomics and place the BRI within the political economy of China's own domestic transformation. Given the BRI's three-decade intended lifespan, with just five years behind it, it is too early to judge the effectiveness of this manifestation of "geoeconomics with Chinese characteristics." Looking ahead, however, we see four recent developments that will have important, if as yet uncertain, impacts.

The first is the strong likelihood that Xi Jinping's model of CCP control over the economy will extend well past the end of his formal second term as president. At the nineteenth NPC in October 2017, CCP members unanimously agreed to incorporate Xi Jinping's "Thought for the New Era of Socialism with Chinese Characteristics" as a "guiding ideology" into China's constitution. As Xi himself put it, only by following the path, theory, system, and culture of Socialism with Chinese Characteristics (his "Four Confidences") will the Communist Party succeed in taking China beyond "standing up" (as it did under Mao), and growing rich (as it did under Deng), to becoming strong under his own leadership. Xi's tenure has been marked by the steady increase of the oversight and influence of the CCP over virtually all areas of the Chinese economy, and this trend is set to continue. This will give the Chinese government a greater ability to control and direct the actions of the most significant sectors and companies in the Chinese economy, although that may come at the cost of lower economic growth, as that control is likely to stymie some of the much-needed liberalizing reforms. This, in turn, will make it increasingly difficult for China to convince the rest of the world that its approach to global economic development is compatible with the liberal, rules-based order, undermining its objective of resolving fractious relationships in the process.

The second development is the election of an unconventional president of the United States. While the Obama administration reacted to China's growing economic strength in unambiguous and conventional geoeconomic terms—characterizing the TPP as a response to China's perceived attempt to rewrite global trade rules—it is hard to find any evidence that Trump thinks geoeconomically at all. Rather than use economic leverage for strategic ends, Trump's "fair trade" agenda is based on short-term mercantilist measures, even at the costs of significant American strategic interests. His previous fixation on the bilateral deficit with China has now expanded to viewing the whole world as being somehow exploitative and unfair toward the United States, a point he makes (time and again) through his preferred medium, the tweet:

> We are on the losing side of almost all trade deals. Our friends and enemies have taken advantage of the US for many years. Our Steel and Aluminum industries are dead. Sorry, it's time for a change! MAKE AMERICA GREAT AGAIN![72]

President Xi's pledge to "address problems facing the global and regional economy, create fresh energy for pursuing inter-connected development and make the Belt and Road Initiative deliver greater benefits to people of countries involved"[73] is decidedly more appealing than Trump's, despite any reservations outlined earlier. This alone suggests that in the unfolding game of geoeconomic rivalry between the world's two superpowers, China is currently playing the stronger hand. Whether this remains the case into the future will depend on domestic developments in both countries but it is hard to envisage the United States devising a geoeconomic strategy that could outdo the BRI and prevent China's rise to the top.

Moreover, Trump's mercantilist tantrums contribute powerfully to the third development that will affect the progress of the BRI: the gradual debilitation of the institutions that have underpinned the global economic order since the Second World War. Even before Trump's election, under the liberal internationalist Obama, international institutions were increasingly falling prey to tensions between established and emerging powers. Trump has added dysfunction to this mix, sowing dissension into discussions between even its closest allies. This was seen at the G7 Summit in June 2018, at which the Trump administration objected to the inclusion of the phrase "rules-based order" in the summit communiqué, leading European Council president Donald Tusk to say that "the rules-based international order is being challenged, quite surprisingly, not by the usual suspects, but by its main architect and guarantor, the US."[74] This is not to say that China poses no challenge to that order. Indeed, as our discussion earlier has revealed, it clearly does. But these challenges are secondary to the far more pressing one of how the status quo can possibly be maintained when its leader appears to have deserted ship.

This brings us to the final element that will shape the future of the BRI—the emergence and strengthening of other regional alliances. One of these is the SCO, a regional bloc now comprising China, India, and Russia, as well as Pakistan, Kazakhstan, Kyrgyzstan, Uzbekistan, and Tajikistan. With the exception of India, the political systems of this bloc of countries are distinctly at odds with the centuries old objective of liberal internationalism.[75] Evident in the discussion of Kazakhstan earlier, they are hence likely to be far more accepting of China's economic model: utilizing state planning to channel investments into predominantly state-owned firms and financed by state-controlled banks. This makes the SCO a highly unlikely contender for upholding the status quo.

On the other hand is the recently resurrected "Quadrilateral Security Dialogue" (the "Quad") involving the United States, Japan, Australia, and India; and the related and renewed promotion of the Indo-Pacific concept. Since Australia and Japan separately began promoting the concept of a strategic realm spanning the Pacific and Indian Oceans at the start of this decade, the concept has now been used—if not in all cases adopted—by India, the United States, Thailand, Vietnam, and Indonesia. While different states seem to have different definitions of the extent and purpose of the Indo-Pacific concept, all who use the term seem to tie it to a vision of a free and open, rules-based trading and maritime order (as is evident, for instance, in the Australian Foreign Policy White Paper).

China has been conspicuously critical of the Indo-Pacific concept, at times labeling it as an attempt to "contain" it. More recently, commentators have labeled the concept and China's "Maritime Silk Road" as head-to-head competitors over the future alignment of maritime Asia. Rather than developing the concept with either of these intentions, it would be far better if all those countries embracing it would live up to the vision that they claim underpins it, while encouraging China to do the same. Given the air of inevitability that we are headed toward China's long-term goal of shifting toward a multipolar world, this would in turn enhance the likelihood that it becomes the kind of world that upholds peaceful coexistence, rather than competition and conflict.

NOTES

1. This chapter draws on and incorporates material previously published as Michael Wesley, "Australia and the Rise of Geoeconomics," *Centre of Gravity Series* No. 29, Canberra: Strategic and Defence Studies Centre, November 2016, http://sds

c.bellschool.anu.edu.au/sites/default/files/publications/attachments/201705/australia_and_the_rise_of_geoeconomics.pdf.

2. Wayne M. Morrison, "China's Economic Rise: History, Trends, Challenges, and Implications for the United States," Congressional Research Service Report 7-5700, 21 October 2015.

3. See, for example, the International Comparison Program, backed by the World Bank and the IMF, predicting that China's nominal GDP surpasses the United States' by 2024. https://www.cnbc.com/2014/09/07/china-to-become-largest-economy-by-2024.html. Other forecasts push this out to 2030 or 2032. See https://www.thesun.co.uk/news/5217296/china-overtake-us-economy-15-years-global-report-2018/ and https://www.cnbc.com/2017/11/09/goldman-sachs-ceo-lloyd-blankfein-chinese-economy-will-surpass-the-us.html.

4. President Trump, "National Security Strategy of the United States of America," ed. The White House, Washington, DC, 2017, p. 2. Department of Defense United States of America, "Summary of the 2018 National Defense Strategy of United States of America. Sharpening the American Military's Competitive Edge," Washington, DC, United States of America, 2018, p. 1.

5. Edward S. Steinfeld, *Playing Our Game: Why China's Rise Doesn't Threaten the West*, Oxford: Oxford University Press, 2010, pp. 25–28.

6. For example Hu Jintao, "Work Together and Help Each Other" Speech to the London G20 Summit, 2 April 2009, http://news.xinhuanet.com/newscenter/200904/03/content_11122834.htm.

7. For example: Ma Zhengang, "Behind the Propagation of 'China Model' by the West," *People's Tribune* (24) (2008), pp. 28–29.

8. F. Leverett and Bingbing Wu, "The New Silk Road and China's Evolving Grand Strategy," *China Journal* 77 (2017), p. 115.

9. Quoted in Neil Thomas, "Rhetoric and Reality: Xi Jinping's Australia Policy," *The China Story Journal*, Australian Centre on China and the World, 15 March 2015, http://www.thechinastory.org/2015/03/rhetoric-and-reality-xi-jinpings-australia-policy/.

10. Edward N. Luttwak, "From Geopolitics to Geo-Economics: Logic of Conflict, Grammar of Commerce," *The National Interest* 20 (Summer 1990), p. 19.

11. Michael Wesley, *Restless Continent: Wealth, Rivalry and Asia's New Geopolitics*, Melbourne: Black Inc Books, 2015.

12. See also Paul Kennedy's *The Rise and Fall of the Great Powers: Economic Change and Military Conflict From 1500 to 2000*, New York: Random House, 1987; and Samuel Huntington's "Why International Primacy Matters," *International Security* 18 (4) (1993). For a succinct summary of these two works and Luttwak's see Sanjaya Baru, "A New Era of Geo-economics: Assessing the Interplay of Economic and Political Risk," IISS Geo-economics and Strategy Programme Seminar, 23–25 March 2012.

13. Ibid., p. 2.

14. Stephen Walt, "Dealing with a Chinese Monroe Doctrine," *New York Times*, 26 August 2013; John Mearsheimer, "Can China Rise Peacefully?" *The National Interest*, 25 October 2014.

15. For the full text see Xi Jinping, "Work Together to Build the Silk Road Economic Belt and the 21st Century Maritime Silk Road" at the Opening Ceremony of the Belt and Road Forum for International Cooperation, *Xinhua.com*, 2017, online at: http://www.xinhuanet.com/english/2017-05/14/c_136282982.htm.

16. The full text of the speech, delivered on 10 April 2018, is available online at: http://www.chinadaily.com.cn/a/201804/10/WS5acc515ca3105cdcf6517425.html.

17. Timothy R. Heath, *China's New Governing Party Paradigm: Political Renewal and the Pursuit of National Rejuvenation*, Farnham: Ashgate, 2014.

18. See Tshering Chonzom Bhutia, "Tibet and China's Belt and Road," *The Diplomat*, 30 August 2016, http://thediplomat.com/2016/08/tibet-and-chinas-belt-and-road/.

19. As described by Huang Yiping, "Understanding China's Belt and Road Initiative: Motivation, Framework and Assessment," *China Economic Review* 40 (C) (2016), pp. 314–321. Huang Yiping, "Huang Yiping Discusses One Belt One Road: He Hopes it Does Not become an International Version of the Western Development Strategy 黄益平谈一带一路：希望不要成为国际版西部大开发," *Sina Finance*《新浪财经》, 30 January 2015. Feng Xingke， "One Belt One Road is an Upgraded Version of the Western Development Strategy 一带一路是西部大开发升级版," *CRI Online*《国际在线, 25 June 2015.

20. See, respectively, "Foreign Minister Wang Yi Answers Journalists' Questions on China's Diplomacy, Foreign Policy and Foreign Relations," *Ministry of Foreign Affairs*, 8 March 2015. Zhang Yesui (Vice Foreign Minister), "The One Belt One Road Initiative is not a Geopolitical Tool," Speech at the China Development Forum, *Xinhua*, 21 March 2015, both discussed in Antoine Bondaz, "Rebalancing China's Geopolitics in One Belt, One Road: China's Great Leap Outward," *European Council on Foreign Relations China Analysis*, June 2015, http://www.ecfr.eu/page/-/China_analysis_belt_road.pdf, p. 3.

21. For further details see David Cohen, "China's 'Second Opening': Grand Ambitions but a Long Road Ahead," in One Belt, One Road: China's Great Leap Outward, *European Council on Foreign Relations China Analysis*, June 2015, online at: http://www.ecfr.eu/page/-/China_analysis_belt_road.pdf, p. 6.

22. Huo Jianguo, "Huo Jianguo: One Belt One Road is a "Strategic Concept" not a "Construction Project" 霍建国："一带一路"是战略构想不是"工程项目," *China Economic Network* 《中国经济网》, 19 March 2015.

23. National Development and Reform Commission (NDRC), "Vision and Actions on Jointly Building Silk Road Economic Belt and 21st-Century Maritime Silk Road," ed. National Development Reform Commission (NDRC) (2015). Full quote "The initiative to jointly build the Belt and Road, embracing the trend towards a multipolar world, economic globalization, cultural diversity and greater IT application, is designed to uphold the global free trade regime and the open world economy in the spirit of open regional cooperation."

24. President of Peoples Republic of China Xi Jinping, "Jointly Shoulder Responsibility of Our Times, Promote Global Growth," At the Opening Session, Of the World Economic Forum Annual Meeting 2017, Davos, 17 January 2017, online at: https://america.cgtn.com/2017/01/17/full-text-of-xi-jinping-keynote-at-the-world-economic-forum.

25. Xi Jinping, "Full Text of Xi Jinping's Report at 19th CPC National Congress," Beijing, China, 2017, http://www.xinhuanet.com/english/special/2017-11/03/c_136725942.htm, p. 6.

26. See Andrew Small, "First Movement: Pakistan and the Belt and Road Initiative," in Roundtable on China's Belt and Road Initiative: Views from along the Silk Road (2017), *Asia Policy* 24 (July), pp. 80–87.

27. Figures from: https://asia.nikkei.com/Politics/International-Relations/Linking-China-to-the-EU-s-gateway-for-exporters, accessed on 20 June 2018.

28. Nargis Kassenova, "China's Silk Road and Kazakhstan's Bright Path: Linking Dreams of Prosperity," in Roundtable on China's Belt and Road Initiative: Views from along the Silk Road (2017), *Asia Policy* 24 (July), pp. 110–116, p. 14.

29. Hu Angang 胡鞍钢, "SOEs Should be the Vanguard of One Belt One Road" 国企将成为一带一路的主力军, *Sina Finance* 《新浪财经》, 17 July 2015.

30. Hongyi Harry Lai, "China's Western Development Program: Its Rationale, Implementation and Prospects," *Modern China* 28 (4) (October 2002).

31. Dai Ze and Zhu Mengnan 戴赜，朱孟楠，"On the Policy of Financial Support of the Western Development Strategy" 轮我国西部大开发中的金融支持政略'，*Shaanxi Trade Journal*《陕西经贸学院报.

32. See, for examples, Ze and Mengnan, "On the Policy of Financial Support of the Western Development Strategy"; Wei Houkai 魏后凯, "A New Stage and New Content for China's Western Development Strategy" 我国西部大开发的新阶段和新内涵'，*China Finance*《中国金融》14 (2004); Wei Houkai and Zhao Yong 魏后凯，赵勇，"An Evaluation and Policy Suggestions for Deepening the Implementation of the Western Development Strategy" 深入实施西部大开发战略评估及政策建议'， *Research on Development*《开发研究1 (2014).

33. John Gallagher and Ronald Robinson, "The Imperialism of Free Trade," *Economic History Review* 6 (1) (1953), pp. 1–15.

34. Albert O. Hirschman, *National Power and the Structure of Foreign Trade*, Berkeley: University of California Press, 1945.

35. Written evidence from Lee Jones, Jinghan Zeng and Shahar Hameiri on China's Belt and Road Initiative, provided to the UK Parliament in December 2017, accessed on 10 June 2018, http://data.parliament.uk/writtenevidence/committeeevidence.svc/evidencedocument/foreign-affairs-committee/china-and-the-international-rulesbased-system/written/75536.html.

36. See the Vision and Actions plan online at: http://en.ndrc.gov.cn/newsrelease/201503/t20150330_669367.html.

37. Zhong Xiuling Li Xing, "Xinjiang Accelerates the Construction of the Core Area of the Silk Road Economic Belt," *Xinjiang Daily*, 19 May 2014.

38. 丝绸之路经济带核心区交通枢纽中心建设规划（2016–2030年）https://eng.yidaiyilu.gov.cn/zchj/dfgg/25503.htm.

39. "One Belt One Road ICT Brigade: Huawei Tours Xinjiang," in Chinese, *CCIDNET*, 18 May 2015.

40. Sany Group, "One Belt One Road" repeat orders through the roof—overseas business up 25 percent, in Chinese, *d1cm.com*, 11 November 2015.

41. "China Communications Construction Company Chairman: Enterprises Can Realise 'Going Overseas Together' in 'One Belt One Road' Construction" (in Chinese), *Xinhua*, 23 May 2015.

42. Cited in Angang 胡鞍钢, "SOEs Should be the Vanguard of One Belt One Road."

43. Ibid.

44. For further discussion on this point, see Lee Jones and Yizheng Zou, "Rethinking the Role of State-Owned Enterprises in China's Rise," *New Political Economy* 22 (6), pp. 743–760.

45. Jones and Zou, "Rethinking the Role of State-Owned Enterprises in China's Rise."

46. The "Chinese Exploration" of Development Finance—an interview with China Development Bank Chairman Chen Yuan 开发性金融的"中国探索"——访国家开发银行董事长陈元', Gong Wen 龚雯, *Renmin Wang* 人民网, 3 September 2012, http://www.people.com.cn/n/2012/0904/c15373-18917482.html.

47. H. Sanderson and M. Forsythe, *China's Superbank: Debt, Oil and Influence: How China Development Bank is Rewriting the Rules of Finance*, Wiley-Bloomberg Press, 2013. See also Liao Fan, "Quench a Thirst with Poison?—Local Government Financing Vehicles' Past, Present and Future," *Parker School of Foreign and Comparative Law*, available online at: http://web.law.columbia.edu/parker-school/chinese-state-capitalism-workshop/papers/quench-thirst-poison-local-government-financing-vehicles-past-present-and-future-liao-fan.

48. Wang Wensong: The China Development Bank has a big role to play in assisting "One Belt One Road" Construction 王文松：国家开发银行助推"一带一路"建设大有可为," Wang Wensong 王文松, *Xinhua Education* 新华教育, 24 May 2015, online at: http://news.xinhuanet.com/live/2015-05/24/c_127835411.htm.

49. G. John Ikenberry and Darren Lim, "China's Emerging Institutional Statecraft: The Asian Infrastructure Investment Bank and the Prospects for Counter-Hegemony," *Projects on International Order and Strategy*, Brookings Institution, April 2017, p. 14.

50. Ibid., p. 11.

51. For more details, see Ikenberry and Lim, "China's Emerging Institutional Statecraft"; and Shahar Hameiri and Lee Jones, "China Challenges Global Governance? Chinese International Development and the AIIB," *International Affairs* 94 (3) (2018), pp. 575–593.

52. "One Belt One Road Six Segments Revealed: CDB to Invest Nearly $US 1 trillion" (in Chinese), *21 Century Economic Herald*, 28 May 2015.

53. See "Behind China's $1 trillion Plan to Shake up the Economic Order," 13 May 2017, online at: https://www.nytimes.com/2017/05/13/business/china-railway-one-belt-one-road-1-trillion-plan.html.

54. Peter Hartcher, "Beijing Uses Infrastructure as Friendly Forerunner to Political Power," *Sydney Morning Herald*, 18 June 2018, online at: https://www.smh.com.au/national/beijing-uses-infrastructure-as-friendly-forerunner-of-political-power-20180618-p4zm7t.html.

55. "Australia Least Friendly Country Towards China in 2017: Poll," *Global Times*, 27 December 2017, online at: http://www.globaltimes.cn/content/1082374.shtml.

56. Australian Foreign Policy White Paper 2017, online at: https://www.fpwhitepaper.gov.au/foreign-policy-white-paper/chapter-three-stable-and-prosperous-indo-pacific/geo-economic-competition.

57. "Chinese Investment in Australia Falls as Political Debate Hits Confidence," *The Conversation*, 13 June 2018, http://theconversation.com/chinese-investment-in-australia-falls-as-political-debate-hits-confidence-98144.

58. David Wroe, "Australia will Compete with China to Save Pacific Sovereignty, Says Bishop," *Sydney Morning Herald*, 18 June 2018, online at: https://www.smh.com.au/politics/federal/australia-will-compete-with-china-to-save-pacific-sovereignty-says-bishop-20180617-p4zm1h.html.

59. Harsh Pant and Ritika Passi, "India's Response to China's Belt and Road Initiative: A Policy in Motion," in Roundtable on China's Belt and Road Initiative: Views from along the Silk Road (2017), *Asia Policy* 24 (July), pp. 88–95. p. 89.

60. As explained in the Indian media at the time, noted by Blackwill and Harris, p. 127.

61. "China Fails to Get Indian Support for Belt and Road Project Ahead of Meeting between Xi, Modi," *The Straits Times*, 24 April 2018, online at: https://www.straitstimes.com/asia/east-asia/china-fails-to-get-indian-support-for-belt-and-road-project-ahead-of-meeting-between.

62. Hidetaka Yoshimatsu, "Japan, Globalization, and East Asian Dynamism," in Jan Nederveen Pieterse and Jongtae Kim (eds), *Globalization and Development in East Asia*, London: Routledge, 2012, p. 131.

63. See Shashank Joshi, "With an Eye on Beijing, India and Japan Double Down," *Lowy Institute Interpreter*, 15 September 2017, online at: https://www.lowyinstitute.org/the-interpreter/eye-beijing-india-and-japan-double-down; and the India-Japan Joint Statement, online at: http://www.mea.gov.in/bilateral-documents.htm?dtl/28946/IndiaJapan_Joint_Statement_during_visit_of_Prime_Minister_of_Japan_to_India_September_14_2017.

64. "Government Seeking Involvement in China's Belt and Road Plans," *The Japan News*, 18 June 2018, online at: http://the-japan-news.com/news/article/0004520406.

65. International Crisis Group, "Central Asia's Silk Road Rivalries," Report No. 245, Europe and Central Asia (2017), online at https://www.crisisgroup.org/europe-central-asia/central-asia/245-central-asias-silk-road-rivalries?utm_source=SupChina&utm_campaign=e446db5b79-20170727-343AHappyStoryTibetanPlateau&utm_medium=email&utm_term=0_caef3ab334-e446db5b79-164871129.

66. Sebastien Peyrouse, "The Evolution of Russia's Views on the Belt and Road Initiative," in Roundtable on China's Belt and Road Initiative: Views from along the Silk Road (2017), *Asia Policy* 24 (July), pp. 96–102.

67. "China's Xi Awards 'Best Friend' Putin Friendship Medal, Promises Support," *Reuters*, 8 June 2018, online at: https://www.reuters.com/article/us-china-russia/chinas-xi-awards-best-friend-putin-friendship-medal-promises-support-idUSKCN1J41RO.

68. "Vladimir Putin Names India, China and Russia as 'Major Players' in Shanghai Cooperation Organisation," *Hindustan Times*, 6 June 2018, online at: https://

www.hindustantimes.com/world-news/vladimir-putin-names-india-china-and-russia-as-major-players-in-sco/story-mJPPPBu2fXg7VHtg2hRwKM.html.

69. Zhao Hong, "Japan and China: Competing for Good Relations with Myanmar," *Journal of East Asian Affairs* 28 (2) (Fall/Winter 2014), pp. 1–24.

70. Keith Johnson, "China, Sri Lanka and the Maritime Great Game," *Foreign Policy*, 12 February 2015, online at: http://foreignpolicy.com/2015/02/12/china-sri-lanka-and-the-maritime-great-game-silk-road-xi-port/.

71. Ben Bland, "China's South-East Asia Threatened by New Malaysia Regime," *Financial Times*, 15 May 2018, online at: https://www.ft.com/content/94906ad4-57eb-11e8-bdb7-f6677d2e1ce8.

72. See Jane Golley and Adam Ingle, "The Belt and Road Initiative: How to Win Friends and Influence People," in *China Story Yearbook 2017: Prosperity,* ANU Press, Canberra, online at: http://press-files.anu.edu.au/downloads/press/n4224/pdf/ch02.pdf.

73. For the full text, see https://america.cgtn.com/2017/01/17/full-text-of-xi-jinping-keynote-at-the-world-economic-forum.

74. Michael Shear, "Trump Attends G-& with Defiance, Proposing to Readmit Russia," *New York Times*, 8 June 2018, online at: https://www.nytimes.com/2018/06/08/world/americas/trump-g7-trade-russia.html.

75. As discussed at length in G. John Ikenberry, "The End of Liberal International Order?" *International Affairs* 94 (1) (2018), pp. 7–23.

Chapter 6

The Environmental and Social Safeguard Policies of the Belt and Road Initiative

The Geopolitical Implications

Brooke Wilmsen, Andrew van Hulten,
Xiao Han, and David Adjartey

When first announced by President Xi Jinping in 2013, the Belt Road Initiative (BRI) was portrayed as an infrastructure investment project established to connect China to Asia and Europe through a wide range of road, rail, and port projects. In the intervening years, however, the variety of projects included under the BRI banner has blossomed to include projects such as the BRI Fashion Week in Guangzhou,[1] a theme park on the Gold Coast of Australia,[2] and a high-tech city on Melbourne's western fringe.[3] The number of actors involved in the initiative has also grown rapidly. More than a hundred countries have expressed interest in participating in the BRI,[4] many of which have only tenuous interests in infrastructure investment in Asia and Europe. For example, in early 2018, China invited Latin American and Caribbean countries to participate in the BRI. Meanwhile, multilateral financial institutions, including the World Bank and Asian Development Bank (ADB), have agreed to cofinance BRI projects. Bolstering the multilateral credentials of the initiative, in 2016, the Chinese government established the Asian Infrastructure Investment Bank (AIIB), which now has eighty-eight members.[5] Of the OECD countries, the United States is a notable exception. Finally, a multitude of private and state-owned firms—Chinese or otherwise—will be involved in financing and implementing projects on the ground.

This ever-growing list of participants—not to mention the uncertain status of many of the announced projects—complicates the task of unpacking

China's geopolitical motivations for pursuing the BRI. Several recurring themes emerge, however, from the existing literature. Many commentaries portray the BRI as a tool of state propaganda. As Jonathan Hillman states, "By design, the BRI is more a loose brand than a program with strict criteria."[6] Others describe it is an umbrella or "Christmas tree"[7] under which all of China's overseas investments can be gathered for public display. Other accounts portray the BRI more as a *re*branding exercise; a co-optation and refinement of Jiang Zemin's "Going Out" policy by Xi Jinping, which encouraged the internationalization of Chinese firms since the early 2000s.[8] Another theme focuses on how the Chinese government is using the BRI to address domestic economic and political problems. In these accounts, the BRI is a tool to soak up excess capacity in heavy industries like steel and coal while supporting employment; reinvest China's huge foreign exchanges in high-return assets; and drive China's ecological modernization by paving the way for firms to relocate their most polluting, low-valued activities elsewhere in Asia.[9] Some go so far as to describe the BRI as "a domestic policy with geostrategic consequences rather than a foreign policy."[10] Other threads focus on how China, through the BRI and AIIB, is beginning to challenge the normative dominance of multilateral institutions such as the World Bank and International Monetary Fund, seen by the Chinese government as serving Western norms and interests.[11]

All of these threads analyze the motivations of the Chinese state through the lens of soft power. There is, however, growing interest in the hard power implications of the BRI. In early 2018, for example, the Australian government expressed concern about the high level of debt some Pacific Island countries have incurred to the Chinese government, which could generate financial crises and political turmoil.[12] Peter Cai reports nearly two-thirds of BRI countries have a sovereign credit rating below investable grade.[13] Hurley et al. identify eight BRI countries at risk of debt default based on the *existing* pipeline of projects.[14]

Another concern is that BRI projects—and the associated debt—provide China with a surreptitious way of extending its military footprint. The port of Hanbanbota in Sri Lanka, for example, was financed using Chinese debt and built by China Communications Construction Company (CCCC). When the Sri Lankan government was unable to service this debt, the Chinese government acquired an 80 percent stake in the port and, subsequently, acquired a ninety-nine-year lease over the port facilities.[15] These sorts of outcomes may also generate protests and violent resistance, especially in neighboring countries where tensions exist over China's treatment of its Uighur minority.[16]

Whether these risks materialize will depend, in large part, on the quality of individual BRI projects, in particular, whether they bring benefits to local populations and "pay for themselves" by increasing economic productivity.

In this chapter we analyze a specific subset of risks with geopolitical implications, namely the risk that BRI projects will cause harm to local populations due to inadequate environmental and social protection standards.[17] The environmental and social risks of large infrastructure projects are well established, and the major multilateral institutions and many national governments have developed laws, regulations, and standards of best practice to mitigate these risks.[18] We assess these risks with regards to the BRI by reviewing the environmental and social risk management frameworks of recipient countries, Chinese firms operating abroad, and the major multilateral institutions, including the newly created AIIB. To assess the likelihood of these laws and guidelines being translated into practice, we review the literature that explores the social and environmental practices of Chinese banks and firms operating abroad, and present a case study of the Chinese-funded Bui Dam project in Ghana. We conclude by discussing, albeit tentatively, the geopolitical implications of our findings.

COUNTRY STANDARDS

China pursues a policy of noninterference with regards to its official development assistance and other foreign investment activities.[19] The State Council declares, "When providing foreign assistance, China adheres to the principles of not imposing any political conditions, not interfering in the internal affairs of the recipient countries and fully respecting their right to independently choosing their own paths and models of development."[20] Developing countries often favor the Chinese approach because it "comes without Western lectures about governance and human rights"[21] and eschews the cumbersome social, environmental, and accountability standards of Western donors.[22] Others argue that China invokes the sanctity of state sovereignty in order to willfully ignore the human rights abuses, corruption, and social and environmental implications of overseas projects in order to preserve the cost-competitiveness of Chinese firms.[23]

In the early years of the BRI, at least, China will continue its noninterference policy. The BRI Vision Statement offers no specific guidance to Chinese investors on how they should deal with social and environment issues generated by the BRI projects. As such, where BRI projects are funded *solely* by Chinese banks and implemented by Chinese construction firms, the burden of managing environmental and social risks will fall to recipient countries. Moreover, it is the responsibility of the recipient country to knock back funding when they do not have the capacity to manage these risks. This brings into sharp focus the social and environmental protection frameworks of the countries participating in the BRI.

Commentators have argued the environmental and social protection frameworks of many BRI member countries, especially in Central Asia, are inadequate.[24] The social and environmental risks of large-scale infrastructure projects are many and varied and include the loss of biodiversity, land and water contamination, habitat loss and fragmentation, social fragmentation and conflict, the increased prevalence of disease, and forced displacement. Analyzing all of these risks is beyond the scope of this chapter. In the following analysis, we focus on an important social risk—involuntary resettlement—as a case in point. We assess the degree to which BRI countries are compliant with the ADB's *Involuntary Resettlement Guidelines*—an important international standard in this area—by encoding and mapping each country's most recently published compliance report.[25] Among other things, these reports assess whether a country has laws and regulations in place to ensure people displaced by large infrastructure projects play an active role in their own resettlement and are properly compensated for any livelihood losses. Our results are displayed in figure 6.1.

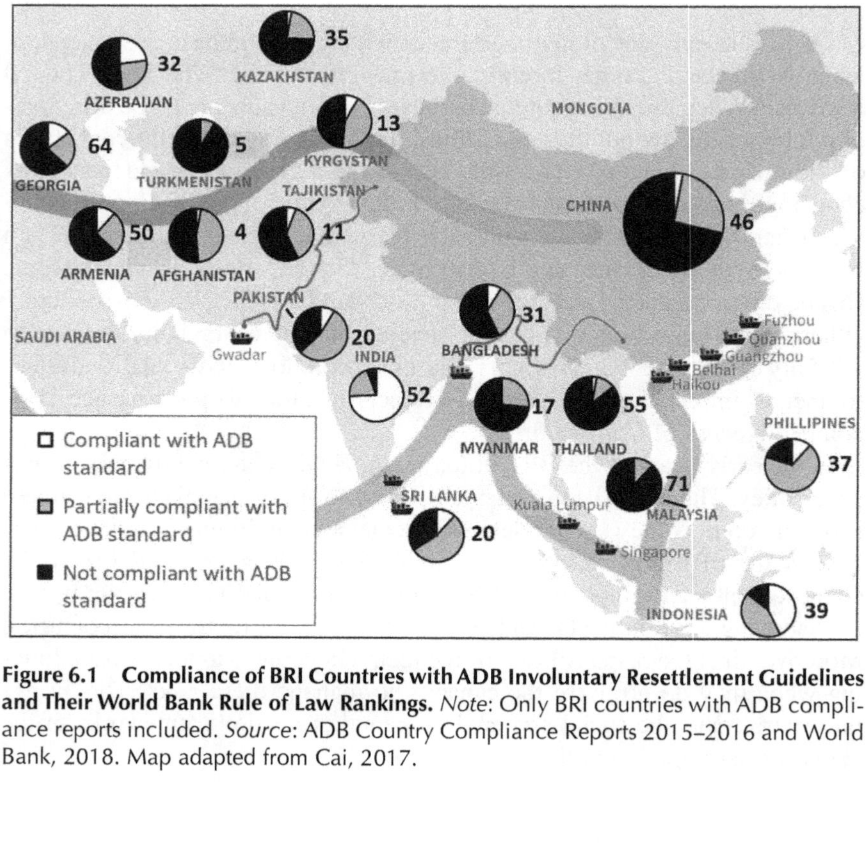

Figure 6.1 Compliance of BRI Countries with ADB Involuntary Resettlement Guidelines and Their World Bank Rule of Law Rankings. *Note*: Only BRI countries with ADB compliance reports included. *Source*: ADB Country Compliance Reports 2015–2016 and World Bank, 2018. Map adapted from Cai, 2017.

Figure 6.1 demonstrates that many BRI countries, particularly those in Central and South East Asia, are noncompliant with a majority of the ADB guidelines. Indeed, no country, apart from India, is complaint with more than a small fraction of the ADB guidelines. Importantly, China's own resettlement standards are mostly noncompliant with the ADB standards, although significant progress has been made in the area in recent years.[26] This suggests many BRI countries lack the basic legal infrastructure needed to prevent adverse outcomes for local populations forced to make way for BRI projects.

Questions also exist about the capacity of these countries to translate domestic laws and regulation, however flimsy, into practice. To explore this issue, in figure 6.1 we include each country's *Rule of Law Index* ranking, published annually by the World Bank. This measure captures people's perceptions of the quality of a country's legal system and enforcement agencies.[27] It shows that many important BRI countries, especially in Central Asia, are ranked in the bottom deciles by this measure. This suggests that many BRI countries lack the capacity to implement existing laws, and that some laws will be bypassed by corrupt means.[28] A case in point is the Zamfara Dam in Nigeria. Its construction has stalled for at least seven years because elites in the Nigerian government did not follow national regulatory processes or conduct proper consultation with local communities.[29] All of this increases the likelihood that local populations and environments will be adversely affected by BRI projects, especially if China continues its long-standing practice of deferring to local laws and customs.

Poor project outcomes at the local level can generate resentment and protests, if not, outright violence. This is of particular concern in Central Asia, where border disputes and China's treatment of the Uighur minority have heightened tensions with its neighbors. In 2018, for example, protestors in Kyrgyzstan set alight a newly built Chinese gold mine.[30] This followed the suicide bombing of the Chinese embassy in 2016. Meanwhile, in neighboring Kazakhstan, in 2016, protests broke when people grew fearful the government was changing the local land codes so it could sell off their land to Chinese agricultural companies.[31] Of course, these risks must be weighed against the potential benefits of infrastructure projects, such as generating new jobs and increasing private investment in the local economy.

CHINESE STANDARDS

In recent decades, China has enacted a wide range of laws and guidelines that seek to improve the environmental and social risk management practices of Chinese banks and firms. While the strongest of these laws apply only *within* China, the Chinese government has also promulgated a range of (voluntary) guidelines pertaining to the overseas operations of Chinese banks and firms. These guidelines are largely aspirational and rarely translated into practice. While China is likely to persist with its noninterference policy for the foreseeable future, these domestic laws and (voluntary) guidelines are nonetheless important as they provide the Chinese government with the legal mechanisms it needs to force Chinese banks and firms involved in BRI projects to improve their environmental and social risk management practices. The following subsections provide a brief overview of this legal infrastructure, with a particular focus on the laws and guidelines pertaining to the overseas operations of Chinese banks and firms.

CHINESE CONSTRUCTION FIRMS

The Chinese government insists the BRI will be a truly international endeavor that will involve a vast array of non-Chinese firms and banks. To date, however, BRI projects have been dominated by Chinese firms. According to Hillman, of all the contractors involved in Chinese-funded projects completed-to-date, 89 percent were Chinese companies.[32] By contrast, for BRI projects funded by multilateral financial institutions, 29 percent of contracting firms were Chinese, 41 percent were local firms, and 30 percent were from third countries (Ibid). Under the "Going Out" policy, which preceded the BRI, this practice of favoring Chinese contractors was official government policy.[33] Furthermore, the largest contracts tend to go to the largest SOEs, such as China Railway Construction Corp (CRCC), CCCC, and Sinohydro. To date, around 50 SOEs have participated in 1,700 BRI projects.[34] Centrally owned SOEs are regulated by the state-owned Assets Supervision and Administration Commission, giving the State Council significant control over the activities of these firms, including their environmental and social risk management practices.

In recent decades, the Chinese government has gradually improved its *domestic* environmental and social protection laws. In 2003, the *Environmental Impact Assessment Law* was implemented, requiring all medium and large investment projects to undertake environmental impact assessments.[35] Meanwhile, the state agencies responsible for drafting and enforcing environmental regulations have been progressively strengthened, culminating, in 2008, in the creation of the Ministry of Environmental Protection. According to Compagnon and Alejandro, "Chinese environmental legislation is quite strong on paper and more sophisticated than many assume, but its implementation is rather weak, depending on the efforts of local governments and other state agencies."[36] Laws protecting the rights of people displaced by large development projects have also been progressively strengthened.[37] In 2006, for example, new rules were promulgated to protect communities displaced by large hydroelectric dam projects.[38] It remains an open empirical question, however, whether Chinese firms subject to tighter standards at home will also improve their practices abroad.

In this regard, the Chinese government has issued a number of guidelines focused upon the overseas activities of Chinese firms. In 2006, the State Council called on Chinese overseas investors to "fulfil the necessary social responsibility to protect the legitimate rights and interests of local employees, pay attention to environmental resource protection, care and support of the local community and people's livelihood cause."[39] In 2013, the Ministry of Commerce issued *Guidance on Environmental Protection in Foreign Investment and Cooperation* that, among other things, encourages Chinese firms to "abide by the environmental protection laws and regulation of the host country" and to "*learn from* the environmental principles, standards and practices of international organizations and multilateral institutions."[40] Recent guidelines jointly published by the Ministry of Environment Protection and other Chinese environmental agencies encourage Chinese enterprises to "fully understand the environmental standards of China, the country in which the project is located and the international environment and *adopt the highest standards possible* in accordance with the industry characteristics of the project."[41] Leung et al. describe a range of similar guidelines, which reflect the growing concern that poorly executed projects abroad damage the international reputation of the Chinese firms, not to mention the government.[42] This risk is particularly acute with regards to the BRI, given its close association—real and perceived—with the Chinese government. It is important to note, however, that all of these guidelines pertaining to the overseas operations of Chinese firms are nonbinding.[43]

CHINESE BANKS AND FINANCIAL INSTITUTIONS

To date, the majority of finance for BRI projects has been provided by China's largest state-owned banks, in particular, China Development Bank (CDB), Export-Import Bank of China (Eximbank), and the "Big Four" commercial banks. This reflects the Chinese government's long-standing preference to debt-finance overseas development projects. During the "Going Out" years, China developed what became known as the Angola model. Under this model, developing countries were offered cheap loans for infrastructure projects, which would subsequently be built by Chinese construction firms. In the event of a default, the borrowing country would agree to transfer ownership of a natural resource (such as an oil field or mineral deposit) or some other national asset to the Chinese lender. This general model has been refined and extended into the BRI era. The port of Hanbanbota in Sri Lanka, for example, was debt-financed and later acquired by the Chinese government through a debt-for-equity swap.[44]

The aim of the Chinese government is ultimately to cofinance BRI projects with other countries and multilateral institutions like the World Bank. For the foreseeable future, however, China's large banks and other state-controlled financial institutions will continue to finance the majority of BRI projects. This has important implications for environmental and social risk management. Financial institutions play a critical, gatekeeping role in setting and improving environmental and social protection standards, for example, by requiring that project proponents carry out environmental and social impact assessments and developing risk mitigation plans. The most important banks and financial institutions bankrolling the BRI are already subject to a wide range of regulations and guidelines pertaining to their overseas investment activities (see table 6.1). The most important of these are the Green Credit Guidelines (GCG), announced by the China Banking Regulatory Commission (CBRC) in 2012. These guidelines apply to both the domestic and international operations of China's policy banks, commercial banks, rural cooperative banks, and rural credit unions. These guidelines state:

> Banks shall strengthen environmental and social management for proposed overseas projects, ensure project sponsors are compliant with local environmental, land, health and safety laws and regulations in the project country or region. Banks shall publicly commit to adopt relevant international best practices or standards for the proposed overseas project, ensure the proposed project is consistent with international best practices in essence.[45]

In 2014, the CRBC published key performance indicators (KPIs) the banks can use to assess their own progress in meeting the GCGs. While hailing the GCGs as an important advance in the field of sustainable finance, an analysis of several case studies undertaken by the Friends of the Earth concludes, "Chinese banks still struggle to comply with host country laws and regulations, let alone international norms and standards."[46]

Table 6.1 demonstrates the Chinese central government has a high degree of control over the most important Chinese financial institutions funding BRI projects. The two policy banks—CDB and Eximbank—are under the direct jurisdiction of the State Council. Similarly, the "Big Four" commercial banks are centrally owned and regulated by the CBRC, which also reports directly to the State Council. By controlling the flow of finance through these institutions, the Chinese central government can play—if it so chooses—a powerful role in determining the environmental and social risk management practices, even in situations where it has limited control over the Chinese construction firms paid to implement projects (such as SOEs controlled by lower levels of government).

Table 6.1 Regulation Frameworks for Major Chinese Financial Institutions Funding BRI Projects

Funding Institution	*Main Form of Financing*	*Direct Regulatory Body*	*Subject to National Regulations Governing Overseas Environmental and Social Practices*	*Corporate Responsibility Policies*
China Development Bank (CDB)	Loans (non-concessional)	State Council via Board of Supervisors	Yes *GCG* (2012); *Environmental Protection Guide in Foreign Investment Cooperation* (2013); *CSR Guidelines for China's Banking Institutions* (2009).	Yes CDB has issued a range of guidelines, the latest of which is the *Guidance on Environmental Protection and Emissions Reduction Business* (2012)
Export-Import Bank of China (EXIM)	Loans (concessional)	State Council	Yes See above	Yes *Guidelines for ESIAs of the China EXIM Bank Loan Projects (2007)*
Commercial banks including "Big Four" state-owned banks	Loans	CBRC	Yes *GCG* (CBRC); *Guide on Information Disclosure of Listed Companies* (Shanghai Stock Exchange); *Guide on Environmental, Social and Governance Report* (Hong Kong Stock Exchange); *Global Reporting Initiative Sustainability Reporting Guidelines* (GRI4.0)	Yes A range of bank-specific corporate governance policies and guidelines

(*Continued*)

Table 6.1 Regulation Frameworks for Major Chinese Financial Institutions Funding BRI Projects *(Continued)*

Funding Institution	*Main Form of Financing*	*Direct Regulatory Body*	*Subject to National Regulations Governing Overseas Environmental and Social Practices*	*Corporate Responsibility Policies*
Silk Road Fund	Equity	State Council via four major shareholders: State Adm. Foreign Exchange (65 percent), China Investment Corporation (15 percent), EXIM (15 percent), CDB (5 percent)	No details, but presumably subject to the same guidelines as its major shareholders (see CDB and EXIM above).	No details, but states it will comply with international standards and guidelines of countries of investment.
China-ASEAN Investment Corporation Fund	Equity	State Council	No details	Not details. States it will comply with World Bank environmental and social standards
Green Silk Road Equity Fund	Equity	No details. Owned by private investors, including non-Chinese investors	No details	No details
China Insurance Investment Fund	Equity	China Insurance Regulatory Commission	No details	No details

Source: Greenovation hub (2016) and relevant government websites.

Table 1 also reveals that all of the big Chinese banks have published corporate social responsibility (CSR) statements, some of which contain environmental and social risk mitigation provisions.[47] This is part of a broader trend in China. Since the mid-2000s, many corporations in China—state-owned and private—have released CSR statements. A range of empirical studies reveal, however, that the concept remains in its infancy in China. Studies have found that Chinese manager do not consider CRS to be strategically important and regard it mainly as a public relations exercise,[48] especially when it comes to their overseas activities.[49] For instance, Wu et al. found that Chinese contractors place less emphasis on social and environmental issues than other international contractors.[50] Nonetheless, as the Chinese government and Chinese managers grow more concerned about the global reputations of their firms, these CRS statement may play an increasingly important role in improving environmental and social risk management practices.

EMPIRICAL STUDIES

The previous sections demonstrate that the legal and regulatory infrastructure already exists to significantly improve the environmental and social risk management practices of Chinese firms and banks. Further, the State Council has significant capacity to force the most important players involved in the BRI—the large state-owned banks and construction firms—to improve their environmental and social risk management practice. There is great uncertainty, however, about whether—and how—the Chinese government will exercise this power. In the meantime, China is likely to persist with the policies and business practices it developed during the "Going Out" era. In this regard, it is worth reviewing briefly the broad literature that discusses the overseas activities of Chinese firms and banks since the early 2000s.

On behalf of the UNDP, Wang et al. reviewed 384 papers exploring the effects of Chinese investment abroad.[51] The review identified some important recurring themes:

- Developing countries often welcome China's "no-strings attached" approach to providing investment finance, although it is often seen to exacerbate local corruption.
- Chinese investment boosts incomes and lowers poverty while generating income inequality in host communities.
- Chinese companies often ignore social and environmental impacts due to concerns about competitiveness and profitability.
- EIAs conducted by Chinese firms are often inadequate.
- There is no substantial difference between Chinese and OECD firms with regard to their treatment of employees.

- Host communities are particularly concerned about the corruption and environmental damage caused by Chinese investments, particularly in infrastructure, mining, forestry, and agriculture sectors.

Wang et al pointed out, however, that there was a paucity of research comparing the behavior of Chinese and OECD firms. As such, it remains an open empirical question whether Chinese investments produce worse environmental and social outcomes than similar investments sourced from Western countries.

The studies reviewed by Wang et al. focus largely on the "Going Out" era. Empirical studies covering the BRI era are only now beginning to emerge. Notable among these, Friends of the Earth reviewed seven BRI projects funded by Chinese banks and found host-country laws and international norms were violated in all seven case studies.[52] In four cases they found serious flaws in the EIAs carried out prior to finance being secured. This provides some preliminary evidence that the project-level practices developed by Chinese firms during the "Going Out" years are likely to carry over into the BRI era for some years at least.

GLOBAL STANDARDS

Although China will continue to defer to host-country laws for the foreseeable future, global standards will play an increasingly important role in future BRI projects. Many of the (aspirational) guidelines discussed in the previous sections already make reference to important global standards and agreements, such as the Equator Principles, the United Nations Global Compact, and the Global Reporting Initiative.[53] More importantly, the Chinese government has stated that it wants to cofinance more BRI projects multilaterally and bilaterally. The World Bank and Silk Road Fund, for example, are already cofinancing a hydropower project in Pakistan, which will be built by Three Gorges Company, a Chinese state-owned hydropower firm.[54] These sorts of projects will require Chinese banks and firms to learn from—and comply with—the environmental and social safeguard policies of their partner organizations.

The World Bank and the other major multilateral financial institutions require project proponents to comply with a wide range of environmental and social safeguard policies (see table 6.2). Although the World Bank policies are regarded as the "gold standard" in this area,[55] there is a high level of policy convergence between these institutions. World Bank policy, for example, requires detailed environmental impact assessments to be carried out for all projects with significant environmental implications.[56] Other provisions limit the use of pesticides, the destruction of forests and animal habitats, and the like. With regards to the issue of involuntary resettlement, World Bank policy

Table 6.2 Environmental and Social Policies of the Major Multilateral Financial Institutions

Policy Area	*World Bank*	*International Financial Corporation*	*Asian Development Bank*	*African Development Bank*	*European Bank for Reconstruction and Development*	*European Investment Bank*	*Inter-American Development Bank*
Environmental and social assessment	Yes	Yes	Yes	Yes	Yes	Yes	Yes
Pollution prevention	Yes	Yes	Incorporated into ESA	Yes	Yes	Yes	Yes
Biodiversity	Yes	Yes	Incorporated into ESA	Yes	Yes	Yes	Yes
Environmental flow	Yes	None	None	Biodiversity	None	None	None
Involuntary resettlement	Yes	Yes	Yes	Yes	Yes	Yes	Yes
Community impacts	None	Yes	Yes	Incorporatedinto ESA	Yes	Yes	Yes
Workforce environment/ labor conditions	None	Yes	Incorporated into ESA	Yes	None	Yes	None
Indigenous peoples	Yes	Yes	Yes	Incorporatedinto ESA	Yes	Yes	Yes
Cultural heritage	Yes	Yes	Incorporated into ESA	Incorporatedinto ESA	Yes	Yes	Yes

Source: Greenovation Hub, 2016.

requires that resettlement be avoided where possible and, if not, that people be given an active voice in the resettlement process and be left no worse off as a result of their resettlement. A downside of this approach, however, is that poverty is often reinstated rather than alleviated.

ASIAN INFRASTRUCTURE INVESTMENT BANK (AIIB)

In 2014, China—along with Brazil, Russia, India, China, and South Africa—established the New Development Bank to fund development projects around the world and, in 2016, China established the AIIB. These new institutions not only provide developing countries with an important new source of finance, they also provided China with a growing voice in global debates about what constitutes "international best practice."[57]

Given its focus on funding Asian infrastructure investment, the AIIB will play an important role in shaping the environmental and social protection standards applied to BRI projects. Although China dominates the AIIB from a funding and voting perspective—as of September 2016, China holds 29 percent of the total voting power—its governance practices resemble those of the World Bank and similar multilateral institutions. When the AIIB was announced, President Xi Jinping stated the AIIB would adhere to "multinational rules and procedures" and follow the "good practices" of the established multilateral institutions.[58] Furthermore, founding members like Germany, Australia, France, and the United Kingdom are expected to push for high environmental and social risk management standards.[59]

In its first year, the AIIB cofinanced 75 percent of its projects with other institutions, most importantly, the World Bank and ADB.[60] As De Jonge suggests, by "focusing on projects led by other international financial institutions, the AIIB can build up an investment portfolio and a track record, and gain experience in development finance, faster than would be possible if it acted on its own."[61] Many of the AIIB's staff are former ADB employees, which further strengthens these processes of cross-country, inter-institutional learning. Chinese construction firms involved in AIIB projects will also have to improve their environmental and social risk management practices.

In August 2015, the AIIB published its draft environmental and social framework and, after a six-week consultation period, the final version was published. While voicing concerns about this brief consultation period, most commentators agree that the AIIB's standards are roughly equivalent to those of the World Bank and ADB.[62] The AIIB has also announced that projects with significant environmental and social risks will need to carry out detailed risk assessments (like EIAs) and develop risk mitigation plans (including resettlement plans) during the loan application process.[63] The AIIB has also announced tendering policies to ensure non-Chinese firms can compete on an equal footing with (state-owned) Chinese firms for AIIB contracts.[64]

All of this indicates that the Chinese central government is keen to quickly establish the international credentials of the AIIB and, in doing so, create another vehicle through which it can finance BRI projects. While most commentators are optimistic about early efforts to integrate international best practices into the AIIB's day-to-day operations, it will be years before empirical studies can establish whether these efforts will prove effective. It should also be noted that the Bretton Woods institutions, themselves, often fail to translate policy into practice. In 2015, the World Bank admitted that it had failed to follow its own guidelines in a range of big projects.[65] A major reason for this is that project proponents often lack the skills and resources needed to implement environmental and social risk mitigation plans. Another problem, as our case study will reveal, is mock compliance.

CASE STUDY OF THE BUI DAM, GHANA

The Bui Dam project is of interest because it epitomizes China's approach to outbound investment during the "Going Out" era, aspects of which are likely to continue into the BRI period. More importantly, however, the Bui Dam case demonstrates the various ways in which environmental and social concerns can "slip through the cracks" of large infrastructure projects even when stakeholders comply with host-country laws and risk mitigation plans are prepared in accordance with global standard of best practice.

Proposals to build the Bui Dam date back to the 1920s. Over the years, the Ghanaian government made several attempts to build the dam but were never able to secure the necessary finance.[66] In 2001, the World Bank rejected a loan application due to concerns about the project's environmental and social impacts.[67] In 2003, the Ghanaian government requested assistance from the Chinese government to build the Bui Dam. Financing was agreed in 2007, construction began in 2009, and the dam was commissioned in December 2013.

The Bui Dam project embodies many aspects of the so-called Angola model. The Ghanaian government borrowed US$622 million from Eximbank. This debt was secured with claims over Ghana's future cocoa exports.[68] The borrowed money was used to pay Sinohydro, a large state-owned Chinese firm, to construct the dam. The dam was built using a "turn key" contract, which meant that Sinohydro designed and built the dam before handing it over to the Ghanaian government. Responsibility for running the dam was devolved to a newly created agency, the Bui Power Authority (BPA). The BPA was also responsible for resettling the more than 1,200 villagers who had to make way for the project. These arrangements ensured Sinohydro avoided any responsibility for the environmental and social implications of the dam.[69]

Consistent with China's noninterference policy, Sinohydro and Eximbank deferred to Ghana's environmental and social laws. Chinese and global standards, nonetheless, played an important—if ineffective—role. Under Ghanaian law, a full environmental and social impact assessment (ESIA) was needed before the Ghanaian Environmental Protection Agency could issue a project permit.[70] Eximbank's internal guidelines also required an ESIA to be conducted before finance could be approved.[71] To this end, Environmental Resource Management (ERM), an international consultancy firm, was contracted to produce three reports: an ESIA environmental impact assessment, a resettlement plan, and an Environmental and Social Management Plan.[72] This meant, "Sinohydro was contracted to build the dam based on a set of planning documents commissioned and paid for by Ghanaian government agencies and written by European consulting agencies."[73]

ERM's reports were produced in compliance with the relevant World Bank guidelines. The resettlement plan, for example, was prepared in accordance with the World Bank's *Involuntary Resettlement Operational Manual* 4.12, regarded as best practice at the time. The stated aim of ERM's resettlement plan was as follows:

> To ensure that the Bui Dam project improves people's economic opportunities and living conditions and minimises adverse impacts while also providing remedial measures for those adverse impacts that are unavoidable, particularly among the communities most directly affected by resettlement either through physical displacement and or loss of economic resources.[74]

This plan analyzed the livelihood strategies and assets of the displaced households and outlined detailed risk mitigation measures, including the provision of new housing and farmland as well as financial compensation. ERM submitted its work to the Ghanaian government in early 2007.[75] This ended ERM's involvement in the project. It had no ongoing role in advising on—or monitoring—the implementation of the plans it had drafted. Thus, prior to finance being secured, the Chinese and Ghanaian actors went to considerable lengths to (give the appearance) that international best practices were being followed. Afterward, however, responsibility for implementing ERM's recommendations fell to the Ghanaian government, which lacked the human and financial resources—not to mention, political will—to ensure that ERM's plans were properly implemented.

The Bui Dam project produced a wide range of adverse social and environmental impacts.[76] The public consultation process carried out prior to the resettlement of the villagers was cursory and fell short of the World Bank standard, which requires free, prior, and informed consent. The government's promise to build a new city—called Bui City—was never fulfilled. Residents complained that the "BPA took advantage of our ignorance to convince us to agree to relocate."[77] Villagers spoke at length about the loss of critical livelihood assets. Farming-dependent households complained about the loss of land, in particular, the loss of good quality land. Fishing-dependent households lost access to the river. Prior to the dam's construction, the Black Volta River flowed according to the seasons. Afterward, the river flow was greatly reduced, rendering the fisherfolk's traditional methods ineffective. Furthermore, the fisherman could not afford motorized boats to fish upon the lake. As such, many resettled households were struggling to make a living.

While some of these adverse outcomes can be attributed to the failure of the Ghanaian government to implement ERM's plans, other adverse outcomes were poorly anticipated in the planning documents. The project produced a high level of in-migration into the local area, which had a range of flow-on effects. On the dam, for example, local fisherman reported coming into violent conflict with other fisherman who had recently moved into the area. Villagers also spoke about the breakdown of communal norms and power structures. Marriages were put under stress by the inability of men to earn a living from farming and fish as they had done previously. Another manifestation of this impoverishment and the breakdown of traditional power structures was an increase in the rate of teenage pregnancy. A local teacher reported that around 70 percent of girls at the junior school were pregnant. Furthermore, young girls were forming relationships with itinerant workers rather than marrying within their community, in large part, because they lacked other means of supporting themselves.

These poorly anticipated outcomes demonstrate that environmental and social risk management remains an inexact science. World Bank and ADB guidelines still struggle to accommodate—let alone predict and mitigate—a wide range of risks generated by large infrastructure and resettlement projects. This explains, in part, why the World Bank dramatically reduced its spending on infrastructure projects from 70 to 30 percent of its total funding between the 1950s and the 2000s.[78] The Bui Dam case warns against viewing increased involvement of multilateral institutions and the application of "global standards of best practice" as a panacea for dealing with the environmental and social risks—and attendant geopolitical risks—generated by BRI projects.

DISCUSSION AND CONCLUSIONS

The BRI is a moving feast of project proposals, financial institutions, construction firms, and member countries, many of whom are still deciding their actual level of commitment. There is also a great degree of uncertainty about what environmental and social standards will be applied to BRI projects. The existing regulatory terrain is multilayered, comprised of various host-country laws and regulations, Chinese laws and (voluntary) guidelines, and global standards of best practice (which China itself is beginning to adapt and, in some cases, adopt). The geopolitical implications of all this are equally uncertain. Nonetheless, we offer some tentative conclusions.

For the foreseeable future, the vast majority of finance for BRI projects will be provided by the Chinese government, which will encourage Chinese banks and firms to continuing their established practice of deferring to host-country laws and regulations. Our analysis revealed the danger of China's "hands off" approach. Environmental and social protection laws are severely lacking in many BRI member countries, particularly in Central and South Asia. Furthermore, the weak rule of law in many of these countries lowers the likelihood that host-country laws will ever be enforced. All of this raises the risk of adverse project outcomes, especially for local populations displaced by large infrastructure projects and exposed to environmental damage.

It is easy to see how poor project implementation might generate protest, if not violent resistance, especially in neighboring countries where there is a history of border tensions and religious animosity. Violent protests against China's growing influence have already taken place in some of these countries. Indeed, the World Bank's environmental and social safeguard policies emerged from a series of high-profile failed infrastructure projects, most notably, the notorious Narmada Dam in India. Poorly implemented projects not only harm local communities and generate political problems in host countries but also damage the reputations of lenders and donors, eroding the soft power dividends of these "investments." Further geopolitical risk is generated by the rising indebtedness of many BRI countries to China. When debt is squandered on low-return investments (or simply embezzled) financial crises may ensue, generating further geopolitical turmoil. In 1980s and 1990s, Western donors imposed structural adjustment packages on developing countries unable to service their debt. Much of this debt had been extended with geopolitical considerations in mind; in particular, to bolster support for the West during the Cold War era. Many of these structural adjustment programs proved counterproductive, however, exacerbating the economic and political problems of developing countries and further damaging the reputations of Western lenders. Today, China exploits this sad history when it promotes its approach to foreign lending as being both less bureaucratic and less sanctimonious than Western institutions.[79] One wonders, however, whether China risks repeating these same mistakes, given its predilection for debt financing in countries where the rule of law is weak and environmental and social protection laws are inadequate.

The Chinese government understands that poor implementation of BRI projects at the local level may thwart its geopolitical and geoeconomic ambitions. To this end, it has invested heavily in the legal infrastructure required to raise the environmental and social protection standards of Chinese firms. Domestically, at least, China has made great strides in improving its laws and agencies in this area. Indeed, some argue that the BRI paves the way for China to export its dirtiest industries abroad, following in the footsteps of the other advanced economies. The Chinese government has also issued a multitude of (nonbinding) guidelines pertaining to the *overseas* activities of Chinese banks and firms, many of which make reference to key global standards. Meanwhile, Chinese banks and firms are developing their own CSR policies that contain environmental and social provisions. For the time being, however, these government guidelines and CRS policies are largely aspirational, especially when it comes to the activities of Chinese banks and firms abroad. This legal infrastructure is, nonetheless, important: the laws, guidelines, and agencies needed to effect rapid change are already in place.

Global standards like the World Bank's Safeguard Policies will play an increasingly important role in BRI projects. If China wants to cofinance more BRI projects then they will need to comply with the highest standards acceptable to all stakeholders. Through the AIIB, China has revealed a growing appetite for "interventionist" environmental and social standards. The AIIB's environmental and social policies are broadly consistent with those of the World Bank and ADB. While its funding is a small proportion of total BRI funding, the AIIB provides China with a mechanism through which it can learn about—and experiment with—global standards. Furthermore, Chinese banks and firms participating in AIIB projects will be forced to change their internal practices.

The AIIB has some important geopolitical implications too. The AIIB also provides China with a new way of channeling funds to politically sensitive projects. In this light, the AIIB may provide China with a valuable distancing mechanism, allowing it to progress strategically important projects where local resistance is likely to be high, for example, road projects in Central Asia. Channeling funds through the AIIB will, however, dilute the soft power dividends China receives from such projects. Through the AIIB—and to a lesser degree, the New Development Bank—China has a growing voice in the global conversation about how "international best practice" should be defined and, in doing so, it begins to challenge the normative dominance of the World Bank, IMF, and ADB.

While it is difficult to anticipate the environmental and social consequences of BRI projects, two key points emerge from our analysis. First, the Chinese central government—by virtue of its control over the most important banks and firms involved in the BRI—has the capacity to rapidly raise environmental and social standards. How it exercises this capacity will depend in large part on whether early BRI projects deliver the promised benefits to host countries, as well as how other countries respond to China's growing influence in Asia and the Pacific. Poor environmental and social outcomes will be used by China's critics to undermine the BRI and increase calls for it to comply with international standards.

Second, China has gone to great lengths to maximize its own room to maneuver. It has created a multitude of mechanisms through which it can fund BRI projects, all of which entail different environmental and social standards. This allows China to tailor its approach on a project-by-project basis. Geopolitical considerations will play an important role in this calculation. One might expect, for example, China to fund low-risk projects through the mechanisms it developed during the "Going Out" era. Conversely, China may seek to distance itself from projects in more volatile countries—for example, road and rail projects in Central Asia—by funding them through the AIIB or by cofinancing them with other countries. Finally, this analysis demonstrates that environmental and social risk management standards—both in how they are translated into practice and how they are deployed for propaganda purposes—will play an important role in shaping the geopolitics of the BRI.

NOTES

1. J. Ji-hee, "The belt and road fashion week opens in Guangzhou," *Huffington Post*, December 25, 2017. https://www.huffingtonpost.com/entry/the-belt-and-road-fashion-week-opens-in-guangzhou_us_5a40d339e4b0d86c803c72da. Accessed March 15, 2018.

2. M. Walsh & B. Xiao, "China lists $400m Gold Coast theme park as 'key' part of global initiative," *ABC News*, March 5, 2018. http://www.abc.net.au/news/2018-03-05/china-lists-planned-gold-coast-theme-park-as-a-key-project/9508904. Accessed May 23, 2018.

3. C. Lucas & S. Johanson, "Scientologists linked to China ask state for $1b rail to $31b city," *The Age*, March 28, 2018. https://www.theage.com.au/politics/victoria/scientologists-linked-to-china-ask-state-for-1b-rail-to-31b-city-20180328-p4z6r3.html. Accessed May 10, 2018.

4. Deutsche Bank, *One Belt, One Road: Moving Faster than Expected*. September 17, 2017. https://www.dbs.com.sg/treasures/templatedata/article/generic/data/en/GR/092017/170927_insights_one_belt_one_road_moving_faster_than_expected.xml. Accessed September 26, 2018.

5. AIIB, "Members and prospective members of the bank," 2018. https://www.aiib.org/en/about-aiib/governance/members-of-bank/index.html. Accessed May 10, 2018.

6. J. Hillman, "China's Belt and Road Initiative: Five years later," *Testimony to the U.S.-China Economic and Security Review Commission*, January 25, 2018. https

://www.csis.org/analysis/chinas-belt-and-road-initiative-five-years-later-0. Accessed May 22, 2018.

7. C. Clover & L. Hornby, "China's great game: Road to a new empire," *Financial Times*, October 12, 2015. https://www.ft.com/content/6e098274-587a-11e5-a28b-50226830d644. Accessed May 23, 2018.

8. Friends of the Earth, "China's Belt & Road Initiative: An introduction," 2016. https://foe.org/resources/chinas-belt-road-initative/. Accessed May 23, 2018.

9. See Y. Wang, "Offensive for defensive: The Belt and Road Initiative and Chinas new grand strategy," *The Pacific Review*, 29(3), 2016, pp. 455–463; E. T. Yeh, "Introduction: The geoeconomics and geopolitics of Chinese development and investment in Asia," *Eurasian Geography and Economics*, 57(3), 2016, pp. 275–285; A. De Jonge, "Perspectives on the emerging role of the Asian Infrastructure Investment Bank," *International Affairs*, 93(5), 2017, pp. 1061–1084; P. Cai, "Understanding China's Belt and Road Initiative," 2017. https://www.lowyinstitute.org/publications/understanding-belt-and-road-initiative. Accessed May 23, 2018; Deloitte, "Embracing the BRI ecosystem in 2018," April 4, 2018. https://www2.deloitte.com/cn/en/pages/soe/articles/embracing-the-bri-ecosystem-in-2018.html. Accessed May 23, 2018. See also E. F. Tracy, E. Shvarts, E. Simonov & M. Babenko, "China's new Eurasian ambitions: The environmental risks of the Silk Road Economic Belt," *Eurasian Geography and Economics*, 58(1), 2017, pp. 56–88.

10. Cited in Deloitte, "Embracing the BRI ecosystem in 2018," 2018, p. 9.

11. R. Biswas, "Reshaping the financial architecture for development finance: The new development banks," *LSE Global South Unit Working Paper Series,* No. 2, 2015. http://eprints.lse.ac.uk/61120/. Accessed May 23, 2017. See also S. Griffith-Jones, L. Xiaoyun & S. Spratt, "The Asian Infrastructure Investment Bank: What can it learn from, and perhaps teach to, the multilateral development banks?" *IDS Evidence Report*. No. 179, 2016. https://www.ids.ac.uk/publication/the-asian-infrastructure-investment-bank-what-can-it-learn-from-and-perhaps-teach-to-the-multilateral-development-banks. Accessed May 23, 2018.

12. Fergus Hunter, "Australia does not want the Pacific's debt burden to increase: Concetta Fierravanti-Wells," *Sydney Morning Herald*, April 11, 2018. https://www.smh.com.au/politics/federal/australia-does-not-want-the-pacific-s-debt-burden-to-increase-concetta-fierravanti-wells-20180411-p4z8z5.html. Accessed May 23, 2018. See also M. Wenbridge, "Australia lashes out at China's 'useless' Pacific projects," *Financial Times,* January 10, 2018. https://www.ft.com/content/9bd0cb6a-f5a6-11e7-8715-e94187b3017e. Accessed May 22, 2018.

13. Cai, "Understanding China's Belt and Road Initiative," 2017.

14. J. Hurley, S. Morris & G. Portelance, "Examining the debt implications of the Belt and Road Initiative from a policy perspective," Center for Global Development, 2018. https://www.cgdev.org/sites/default/files/examining-debt-implications-belt-and-road-initiative-policy-perspective.pdf. Accessed May 23, 2018.

15. K. Stacey, "China signs 99-year lease on Sri Lanka's Hambantota port," *Financial Times*, December 11, 2017. https://www.ft.com/content/e150ef0c-de37-11e7-a8a4-0a1e63a52f9c. Accessed May 23, 2018.

16. J. Farchy, "China seeking to revive the Silk Road," *Financial Times*, May 10, 2016. https://www.ft.com/content/e99ff7a8-0bd8-11e6-9456-444ab5211a2f.

Accessed May 23, 2018. See also C. Shephard & J. Farchy, "Chinese embassy in Kyrgyzstan hit by suicide bomb attack," *Financial Times*, August 30, 2016. https://www.ft.com/content/23243e7e-6e82-11e6-9ac1-1055824ca907. Accessed May 23, 2018. R. Dellios & R. Ferguson, "The human security dimension of China's belt and road initiative," *Journal of Management and Sustainability*, 7(3), 2017, p. 481; and J. Eisenman & D. Stewart, "China's new Silk Road is getting muddy," *Foreign Policy*, January 9, 2017. http://foreignpolicy.com/2017/01/09/chinas-new-silk-road-is-getting-muddy/. Accessed May 22, 2018.

17. Friends of the Earth, "China's Belt & Road Initiative," 2016; Tracy et al., "China's new Eurasian ambitions," 2017; and Dellios & Ferguson, "The human security dimension," 2017.

18. Tracy et al. "China's new Eurasian ambitions," 2017; and F. Vanclay, "Project-induced displacement and resettlement: From impoverishment risks to an opportunity for development?" *Impact Assessment and Project Appraisal*, 35(1), 2017, pp. 3–21.

19. Griffith-Jones et al., "The Asian Infrastructure Investment Bank," 2016; A. Isaksson & A. Kotsadam, "Chinese aid and local corruption," *Journal of Public Economics*, 159, 2017, pp. 146–159; and A. Dreher, A. Fuchs, B. Parks, A. M. Strange & M. J. Tierney, "Apples and dragon fruits: The determinants of aid and other forms of state financing from China to Africa," *International Studies Quarterly*, 62(1), 2018, pp. 182–194.

20. State Council, "China's foreign aid," July 10, 2014. http://www.globaltimes.cn/content/869784.shtml. Accessed May 23, 2018.

21. "The Beijing consensus is to keep quiet," *Economist*, May 8, 2010. https://www.economist.com/node/16059990. Accessed May 23, 2018.

22. Griffith-Jones et al., "The Asian Infrastructure Investment Bank," 2016; Dreher et al. "Apples and dragon fruits," 2018; and D. Dollar & J. Thornton, "Is China's development finance a challenge to the international order?" *Brookings Institution*, November 28, 2017. https://www.brookings.edu/research/is-chinas-development-finance-a-challenge-to-the-international-order/. Accessed May 23, 2018.

23. D. Brautigam, "Chinese development aid in Africa what, where, why, and how much?" in Jane Golley & L. Song (eds.), *Rising China: Global Challenges and Opportunities*. Canberra: Australian National University Press, 2011, pp. 203–222; M. Condon, "China in Africa: What the policy of nonintervention adds to the Western development dilemma," *Praxis*, 28, 2012, pp. 5–25; Tracy et al., "China's new Eurasian ambitions," 2017.

24. Friends of the Earth, "China's Belt & Road Initiative," 2016; Tracy et al., "China's new Eurasian ambitions," 2017; Dellios & Ferguson, "The human security dimension," 2017.

25. ADB, "Country Safeguard Systems," 2018. https://countrysafeguardsystems.net/. Accessed May 23, 2018.

26. M. Cernea, "The state and involuntary resettlement: Reflections on comparing legislation on development-displacement in China and India," in F. Padovani (ed.), *Development-Induced Displacement in India and China: A Comparative Look at the Burdens of Growth*. Lanham: Lexington Books, Rowman & Littlefield Publishers,

2016, pp. vii–lii; Brooke Wilmsen, M. Webber & Y. Duan, "Development for whom? Rural to urban resettlement at the Three Gorges Dam, China," *Asian Studies Review*, 35(1), 2011, pp. 21–42; and Brooke Wilmsen, "After the deluge: A longitudinal study of resettlement at the Three Gorges Dam, China," *World Development*, 84, 2016, pp. 41–54.

27. D. Kaufmann, A. Kraay & M. Mastruzzi, "The worldwide governance indicators: Methodology and analytical issues," *Hague Journal on the Rule of Law*, 3(2), 2011, pp. 220–246.

28. Dellios & Ferguson, "The human security dimension," 2017.

29. O. Felix, M. Tan-Mullins, G. Mohan, G. Siciliano, and F. Urban, "Hope, politics and risk: The case of a Chinese dam in Nigeria," *Energy and Environment Research*, 7(2), 2017, pp. 1–13.

30. M. Levina, "Kyrgyzstan: China demands to protect investor after locals burnt gold-processing plant," April 13, 2018. https://www.timesca.com/index.php/news/19611-kyrgyzstan-china-demands-to-protect-investor-after-locals-burnt-gold-processing-plant. Accessed May 22, 2018.

31. Farchy, "China seeking to revive the Silk Road," 2016.

32. Hillman, "China's Belt and Road Initiative," 2018.

33. Y. Sun, "China's aid to Africa: Monster or messiah?" *Brookings Institution*, February 7, 2014. http://www.brookings.edu/research/opinions/2014/02/07chinaaidtoafricasun. Accessed May 22, 2018.

34. Deloitte, "Embracing the BRI ecosystem in 2018," 2018.

35. C. Maurin & P. Yeophantong, "Going global responsibly? China's strategies towards 'sustainable' overseas investments," *Pacific Affairs*, 86(2), 2013, pp. 281–303.

36. D. Compagnon & A. Alejandro, "China's external environmental policy: Understanding China's environmental impact in Africa and how it is addressed," *Environmental Practice*, 15(3), 2013, pp. 220–227.

37. O. Hensengerth, "Chinese hydropower companies and environmental norms in countries of the global South: The involvement of Sinohydro in Ghana's Bui Dam," *Environment, Development and Sustainability*, 15(2), 2013, pp. 285–300; Cernea, "The state and involuntary resettlement," 2016.

38. K. McDonald, P. Bosshard & N. Brewer, "Exporting dams: China's hydropower industry goes global," *Journal of environmental management*, 90, 2009, pp. 294–302.

39. Cited in P. Bosshard, "China's environmental footprint in Africa," *China in Africa Policy Briefing*, 3, 2008, pp. 1–12.

40. MOFCOM, "MOFCOM and MEP jointly issued guidance on environmental protection in foreign investment and cooperation," 2013. http://english.mofcom.gov.cn/article/newsrelease/significantnews/201303/20130300043146.shtml. Accessed May 23, 2018. Emphasis added.

41. Green Finance Committee, "Environmental risk management initiative for China's overseas investment," September 2017. http://unepinquiry.org/wp-content/uploads/2017/09/Environmental-Risk-Management-Initiative-for-China---s-Overseas-Investment.pdf. Accessed May 22, 2018. Emphasis added.

42. D. Leung, Y. Zhao, A. Ballesteros & T. Hu, "Environmental and social policies in overseas investments: Progress and challenges in China," Washington, DC: World Resources Institute Issue Brief, 2013. http://www.wri.org/sites/default/files/pdf/environmental_and_social_policies_in_overseas_ investments_china.pdf. Accessed May 22, 2018.

43. Maurin & Yeophantong, "Going global responsibly?" 2013; and Z. Chun, "China on path to greener foreign investment," *China Dialogue*, March 10, 2017. https://www.chinadialogue.net/article/show/single/en/10117-China-on-path-to-greener-foreign-investment-. Accessed May 22, 2018.

44. J. Hillman, "Game of loans: How China bought Hambantota," *CSIS*, April 2, 2018. https://www.csis.org/analysis/game-loans-how-china-bought-hambantota. Accessed May 23, 2018.

45. CBRC, "Green credit guidelines," 2012. www.cbrc.gov.cn/chinese/files/2012/E9F158AD3884481DBE005DFBF0D99C45.doc. Accessed May 23, 2018.

46. Friends of the Earth, "Investing in a green belt and road? Assessing the implementation of China's Green Credit Guidelines," 2017. https://foe.org/resources/investing-green-belt-road-assessing-implementation-chinas-green-credit-guidelines-abroad/. Accessed May 23, 2018.

47. M. Davies, P. Draper & H. Edinger, "Changing China, changing Africa: Future contours of an emerging relationship," *Asian Economic Policy Review*, 9(2), 2014, pp. 180–197.

48. L. Lin, "Corporate social responsibility in Africa: Window dressing or structural change?" *Berkeley Journal of International Law*, 28 (1), 2010, pp. 64–100; and S. Cheng & G. Liang, "Social responsibility of Chinese investment in Africa: What does it mean for EU-China cooperation on development policy towards Africa?" https://www.ictsd.org/bridges-news/trade-negotiations-insights/news/social-responsibility-of-chinese-investment-in-africa. Accessed May 23, 2018.

49. Maurin & Yeophantong, "Going global responsibly?" 2013.

50. C. Wu, D. Fang, P. Liao, J. Xue, Y. Li & T. Wang, "Perception of corporate social responsibility: The case of Chinese international contractors," *Journal of Cleaner Production*, 107, 2015, pp. 185–194.

51. Wang et al., "Offensive for defensive," 2016.

52. Friends of the Earth, "Investing in a green belt and road?" 2017.

53. Greenovation Hub, "Exploring the overseas environmental and social risk management by financial institutions under "The Belt and Road" Initiative," 2016. http://www.ghub.org/en/archives/1294. Accessed May 22, 2018.

54. Jim Yong Kim, "Remarks of World Bank group president Jim Yong Kim at the Belt and Road forum for international cooperation—Opening plenary session," *World Bank*, May 14, 2017. http://www.worldbank.org/en/news/speech/2017/05/14/remarks-of-world-bank-group-president-jim-yong-kim. Accessed May 21, 2018.

55. Dollar & Thornton, "Is China's development finance," 2017.

56. Griffith-Jones et al., "The Asian Infrastructure Investment Bank," 2016.

57. Biswas, "Reshaping the financial architecture for development finance," 2015; Griffith-Jones et al., "The Asian Infrastructure Investment Bank," 2016; and UNDP, "The Belt and Road Initiative: A news means to transformative global governance

towards sustainable development," 2017. http://www.cn.undp.org/content/china/en/home/library/south-south-cooperation/a-new-means-to-transformative-global-governance-towards-sustaina.html. Accessed May 22, 2018.

58. D. Junio, "Asian Infrastructure Investment Bank: An idea whose time has come?" *The Diplomat*, 4, 2014. https://thediplomat.com/2014/12/asian-infrastructure-investment-bank-an-idea-whose-time-has-come/. Accessed May 22, 2018.

59. Tracy et al., "China's new Eurasian ambitions," 2017.

60. G. Earl, "Economic diplomacy brief: Infrastructure and trade," *The Interpreter*, 2 August 2018, https:www.lowyinstitute.org/the-interpreter/economic-diplomacy-brief-infrastructure-and-trade/.

61. A. De Jonge, "Perspectives on the emerging role of the Asian Infrastructure and Investment Bank", *International Affairs*, 93(5), 2016, p. 1075.

62. S. Griffith-Jones, L. Xiaoyun, S. Spratt, "The Asian Infrastructure and Investment Bank: What can it learn from, and perhaps teach to, the the Multilateral Development Banks?," *Institute of Development Studies Evidence Report*, 179, https://www.ids.ac.uk/publications/the-asian-infrastructure-and-investment-bank-what-can-it-learn-from-and-perhaps-teach-the-multilateral-development-banks/ ; Greenovation Hub, "Exploring the overseas environmental and social risk management," 2016; R. Hanlon, "Thinking about the Asian Infrastructure Investment Bank: Can a China-led development bank improve sustainability in Asia?" *Asia & the Pacific Policy Studies*, 4(3), 2016, pp. 541–554; and Tracy et al., "China's new Eurasian ambitions," 2017.

63. Hanlon, "Thinking about the Asian Infrastructure Investment Bank," 2016.

64. Griffith-Jones et al., "The Asian Infrastructure Investment Bank," 2016.

65. M. Callaghan & P. Hubbard, "The Asian Infrastructure Investment Bank: Multilateralism on the Silk Road," *China Economic Journal*, 9(2), 2016, pp. 116–139.

66. O. Hensengerth, "Chinese hydropower companies and environmental norms in the global south: The involvement of Sinohydro in Ghana's Bui dam," *Environment, Development and Sustainability*, 15(2), 2013, pp. 285–300; F. Urban, J. Nordensvard, G. Siciliano & B. Li, "Chinese overseas hydropower dams and social sustainability: The Bui Dam in Ghana and the Kamchay Dam in Cambodia," *Asia & the Pacific Policy Studies*, 2(3), 2015, pp. 573–589; and P. Obour, K. Owusu, E. Agyeman, A. Ahenkan & A. Madrid, "The impacts of dams on local livelihoods: A study of the Bui Hydroelectric Project in Ghana," *International Journal of Water Resources Development*, 32(2), 2016, pp. 286–300.

67. C. Benjamin, "$25 million seed money for Bui city," *The Statesman*, September 12, 2007. http://chrisbenjaminwriting.com/25m-seed-money-for-bui-city/. Accessed May 12, 2018.

68. X. Han, *Money Markets and Hydropower: Chinese Dam Construction in Africa*, Doctoral Thesis, The University of Melbourne, 2018.

69. Hesengerth, "Chinese hydropower companies"; Urban et al., "Chinese overseas hydropower dams and social sustainability," 2015.

70. Han, *Money Markets and Hydropower*, 2018.

71. J. Kirchherr, T. Disselhoff & K. Charles, "Safeguards, financing, and employment in Chinese infrastructure projects in Africa: The case of Ghana's Bui Dam," *Waterlines*, 35(1), 2016, pp. 37–58.

72. ERM, "Resettlement Planning Framework (RPF) for the Bui Hydropower Project," 2007. http://www.dialoguebarrages.net/fr/ressources-et-documents/etudes-d-impact/doc_download/28-resettlement-planning-framework-rpf-for-the-bui-hydropower-project. Accessed May 18, 2018. See also Han, *Money Markets and Hydropower*, 2018.

73. Hensengerth, "Chinese hydropower companies and environmental norms," 2013, p. 292.

74. ERM, "Resettlement Planning Framework (RPF) for the Bui Hydropower Project," 2007, p. 14.

75. C. Sutcliffe, "Interviews with people to be affected by Bui da: A field report," Unpublished paper, 2007. https://www.internationalrivers.org/sites/default/files/attached-files/bui_field_report.pdf. Accessed May 12, 2018.

76. Brooke Wilmsen, D. Adjartey & A. van Hulten, "Challenging the risks-based model of involuntary resettlement using evidence from the Bui Dam, Ghana," *International Journal of Water Resources Development*, World Bank, 2018.

77. Wilmsen et al., "Challenging the risks-based model of involuntary resettlement," 2018.

78. Dollar & Thorton, "Is China's development finance," 2017; see also Griffith-Jones, 2016.

79. Shephard & Farchy, "Chinese embassy in Kyrgyzstan hit by suicide bomb attack," 2016; Levina, "Kyrgyzstan: China demands to protect investor after locals burnt gold-processing plant," 2018.

Chapter 7

China's Relationship with Egypt and Oman

A Strategic Framework for the Implementation of China's Maritime Silk Road Initiative

Mordechai Chaziza

INTRODUCTION

The purpose of this chapter is to analyze the geostrategic value of Oman and Egypt in the construction and realization of China's new Maritime Silk Road Initiative (MSRI), a component of the Belt and Road Initiative (BRI), which is the most ambitious Chinese integration project to date, linking Asia with Europe and Africa along the land-and sea-based Silk Road. China's relationship with both countries and their critical role in the MSRI merits attention, given the steady development of their political and economic exchanges in mutual trade and investment. Moreover, as described in this chapter, these countries represent an important hub in the construction and realization of the MSRI projects.

In the second decade of the twenty-first century, the Middle East represents four major priorities for China's foreign policy. Foremost among these priorities is the critical importance of the region as a source of imported energy and for Chinese trade and investment. As the world's largest consumer of energy overall and second-largest importer of crude oil, safeguarding a stable flow of crude oil from the region is a paramount concern.[1] Second, the region is also a key part of China's BRI, especially for its twenty-first-century Maritime Silk Road component. In the past, Beijing considered the Middle East a peripheral and relatively insignificant region of the world, whereas now it is regarded as a vital geostrategic global crossroads, and the PRC's most important region beyond its own Asia Pacific neighborhoods for the realization of the BRI. Finally, Beijing views the region as an arena of great power competition in which a rising power such as China must be seen as a player.[2]

In recent years, China has been seeking to deepen its global centrality by connecting to Asia, Europe, and Africa through physical infrastructural investments in ports and pipelines, high-speed rail, and other utilities, with associated bilateral trade and investments in key states along the land-and sea-based Silk Road. Accordingly, China has vigorously pursued close diplomatic and economic interactions with numerous MSRI-participant Middle East countries. The Middle East countries, for their part, view BRI projects as a way to create new partnerships and expand avenues for trade. Aspiring to maximize the gains derived from cooperation in BRI activities and projects, they now regularly negotiate to bring the BRI projects to fruition and to offer economic opportunities and incentives to foreign investors.[3]

Egypt and Oman are both positioned to play a critical role in China's expanding footprint in the Middle East. Oman's advantageous maritime location, influence in energy markets, and independent foreign policy all make it an attractive partner for China and of vital strategic significance in the construction and realization of the MSRI by turning it into a center of global trade and manufacturing. As for Egypt, it has been elevated to a springboard position in China's MSRI aspirations because of its strategic geographic location along the Suez Canal and its pivotal role in promoting China's relations with the African continent.

The Twenty-First-Century MSRI

China's most significant twenty-first-century diplomatic and economic activity is the launching of the Silk Road initiative that has become the flagship foreign policy effort of the Xi administration. China's BRI is comprised of two components: the Silk Road Economic Belt (SREB) and the MSRI. The former links Beijing with Central Asia, the Middle East, and Europe on land, while the latter unites the major maritime trade routes of Africa, Europe, and Oceania as well as South and Southeast Asia. The two schemes are inseparable, and the PRC's goal is their parallel implementation.[4]

The BRI projects are organized along seven corridors, which encompass as many as seventy-two countries. Overall, the seventy-two BRI countries cover two-thirds of the world's population, 40 percent of the global gross national product, and an estimated 75 percent of known energy reserves.[5] The global infrastructure investment needed to support the currently expected rates of economic growth is between $3.3 trillion and $6.3 trillion annually.[6] Furthermore, it has the potential to establish a new order not only in Eurasia but in the entire international system as well.[7]

Under the strategic framework of the MSRI, China has been buying up the development and operational rights to a chain of ports that stretch from the southern regions of Asia to the Middle East, Africa, Europe, and even South America. According to the *Financial Times*, China has spent billions expanding its port network to secure sea-lanes and establish itself as a maritime power.[8] As of the end of 2017, China has reportedly invested more than $143 billion in its BRI partners, and the total volume of trade between China and other BRI countries has exceeded $3 trillion.[9] Chinese firms have also established more than fifty economic and trade zones in more than thirty countries.[10]

The MSRI is a massive scheme to connect wide swaths of East, Southeast, South, and West Asia through the building of enormous amounts of hard infrastructure, such as high-speed railways, highways and truck roads, air and sea ports, utility stations and power grids, oil and natural gas pipelines, and telecommunication networks. The MSRI also will entail the construction of large industrial parks and special economic zones (SEZs) coupled with manufacturing plants within these areas.[11]

The MSRI is also designed to secure China's maritime energy supply chain across the Indian Ocean region and the South China Sea. The majority of Beijing's seaborne energy imports pass through these regions; thus, China attaches great importance to the security of the sea lines of communication and to ensuring unimpeded access in these two areas.[12] Beijing's dependence on import of foreign oil and gas is great and so crucial for its continued growth that obtaining reliable transport routes and diversifying transport routes by procuring oil and natural gas from the energy-rich Central Asian or the Middle East through the construction of the land- and sea-based Silk Road are of critical importance to Beijing's energy security.[13]

Hence, Beijing has vigorously pursued close diplomatic and economic interactions with numerous participating Middle East countries that viewed MSRI projects as a way to boost new partnerships and avenues for trade. Consequently, China and Middle East countries, which want to maximize the gains derived from cooperation in MSRI activities and projects, are constantly on the lookout for cooperative ventures to promote the realization of the MSRI projects and to create new economic opportunities and incentives for foreign investment.[14]

The purpose of this chapter is to analyze the critical role and the strategic geographical value of each country, Oman and Egypt, in the construction and realization of the new MSRI. In this sense, China's approach toward Oman and Egypt is an interesting case study since Beijing considers both countries as key partners in realizing the MSRI and expanding its maritime presence in the Mediterranean Sea, Arabian Sea, and Indian Ocean for economic, political, and security reasons.

China and Oman

The Persian Gulf constitutes a unique geostrategic position, as it connects three continents: Europe, Asia, and Africa, which gives it a vital significance and value to the materialization of China's BRI.[15] Oman is situated on the axis of the Indian Ocean and Arabian Gulf. As one of member states in the Gulf Cooperation Council (GCC), it will be of immense strategic value to China's efforts to revive ancient maritime trade routes, acting as a regional hub between Asia and GCC states and boasting accessible trade routes and speedy transit times to the world's most attractive emerging markets.[16] China seeks to strengthen the mutual interdependency with Oman in various sectors such as energy and investments, to leverage its economic capabilities to realize the successful implementation of the MSRI.

Trade and Investments

For the past few decades, Beijing has looked for alternative energy sources in different parts of the world, such as Central Asia or Africa, yet its dependence on Middle Eastern oil has risen over time. The Middle East is currently the largest exporter of crude oil to China. In 2016, the region accounted for just under half of China's crude oil imports.[17] According to the International Energy Agency estimates, in 2040 the Middle East will provide about half of China's oil supply, and China will consume about a quarter of the region's oil exports.[18]

Beijing's growing reliance on oil imports from the Middle East is a crucial reason for its heavy investment in its twin trade and infrastructure initiatives (SREB and MSRI); these are likely to become linked through ports or pipeline developments, with growing naval access and support facilities to help protect China's energy security. This is also a powerful driver to China's blue-water naval development and power projection capacity through the Indian Ocean, and developing a whole set of strong diplomatic ties with the littoral Indian Ocean countries. Hence, the oil trade is significant and will become increasingly so in Sino-Omani relations.

Since the early 1980s, Oman has been an essential source of imported energy, and became the first Arab nation and member of the GCC to export oil directly to China.[19] Oman is the largest oil and natural gas producer in the Middle East outside the Organization of the Petroleum Exporting Countries. According to the *Oil & Gas Journal*, Oman, with 5.4 billion barrels of estimated proved oil reserves, ranks as the seventh-largest proved oil reserve holder in the Middle East and the twenty-second largest in the world. With rising production, a growing petrochemical sector, and potential resources, Oman is highly dependent on its hydrocarbon sector as a major source of revenue.[20]

Energy cooperation has been the primary axis around which the Sino-Oman partnership revolves.[21]According to the US Energy Information Administration, China is Oman's largest export market and procured 78 percent of the country's crude oil exports in 2016 (China's fourth-largest source of oil imports).[22] According to the latest statistics released by the National Centre for Statistics and Information, China retained its position as the leading destination for Oman's crude oil exports for the first seven months of 2017. China imported 132.67 million barrels of Oman crude, out of the country's 171.90 million barrel exports.[23] Therefore, although most of Oman's exports of liquefied natural gas (LNG) in 2016 were delivered to Japan and South Korea, China as the world's third-largest importer of LNG continues to show interest in the country's natural gas sector.[24]

While the petroleum exports serve as the foundation of Sino-Omani relationships, the recent Chinese massive investments in construction and infrastructure projects will certainly help grow relations further. Such investments could be the key for Oman as it looks to diversify its economy away from reliance on oil and gas. In 2016, China had become the top foreign investor in the Middle East (totaling $39 billion), the growth driven by the Oman projects.[25] The Omani government borrowed $3.6 billion from Chinese financial institutions, the largest loan deal in the Chinese market for a Gulf borrower.[26]

Within the framework of Beijing's BRI, Chinese firms are investing in construction of large industrial parks and SEZs along the tendrils of the MSRI across Asia, the Middle East, and Africa. Duqm, a remote and underutilized Omani port situated 550 kilometers south of the capital, Muscat,[27] is one of Beijing's more ambitious projects,[28] transforming it into a vital nerve center of Sino-Omani global trade and manufacturing.

Oman Wanfang, a consortium of six private Chinese firms, plans to build a $10.7 billion industrial city there. The Chinese consortium has promised to develop at least 30 percent of the Oman Industrial Park in Duqm within five to seven years, and ten Chinese firms have signed land lease agreements for building various projects, totaling an investment of $3.06 billion.[29] The planned Chinese investment is the equivalent of more than half of Oman's stock of foreign direct investment.[30]

The Chinese consortium plans to develop over 11 square kilometers within the giant Duqm SEZ, making the Chinese the largest prospective foreign tenants by far. There will be some thirty-five SEZ projects implemented in the China-Oman industrial park (production of commercial concrete, building materials and related industries, glazed glass, methanol, and other chemicals, solar power units, production of oil and gas tools, as well as products for pipelines and drilling).[31] For Oman, the SEZ project's success is important for its quest to diversify its economy beyond its traditional hydrocarbon sector, in line with Vision 2020.[32]

Duqm is marketing its location as a major attraction, lying on the Arabian Sea between the Gulf of Oman and the Gulf of Aden, and the location of the port and SEZ combo at Duqm fits into the development and realization of China's MSRI.[33] As a politically stable country situated along the Strait of Hormuz, Gulf of Oman, Indian Ocean, and Arabian Sea, Oman is certainly poised to play a critical role in Beijing's expanding footprint in the region and the realization of MSRI.

The Geostrategic Value of Oman

Oman is likewise well positioned to play a significant role in China's efforts to revive ancient maritime trade routes, despite not being directly situated on the BRI's land or maritime trade routes, and it holds high economic and geopolitical stakes in Beijing's planned maritime economic corridor. As State Councilor Wang Yong remarked during his May 2016 visit in the country, Beijing considers Oman a key partner in materializing the BRI, while China would like to make use of its fine production capacity and advanced industrial technologies to help the Gulf country in building up its infrastructures, like high-speed railways, highways, airports, and seaports.[34]

In particular, Oman has immense geostrategic value to realizing China's MSRI. First, Oman is situated in the southeastern Arabian Peninsula adjacent to the Strait of Hormuz, the vital maritime artery between the Persian Gulf and Gulf of Oman and the Arabian Sea and Indian Ocean. Oman shares borders with Saudi Arabia, Yemen, and the United Arab Emirates (UAE), and is situated close to India, Iran, Pakistan, East Africa, and the greater Indian Ocean region, which is a central concern for China's national security. Expanding its presence in Oman will increase Beijing's presence in the Indian Ocean and the Arabian Sea.[35]

Second, Oman's proximity to the Arabian Sea, Gulf of Oman, Persian Gulf, and wider Indian Ocean grants it access to some of the most important energy corridors in the world, enhancing Oman's position in the global energy supply chain. More than 80 percent of the world's seaborne trade in oil transits through Indian Ocean choke points, with 18.5 percent of the total oil trade and 40 percent of worldwide seaborne oil trade passing through the Strait of Hormuz, making it the largest maritime transit zone in the world.[36]

China, with the help of Oman, could achieve effective management and control over the flow of its energy needs, opening a new market and trade routes for Oman and the Middle East, as the MSRI would connect the region's economies with the Southeastern and East Asian economies.[37] Oman's accessible trade routes and fast transit times to the world's most attractive emerging markets make the country an attractive partner for China's MSRI: in terms of transportation connections, Oman is on the major international shipping routes and within two weeks of most major ports. It also has direct trade routes to the growing GCC market, India and Africa. Oman boasts excellent transportation infrastructure and offers three world-class deep-sea ports and five airports as well as a top-class road network.[38]

For instance, China has developed a particular interest in Oman's Sohar Port and Freezone, a deep-water seaport located on the Gulf of Oman in the northwestern part of the country near Oman's border with the UAE, and the associated free trade zone that is counted among the world's largest developments of its kind. Beijing is also keen to benefit from Oman's expansion of road networks and a railway that will integrate Sohar Port and Freezone into existing Omani and GCC state transportation corridors extending into the UAE and Saudi Arabia.[39]

Additionally, the chairman of China Harbour stated that its company together with a Maltese firm, Suez Capital Ltd., wants to invest in the growth of the Port of Sur in Oman. Sur is the nearest point in the Middle East to India (just 600 kilometers to Porbander), and presents an attractive proposition for its significant sea lines, so that traveling from China to Europe will eliminate the need to deviate tens of thousands of miles from the route to travel to the port of Jebel Ali. The port will also minimize the demand for vessels to enter the Straits of Hormuz, thereby saving millions in insurance premiums.[40]

Moreover, China is already heavily involved in developing the Port of Duqm, and many of the extractive industries around it, and would invest $10.7 billion in building a new industrial city. Duqm, which lies on the Arabian Sea, is a potential operating base for Chinese businesses near export markets which they want to develop in the Gulf, the Indian subcontinent, and East Africa. Through Duqm, Oman can become an oil refinery hub for the Gulf region by collaborating with Chinese Maritime Silk Road infrastructural investments.[41] In the end, Oman will become a major link in the MSRI, and the Chinese presence in these key ports facilities in the country will give Beijing a competitive advantage over its rivals (e.g., India) that have established logistical and transportation hubs in the region.[42]

Third, Oman's location opposite Pakistan's Gwadar Port, an important link to China through the China-Pakistan Economic Corridor (CPEC), could make it a major link in connecting Western China's Xinjiang Province to the Indian Ocean. Beijing launched the CPEC as a flagship project of BRI, and if it succeeds, would have strategic value for China since it could open its landlocked western region to the Arabian Sea. The total cost of CPEC projects has gone up from $46 billion to $62 billion, and the expectation is that the cost will soar even further to $100 billion by 2030.[43] The CPEC linking Gwadar thorough Islamabad to Kashgar in China's Xinjiang Province corresponds to the Gulf's maritime route from Kuwait through the Gulf to Gwadar and on to Kashgar.[44]

Finally, Oman's strategic location enables China to leverage its geopolitical influence across the Indian Ocean. This ocean has become the new global center of trade and energy flows, accounting for half the world's container traffic and 70 percent of its petroleum shipments. China's defense white paper, outlining its regional hegemony aspirations and emphasizing a greater focus on the seas, includes an expanded naval role beyond its maritime backyard.[45] Hence, China's facilities in the key strategic Port of Duqm in Oman will be available for military use and logistical support. Through the Port of Duqm, China's influence can be extended beyond the Arabian Peninsula and Persian Gulf to coastal East Africa and Gwadar in Balochistan in modern Pakistan, all areas to be connected by the Maritime Silk Road.

Lately, China has significantly increased deployment of its naval vessels and assets in the Indian Ocean region (IRO).[46] Beijing has also increased its attempts to penetrate into the IRO through its infrastructural investments in a range of facilities (e.g., Pakistan's Gwadar Port and the Ports of Djibouti and Nairobi in the eastern horn of Africa, Sri Lanka's Hambantota Port and investments in Myanmar, and Bangladesh in a range of facilities).[47] All these developments leverage China's presence in the region, project its power, and challenge the existing balance of power in the IRO.[48]

China and Egypt

In recent years, China developed a strategic cooperative relationship with Egypt, one of the most important regional powers that can promote Beijing's aspirations to strengthen its influence and power in the Middle East, expand its commerce activity, and reinforce its strategic standing at the expense of the United States. The two countries are complementary in terms of natural resources, geographic location, industrial structures, and industrialization. Thus, Egypt has emerged as a crucial component of China's MSRI projects due to its strategic location as the main transit point between the Indian Ocean and Mediterranean Sea and its disproportionate influence in Middle East and Africa affairs.

China's aspiration to expand commercial ties globally seeks Egypt's regional influence and geographic location to provide a portal to the African continent's natural resources. Egypt's free trade agreements and customs exemptions afford it many investment and industrialization advantages regarding exports to African markets.[49] Egypt also can provide a gateway for Chinese exports to the European markets, one of the main destinations for Chinese low-cost goods.[50] Chinese investments, particularly in the Suez Canal infrastructure and the Egyptian ports, could further facilitate this commerce.

Trade and Investments

Economic relations between the two countries have witnessed steady development in terms of mutual trade and investment. Bilateral trade between Egypt and China mounted to $11.3 billion in 2016, ranking Egypt as China's third-largest African trade partner. While the bulk of trade between the two countries consists of Chinese exports to Egypt, China's exports to Egypt amounted to $7.6 billion or 13 percent of its overall imports.[51] China's ambassador to Egypt, Song Aiguo, noted that the trade volume between the two countries exceeded $10 billion, stressing that Chinese imports to Egypt tripled in 2017.[52]

During President Xi's historic state visit to Egypt, the two countries signed twenty-one bilateral deals totaling $10 billion to strengthen cooperation in the fields of economic cooperation, funding electricity, energy projects, trade, civil aviation, science, technology, communications, and aerospace. The deals include a $2.7-billion package to build Egypt's new administrative capital, a $1-billion loan, and bilateral cooperation in infrastructure through the Asian Infrastructure Investment Bank. Both countries are also planning together fifteen projects in electricity, infrastructure, and transport with investments that could total $15 billion.[53] Chinese companies view Egypt as a potentially profitable business environment and participate in various major projects in industries such as electricity, petroleum, natural gas, nuclear energy, railways, highways, and more, at a cost estimated at millions of dollars.[54]

Chinese investments in Egypt increased over the last years, amounting to $6 billion including direct and indirect investments in 2017,[55] and Chinese companies established a presence near the Suez Canal and in Egypt's economic zone. In June 2015, Egypt and China signed a framework agreement for the implementation of fifteen projects worth $10 billion, to be funded by Chinese banks and built at least in part by Chinese companies. The projects include the establishment of three power plants, railways linking east Cairo with Tenth of Ramadan City, a multipurpose station in Alexandria Port, and trains, glass, and leather factories, as well as developing Alexandria-Abu Qir railways.[56] The number of Chinese companies operating in Egypt increased from thirty in 2014 to more than 1,220 Chinese companies now operating there in industry, construction, and services.[57]

In March 2015, the Egyptian government announced plans to build a new capital adjacent to Cairo, in a massive new project whose first phase would cost $45 billion and take up to seven years to complete.[58] This new capital project will largely be funded by Chinese state-owned developers.[59] According to Osama Magdoub, Egypt's Ambassador to China, Beijing will invest $11.2 billion in the second phase in the new capital project over the next ten years.[60] Moreover, Chinese companies invest in a variety of key areas in the

Egyptian economy: energy,[61] nuclear energy,[62] solar energy,[63] electricity, transportation, and ports.[64]

According to the *China Global Investment Tracker*, the Chinese poured $13.1 billion into Egypt's economy between 2015 and 2017. Most of the Chinese investments are in the energy sector ($7.4 billion) while the rest was invested in Egypt transport ($3.3 billion).[65] The increased trade and investment are evident politically as well, but economic interests are the primary considerations in the burgeoning comprehensive strategic partnership.

The Geostrategic Value of Egypt

Egypt's strategic location as the main transit point between the Indian Ocean and Mediterranean Sea[66] makes it the "pivot" or "hub" for the realization of MSRI, since the canal reduces the distance between Europe and the Far East by a third, becoming a key link between the Pacific and Indian Oceans. As China's foreign minister Wang Yi said, Egypt is an important partner of China in the construction of China's BRI.[67]

Egypt is viewed as a central pillar of the Arab world, a regional heavyweight in the Middle East and North Africa (MENA), and a key plank of the Maritime Silk Road, thanks to its control of the Suez Canal. This provides a great opportunity for China to build a complementary relationship between the Suez Canal projects and the MSRI. China and Egypt are promoting the MSRI as well as the Suez Canal economic corridor initiatives, because the harbors at both ends of the Suez Canal have a great influence over the Middle East, Africa, and the entire planet in terms of geopolitics and global trade.[68] Egypt is also increasingly important for promoting the MSRI, since the Suez Canal with its Mediterranean Port Said and its southern terminus at Port Tewfiq serves 90 percent of China's foreign maritime trade.[69]

To ensure reliable access for Chinese commercial shipping from the Red Sea to the Mediterranean, China's state-owned shipping companies have invested heavily in ports along the Suez Canal Corridor, from the Gulf of Suez to Port Said. The first significant Chinese investment in Egypt's port infrastructure was made in 2005 by Hutchison Port Holdings, which acquired a 50 percent share in a joint venture with Alexandria Port Authority to construct, operate, and manage two container terminals in the ports of Alexandria and El Dekheila on Egypt's northern Mediterranean coast.[70]

The Suez Canal Container Terminal (SCCT) in Port Said is the biggest transshipment terminal in this part of the Mediterranean. Here, COSCO invested $185.6 million in a joint venture to operate and manage the SCCT in Port Said's East Port, located in the western Sinai Peninsula at the northern end of the canal.[71] The Chinese Harbor State Company (CHEC), a subsidiary of state-owned China Communications Construction Company, invested $219 million to construct a 1,200-meter quay in Port Said's East Port and al-Adabiya Port at the Suez Canal's southern end.[72]

The construction of MSRI routes will open up huge opportunities for China to invest more in Egypt. Beijing is already the largest investor in Egypt's Suez Canal Corridor Project (SCCP), a mega project that Egypt announced in 2014 to build the area along the 190-kilometer canal into an international economic hub, integrating harbor, logistics, trade zones, and industrial parks.[73] China's MSRI can be well bonded with the SCCP. For instance, China's TEDA Corporation, one of the oldest industrial developers in the zone, has been developing an area of over 7 square kilometer in Ain Sokhna district of the Suez Canal Corridor east of Cairo. It has completed its first phase, attracting some sixty-eight enterprises, including Jushi, a fiberglass giant from China. The second phase in the industrial zone started in 2016.[74]

Egypt is one of the five stakeholders who most welcome BRI projects in the MENA region, while China considers Egypt an important hub, as signaled by its becoming the largest foreign investor in the SCZone where eighty-six Chinese companies have invested over $1.1 billion.[75] The Chinese ambassador to Egypt, Song Aiguo, said Chinese companies are interested in building public facilities and industrial parks in the SCZone project, and the investments of Chinese companies in Egypt reached a total of $6.8 billion, most registered in the last five years.[76] In March 2017, China agreed to contribute $64 million to the Egyptian earth observation satellite program (EgyptSat), as part of a $7 billion Chinese grant to develop infrastructure along the SCZone connecting to Beijing's BRI. Beijing also provided a $23 million grant for an Egyptian satellite test, integration, and assembly facility.[77]

In May 2017, China hosted the Belt and Road Forum for International Cooperation (BRF) in Beijing, where the two countries signed six MoUs. The agreements include investments by the China Development Bank and Export-Import Bank of China for a power transmission line in Egypt, a project to develop the El Sukhna Port, and a $500 million loan from the China Development Bank.[78] The *Daily News Egypt* cited a senior Chinese official that the Chinese government is set to pump in some $40 billion into big development projects in Egypt as part of its ambitious BRI through the Silk Road Fund.[79]

While Egypt stands to benefit greatly from its involvement in MSRI, China is aware that once the Suez Canal is upgraded and under Chinese oversight, it will have considerable control, power, and potential to shape security and commercial dynamics in the region. Essentially, through MSRI, China aims to increase its global and regional influence by building new trade networks and creating investment opportunities that are anticipated to alter the global balance of economic power in the long term.[80]

CONCLUSION

This chapter emphasizes the geostrategic value and importance of Egypt and Oman in the construction and realization of China's MSRI as well as the commercial partnerships developing between the countries, which are essential as a strategic framework for MSRI implementation and success. The new economic package offered by the Chinese government through the MSRI projects has been welcomed by Egypt and Oman as an alternative source of investments and an important bridge for connecting their marketers to the world economy.

Oman's strategic geographic location makes it a unique partner for China's MSRI aspirations in the Persian Gulf, the Arab world, the Middle East, and the Indian Ocean. Egypt stands at a critical juncture of the Maritime Silk Road, with the Suez Canal forming the main transit point between the Indian Ocean and the Mediterranean Sea. Without Egypt's partnership, the entire Maritime Silk Road section of the BRI is unviable. The strategic location of these two countries makes them a "pivot" for the entire MSRI project.

The confluence of mutual interests between China and the two countries indicates that the cordial relationships will continue to grow and flourish. However, there are certain constraints and barriers in the Sino-Omani-Egyptian relationships that could prevent or disrupt engagement between the countries. Oman is seeking to benefit from its geographical location to become a vital maritime global trade route but is forced to compete with other GCC countries that are also keen on capitalizing on their logistic hubs to play a more pivotal role in global trade via the region. While Egypt has been trying to market itself as a manufacturing hub for Chinese investors, its difficulties in creating an investment climate and achieving political and security coherence remain a practical hindrance to future Chinese investments.

Moreover, Oman and Egypt have both been strategic allies of the United States since 1980. Oman became the first of the Persian Gulf states to sign a formal accord permitting the US military to use its facilities. Oman has hosted US forces during every US military operation in and around the Gulf since then, and it is a partner in US efforts to counter regional terrorism and related threats. Similarly, Egypt's strategic partnership with the United States has endured successfully for nearly forty years and now is critical not only to the stability of the MENA but also as a bulwark against global terrorism and violent extremism.

There are no indications to suggest that Oman or Egypt is contemplating either making a shift in their traditionally pro-US foreign policy orientation or replacing their Washington ally with China. Therefore, when Beijing invests billions of dollars in Egypt or Oman's economy and infrastructure as part of the implementation of MSRI projects, it must consider the strategic interests of other major powers in the region, especially the United States. Beijing must promote the MSRI projects without challenging American regional dominance, which could provoke Washington to intervene in order to undermine or obstruct the Maritime Silk Road.

Eventually, despite its emerging strategic partnership with Egypt and Oman, China cannot afford to neglect the existence of numerous challenges and obstacles during the implementation of the MSRI projects, especially in calculating only narrow economic interests without considering the strategic interests and commercial concerns of local governments, regional or great powers. China's success in connecting Egypt and Oman within the MSRI will have broad geoeconomic and geostrategic implications, not only for the Middle East but also for the broader Asia region in which the United States and China each seek to assert their sphere of influence.

NOTES

1. Chris Zambelis, "China and the Quiet Kingdom: An Assessment of China-Oman Relations," *China Brief* XV, no. 22 (November 2015): 11–15.

2. Andrew Scobell and Nader Alireza, *China in the Middle East: The Wary Dragon* (Santa Monica, CA: RAND Corporation, 2016).

3. Abigaël Vasselier, "Chinese Perceptions of Country Risks in North Africa," *European Council on Foreign Relations*, June 2017, http://www.ecfr.eu/page/-/China_Analysis_June_2017.pdf.

4. "Full Text: Vision for Maritime Cooperation under the Belt and Road Initiative," *Xinhua*, June 20, 2017, http://news.xinhuanet.com/english/2017-06/20/c_136380414.htm.

5. "Greening the Belt and Road Initiative," *WWF's Recommendations for the Finance Sector – In Conjunction with HSBC*, January 1, 2018, file:///C:/Users/moti/Downloads/greening-the-belt-and-road-initiative.pdf.

6. Jane Perlez and Yufan Huang, "Behind China's $1 Trillion Plan to Shake Up the Economic Order," *The New York Times*, May 13, 2017, https://www.nytimes.com/2017/05/13/business/china-railway-one-belt-one-road-1-trillion-plan.html?mcubz=3.

7. Jean-Marc F. Blanchard and Colin Flint, "The Geopolitics of China's Maritime Silk Road Initiative," *Geopolitics* 22, no. 2 (April 2017): 223–225.

8. James Kynge, Chris Campbell, Amy Kazmin, and Farhan Bokhari, "How China Rules the Waves," *Financial Times*, January 12, 2017, https://ig.ft.com/sites/china-ports/.

9. Guo Han and Zhou Zhan, "China's Strategic Vision: Five Years On and Looking Ahead," *ICAS BULLETIN: Institute for China-America Studies*, November 1, 2017, http://chinaus-icas.org/wp-content/uploads/2017/11/November-1-Bulletin.pdf.

10. "Greening the Belt and Road Initiative: The WWF's Recommendations for the Finance Sector in Partnership with HSBC", 1 January 2918, https://www.sustainablefinance.hsbc.com/reports/greening-the-belt-and-road-intiative

11. Blanchard and Flint, "The Geopolitics of China's," 223–225.

12. Christopher Len, "China's 21st Century Maritime Silk Road Initiative, Energy Security and SLOC Access," *Maritime Affairs: Journal of the National Maritime Foundation of India* 11, no. 1 (June 2015): 1–18.

13. Tai Hwan Lee, "One Belt, One Road Strategy and Korean-Chinese Cooperation," *The Newsletter*, No. 74, 2016, https://iias.asia/sites/default/files/IIAS_NL74_16-1.pdf.

14. Sumedh Anil Lokhande, "China's One Belt One Road Initiative and the Gulf Pearl Chain," *China Daily*, June 5, 2017, http://www.chinadaily.com.cn/opinion/2017beltandroad/2017-06/05/content_29618549.htm.

15. Ibid.

16. Giorgio Cafiero and Daniel Wagner, "What the Gulf States Think of 'One Belt, One Road,'" *The Diplomat*, May 24, 2017, https://thediplomat.com/2017/05/what-the-gulf-states-think-of-one-belt-one-road/.

17. Tsvetana Paraskova, "China's Becomes World's Next Top Oil Importer," *Oil Price*, February 6, 2018, https://oilprice.com/Energy/Crude-Oil/Chinas-Becomes-Worlds-Next-Top-Oil-Importer.html.

18. Michael Lelyveld, "China's Oil Import Dependence Climbs as Output Falls," *Radio Free Asia*, December 4, 2017, https://www.rfa.org/english/commentaries/energy_watch/chinas-oil-import-dependence-climbs-as-output-falls-12042017102429.html.

19. Mahmoud Ghafouri, "China's Policy in the Persian Gulf," *Middle East Policy Council* 16, no. 2 (Summer 2009): 80–92.

20. Muhammad Zulfikar Rakhmat, "Oman- Overview," *US Energy Information Administration (EIA)*, August 25, 2017, https://www.eia.gov/beta/international/analysis.cfm?iso=OMN.

21. Muhammad Rakhmat, "Exploring the China and Oman Relationship," *The Diplomat*, May 10, 2014, https://thediplomat.com/2014/05/exploring-the-china-and-oman-relationship/.

22. "Oman-: Overview", US Energy Information Administration, https://www.eia.gov/beta/international/country/php?iso=OMN.

23. "China Remains Oman's Top Crude Oil Export Market," *Hellenic Shipping News*, August 28, 2017, https://www.hellenicshippingnews.com/china-remains-omans-top-crude-oil-export-market/.

24. "Country Analysis Brief: Oman," *US Energy Information Administration (EIA)*, August 25, 2017, http://www.marcon.com/library/country_briefs/Oman/oman.pdf.

25. "China is Largest Foreign Investor in Middle East," *The Middle East Monitor*, July 24, 2017, https://www.middleeastmonitor.com/20170724-china-is-largest-foreign-investor-in-middle-east/.

26. Jiang Yan, "LPC-Oman Raising US$3.6bn from Chinese Banks," *Reuters*, May 9, 2017, https://www.reuters.com/article/oman-loans/lpc-oman-raising-us3-6bn-from-chinese-banks-idUSL4N1IB3TW.

27. Nawied Jabarkhyl, "Oman Counts on Chinese billions to Build Desert Boomtown," *Reuters*, September 5, 2017, https://www.reuters.com/article/us-oman-china-investment/oman-counts-on-chinese-billions-to-build-desert-boomtown-idUSKCN1BG1WJ.

28. Wade Shepard, "Why China is Building a New City Out in the Desert of Oman," *Forbes*, September 8, 2017, https://www.forbes.com/sites/wadeshepard/2017/09/08/why-china-is-building-a-new-city-out-in-the-desert-of-oman/#6d3249316b2f.

29. A. E. James, "Oman Wanfang Plans OMR400m Infrastructure Investment in Duqm," *Times of Oman*, May 8, 2017, http://timesofoman.com/article/108565/Business/Oman-Wanfang-plans-OMR400m-infrastructure-investment-in-Duqm.

30. "Oman: Foreign Investment," *Santander Trade Portal*, November 2017, https://en.portal.santandertrade.com/establish-overseas/oman/investing-3.

31. "Oman Wanfang Plans 25 New Projects in Duqm," *Times of Oman*, August 12, 2017, http://timesofoman.com/article/114777/Business/Oman-Wanfang-plans-25-new-projects-at-Duqm.

32. "Oman's 2020 Vision," *Arabian Business*, March 10, 2010, http://www.arabianbusiness.com/oman-s-2020-vision-89986.html.

33. Nawied Jabarkhyl, "Oman Counts on Chinese billions to build desert boom town". Reuters, 5 September 2017, https://www.reuters.com/article/us-china-oman-investment/oman-counts-on-chinese-investment-to-build-desert-boomtown-idUSKCN1BJ1WJ.

34. "China Considers Oman Key Partner for Belt and Road Initiative," *The State Council: The People's Republic of China*, May 24, 2016, http://english.gov.cn/state_council/state_councilors/2016/05/24/content_281475356198114.htm.

35. Zambelis, "China and the Quiet Kingdom," 11–15.

36. "Maritime Chokepoints are Critical to Global Energy Security," *US Energy Information Administration (EIA)*, August 1, 2017, https://www.eia.gov/todayinenergy/detail.php?id=32292#.

37. Lokhande, "China's One Belt One Road Initiative."

38. "Logistics has a Key Role in Oman's Development," *The Business Times*, November 20, 2017, http://www.businesstimes.com.sg/hub/oman-national-day/logistics-has-a-key-role-in-omans-development.

39. Zambelis, "China and the Quiet Kingdom," 11–15.

40. Shiv Shankaran Nair, "One Belt One Road to Invest in Omani Port," *Medium*, November 9, 2017, https://medium.com/@ShivNair/shiv-nair-one-belt-one-road-to-invest-in-omani-port-478b82c82a6.

41. Giorgio Cafiero, "Why China's Investment in Oman Matters," *The New Arab*, October 7, 2017, https://www.alaraby.co.uk/english/comment/2017/10/17/why-chinas-investment-in-oman-matters.

42. Sarah Townsend, "Oman 'to Look East' to China, India for Future Investment," *Arabian Business*, October 2, 2017, http://www.arabianbusiness.com/industries/banking-finance/380125-oman-to-look-east-to-china-india-for-future-investment.

43. "China's Investment in CPEC Set to Cross $100 billion by 2030,"*Pakistan Today*, February 9, 2018, https://profit.pakistantoday.com.pk/2018/02/09/chinas-investment-in-cpec-set-to-cross-100-billion-by-2030/.

44. "PM's Aide Says Pakistan Eyeing to be Gateway to Oman, China," *Daily Times*, September 4, 2016, https://dailytimes.com.pk/59279/pakistan-eyeing-to-be-gateway-to-oman-and-china-sartaj-aziz/.

45. Brahma Chellaney, "China's Indian Ocean Strategy," *The Japan Times*, June 23, 2015, https://www.japantimes.co.jp/opinion/2015/06/23/commentary/world-commentary/chinas-indian-ocean-strategy/#.WumFYoiACUk.

46. Rahul Singh, "From Submarines to Warships: How Chinese Navy is Expanding its Footprint in Indian Ocean," *Hindustan Times*, July 5, 2017, https://www.hin

dustantimes.com/india-news/from-submarines-to-warships-how-chinese-navy-is-expanding-its-footprint-in-indian-ocean/story-QeJp31UtBphNjya2z8L7gM.html.

47. Baljit Singh Mann, "Changing Dynamics of India's Indian Ocean Policy," *Maritime Affairs: Journal of the National Maritime Foundation of India* 13, no. 2 (January 2018): 11–22.

48. R. Sidda Goud and Manisha Mookerjee, Eds., *China in the Indian Ocean Region: Changing Geopolitics and Challenges* (Hyderabad: Allied Publishers Ltd, 2015).

49. Christina Lin, "China's Strategic Shift toward the Region of the Four Seas: The Middle Kingdom Arrives in the Middle East," *Middle East Review of International Affairs* 17, no. 1 (April 2013): 2.

50. "Countries and Regions: China," *European Commission*, March 9, 2016, http://ec.europa.eu/trade/policy/countries-and-regions/countries/china/.

51. "Bilateral Trade between Egypt and China in 2016," *Trade Map, International Trade Centre*, https://www.trademap.org/(S(ec0tv1owkbgfvl3bj4qz0w1w))/Bilateral.aspx?nvpm=1|818||156||TOTAL|||2|1|1|2|1.

52. Hassanein Tayea, "Egypt-China Volume Trade Exchange Exceeds $10 bln," *El-balad*, March14, 2018, http://en.el-balad.com/2372018.

53. Noueihed Lin and Ali Abdelaty, "China's Xi Visits Egypt, Offers Financial, Political Support," *Reuters*, January 21, 2016, http://www.reuters.com/article/us-egypt-china-idUSKCN0UZ05I.

54. Liqiang Hou, "Chinese Companies Boost Operations in Egypt," *China Daily*, February15, 2016, http://www.chinadaily.com.cn/business/2016-02/15/content_23481956.htm.

55. "Chinese Investments in Egypt Reach $6 billion," *Egypt Today*, December 11, 2017, https://www.egypttoday.com/Article/3/36470/Chinese-investments-in-Egypt-reach-6-billion.

56. "Egypt Enters into Initial Deal for 15 Projects Worth $10 bln with China-Minister," *Reuters*, June 16, 2015, http://www.reuters.com/article/egypt-investment-china-idUSL5N0Z14NG20150615.

57. "China's Investments in Egypt Amount to $477 million," *AMEinfo*, June 8, 2015, http://ameinfo.com/money/economy/chinas-investments-in-egypt-amount-to-477-million/.

58. "Egypt Plans New Capital Adjacent to Cairo," *Al Jazeera*, March 14, 2015, http://www.aljazeera.com/news/2015/03/egypt-plans-capital-adjacent-cairo-150314014400946.html.

59. Kieron Monks, "Egypt is Getting a New Capital – Courtesy of China," *CNN*, October 10, 2016, http://edition.cnn.com/style/article/egypt-new-capital/index.html.

60. "China to Invest $11.2 billion in Projects for Egypt's New Administrative Capital," *Egypt Independent*, September 4, 2017, http://www.egyptindependent.com/china-invest-11-2-billion-projects-egypts-new-administrative-capital/.

61. Emma Scott, "China-Egypt Trade and Investment Ties- Seeking a Better Balance," *The Centre for Chinese Studies*, June 2015, http://www.ccs.org.za/wp-content/uploads/2015/06/CCS_PB_China_Egypt_Trade_Ties_Emma_Final_2015.pdf.

62. "CNNC, Egypt Ink MOU on Nuclear Cooperation," *Xinhua Finance*, April 1, 2015, http://en.xinfinance.com/html/Industries/Utilities/2015/74201.shtml.

63. "Yingli Will Build 500MW Solar PV Project in Egypt," *OFweek*, February 10, 2015, http://en.ofweek.com/news/Yingli-will-build-500MW-solar-PV-project-in-Egypt-25326.

64. "Investment Ministry Signs MoU with China Exim Bank to Support Development Projects," *Daily News*, August 29, 2017, https://dailynewsegypt.com/2017/08/29/investment-ministry-signs-mou-china-exim-bank-support-development-projects/.

65. "Chinese Investments & Contracts in Egypt 2015–2017," *China Global Investment Tracker*, 2017, https://www.aei.org/china-global-investment-tracker/.

66. Sharon Li and Colin Ingram, *Maritime Law and Policy in China* (New York: Routledge-Cavendish, 2002).

67. "China, Egypt Eye Belt and Road Cooperation," *Xinhua*, April 24, 2017, http://news.xinhuanet.com/english/2017-04/25/c_136232916.htm.

68. "China to Establish 50 Factories Near Suez Canal," *CNTV*, August 7, 2015, http://en.people.cn/business/n/2015/0807/c90778-8933176.html.

69. Li and Ingram, "Maritime Law and Policy in China."

70. Oded Eran, "China Has Laid Anchor in Israel's Ports," *Strategic Assessment* 19, no. 1 (April 2016): 51–59.

71. Scott, "China-Egypt Trade and Investment Ties."

72. Emma Scott, "China's Silk Road Strategy: A Foothold in the Suez, but Looking to Israel," *China Brief* 14, no. 19 (October 2014): 10–14.

73. Ahmed Farouk Ghoneim, "Egypt's Suez Canal Corridor Project," *Middle East Institute*, August 19, 2014, https://www.mei.edu/content/at/egypts-suez-canal-corridor-project; "China Now Biggest Investor in Suez," *China Daily*, March 23, 2017, http://www.chinadaily.com.cn/business/2017-03/23/content_28648386.htm.

74. Zhao Hong, "Egypt Announces New Chinese Investments in Textile," *China Daily*, April 5, 2017, http://www.chinadaily.com.cn/business/2017-04/05/content_28803966.htm.

75. "Video: Chinese Investment Boosts Suez Canal Economic Zone," *Arab Finance*, March 26, 2017, https://www.arabfinance.com/2015/pages/news/newsdetails.aspx?Id=385421&lang=en.

76. "Chinese Firms Eye Investing in New Admin Capital: Ambassador," *Egypt Today*, August 29, 2017, https://www.egypttoday.com/Article/3/20062/Chinese-firms-eye-investing-in-New-Admin-Capital-Ambassador.

77. "China Grants Egypt $US 71 million for Satellite Project, Vocational Training Centre," *Egyptian Streets*, March 22, 2017, https://egyptianstreets.com/2017/03/22/china-grants-egypt-us-71-for-satellite-project-vocational-training-centre/.

78. "Full Text: List of Deliverables of Belt and Road Forum," *Xinhua*, May 15, 2017, http://www.xinhuanet.com/english/2017-05/15/c_136286376.htm.

79. "China to Invest $40bn in Egypt Development Projects," *Trade Arabia*, May 16, 2017, http://www.tradearabia.com/news/CONS_325023.html.

80. Mandira Bagwandeen, "The African Link in China's OBOR Initiative," *Center for Chinese Studies*, May 15, 2017, http://daofeiconsults.com/wpcontent/uploads/2015/05/CCS_Commentary_Africa_OBOR_15MAY2017.pdf.

Section III

BRI AND INDO-PACIFIC STRATEGIC ACTORS

Chapter 8

India and the Belt and Road Initiative

From Critic to Competitor

Ian Hall

On May 13, 2017, on the eve of the Belt and Road Forum (BRF) in Beijing, a spokesperson for India's Ministry of External Affairs issued a blunt statement on the People's Republic of China's (PRC) Belt and Road Initiative (BRI).[1] It noted New Delhi's long-standing concerns about the China Pakistan Economic Corridor (CPEC), which runs through territory administered by Pakistan as Gilgit-Baltistan, and which India claims as part of Jammu and Kashmir.[2] Then, in a departure from India's approach to the BRI up to that point, the statement also offered a detailed and pointed critique of the wider endeavor. It observed that, in India's view,

> connectivity initiatives must be based on universally recognized international norms, good governance, rule of law, openness, transparency and equality. Connectivity initiatives must follow principles of financial responsibility to avoid projects that would create unsustainable debt burden for communities; balanced ecological and environmental protection and preservation standards; transparent assessment of project costs; and skill and technology transfer to help long term running and maintenance of the assets created by local communities.[3]

Since these principles were not in operation, in New Delhi's view—and because India believes that the PRC is refusing to "engage in a meaningful dialogue" on the BRI—the spokesperson confirmed that an Indian representative would not attend the BRF.[4]

This Indian statement was both unanticipated and unusual.[5] It deviated from New Delhi's typical approach to Sino-Indian bilateral diplomacy since the normalization of relations in the late 1980s, which has been to handle significant disagreements quietly and privately.[6] New Delhi's public rebuff to Beijing and its refusal to participate in the BRF also set it apart from like-minded Indo-Pacific states with reservations about the initiative, including Australia, Japan, Singapore, and the United States. Unlike India, those states all sent representatives to Beijing—albeit not heads of state or government—and issued lukewarm statements following the event that generally eschewed overt criticism. Australia, for example, sent its Trade Minister, Steven Ciobo, who subsequently expressed support for the idea of improved connectivity, as well as the hope that the BRI would employ a "transparent, collaborative and planned approach" in attempting to achieve it.[7]

Moreover, the May 2017 statement was followed by a welter of criticism from Indian observers of the BRI. Many argued that the BRI was a neo-imperial scheme to facilitate the imposition of a Beijing-centric regional order, brought about by the imposition of chronic indebtedness on weaker states. For all this criticism, however, this chapter observes that this Indian response was not a function of some kind of reflexive anticapitalist sentiment. While New Delhi did not issue any new statements that extended or elaborated upon the May 2017 statement,[8] and began to discuss both strategies for dissuading regional states, especially in South Asia, from engaging too deeply in the BRI, to also started to engage more positively and urgently with alternative infrastructure initiatives, including those to be delivered in bilateral partnership with Japan, and more recently with the other three "Quad" states: Australia, Japan, and the United States.

This chapter explores the grounds for India's opposition to the BRI, which is expressed in unusually strong language when seen in the wider context of Sino-Indian relations, and the reasons for the emergence of India as a putative competitor to China in the delivery of regional connectivity. It argues that while India has a mixed record in delivering high-quality, affordable, and functional infrastructure, both domestically and internationally, these new moves are significant and could well be consequential. There is evidence that India's ability to build infrastructure and improve connectivity is improving and that it may be able to deliver better results in partnership with others, notably Japan, which are leading players in regional development.

To make this case, this chapter is divided into four parts. The first traces India's responses to the BRI as it evolved between September and October 2013, when it was first proposed by Chinese president Xi Jinping, and the BRF in May 2017. The second takes a step back to explore India's wider approach to the various challenges that China poses, putting its BRF statement into context. The third section looks in detail at the arguments that undermined and accompanied India's official response to the BRF invitation. And the fourth and final part explores some of the alternative infrastructure and connectivity projects India is now working on with various regional partners.

WRESTLING WITH OBOR

The "One Belt, One Road" (OBOR) scheme, later rebranded the BRI, emerged at an inopportune time for India, in late 2013.[9] A General Election loomed in April and May of the following year,[10] and Manmohan Singh's Congress-dominated United Progressive Alliance (UPA) government, beset by accusations that it had badly underperformed in office, as well as multiple corruption allegations, was tired and lackluster.[11] New Delhi did, however, convey a guardedly positive response to Beijing's initial approaches on improving regional connectivity. In December 2013, India signed up to the BCIM corridor intended to link Kunming to Kolkata via Mandalay and Dhaka, at that point conceived as a discrete (that is, non-OBOR/BRI) project. During a meeting with Chinese special representative Yang Jiechi three months later, in February 2014, Singh also welcomed the idea of the overland New Silk Road Initiative.[12] The prime minister (PM) and his officials were not drawn, however, on the question of the maritime component of the BRI, offering no public comment on the Maritime Silk Road (MSR) during or after the meeting.[13]

The advent of the new Bharatiya Janata Party (BJP)-led government in May 2014 did not bring any immediate change to these positions, despite, on the one hand, public prompting from the Chinese ambassador in a newspaper editorial published during the election campaign,[14] and on the other, signs that Narendra Modi and his team were more skeptical about China and its intentions toward India than their predecessors.[15] Instead, for the first few months of Modi's term in office, India kept its counsel and delayed making decisions. In late June 2014, during Vice President Hamid Ansari's visit to China, Beijing again sought India's backing for the MSR but was met with a polite request for more detail on its plans.[16] Another plea—this time for an endorsement of the full BRI—was made by the Chinese foreign ministry in August 2014, in interviews given to Indian journalists in Beijing, in advance of Xi Jinping's state visit to India the following month.[17] This approach was also rebuffed, with no mention of the BRI made in the lengthy joint statement issued following the meeting, apart from a reference to the two countries' shared commitment to the BCIM project.[18]

This refusal to endorse the BRI occurred at a time in which there was a marked cooling of bilateral relations, during the second half of 2014. In the run-up to Xi's trip to India that September, as Kanti Bajpai notes, Beijing and New Delhi both assumed tougher stances toward one another.[19] On the Indian side, this was achieved by way of a series of high-level visits to states with their own differences with China: Modi went to Japan from August 31 to September 3, while External Affairs Minister Sushma Swaraj and then-president Pranab Mukherjee went to Vietnam. On the Chinese side, the signaling was less subtle: a week before the Xi visit, units of the People's

Liberation Army (PLA) entered Indian-controlled territory claimed by China in Ladakh, Jammu and Kashmir. This intrusion met with a sharp response from New Delhi. Modi ordered three battalions of Indian troops into the area and then—in an unusual move for an Indian PM—he publically criticized the PLA incursion during a joint press conference held with Xi during the latter's visit.[20]

The final straw for New Delhi was, however, yet to come. In April 2015, Xi made a state visit to Pakistan. There he unveiled the US$46bn CPEC project (now valued at some US$64bn),[21] and confirmed that it was a central component of the OBOR/BRI scheme.[22] This announcement cast a pall over Modi's reciprocal trip to China the following month.[23] In response, in Beijing, the Indian PM reportedly lodged a formal protest about the CPEC, noting that the planned road and rail corridor passed through territory India regards as its own.[24] In the weeks that followed, New Delhi also began to draw unfavorable contrasts between BRI and other Chinese-led initiatives that it supports, such as the Asian Infrastructure Investment Bank (AIIB), and BRICS projects like the New Development Bank (NDB). In comments made in Singapore in July 2015, for example, then-Indian foreign secretary Subrahmanyam Jaishankar argued that unlike the AIIB and the NDB, which were created by multilateral negotiations, and which are governed multilaterally, the BRI is a unilateral, "national Chinese initiative" "devised" to serve its "national interest."[25]

This pattern of Indian behavior did not change between mid-2015 and the eve of the BRF in May 2017, despite considerable Chinese efforts to woo Indian scholars and think tank analysts over to more positive assessments through a series of BRI-focused dialogues and conferences. A lively discussion about the initiative did occur outside government, with some prominent voices urging that India try to find a way to use it to its advantage.[26] But at the official level, India mostly "maintained coy and studied silence," criticizing the BRI only indirectly, aside from formulaic protests about the CPEC and the road and rail corridor through Pakistani-administered Kashmir.[27] Modi, his external affairs minister Swaraj, and foreign secretary Jaishankar remained diplomatic, but firm, continuing to welcome for greater "connectivity" in South Asia and the Indian Ocean but insisting that it be developed "through consultative processes," not unilateral decisions, and arguing that connectivity initiatives should not become exercises in "hard-wiring" designed to limit the autonomy of involved states.[28]

MANAGING CHINA

New Delhi's highly critical public statement of May 2017 extended these specific criticisms of the BRI and added to them. It also signaled the end of

India's three-and-a-half years of fence sitting on the Chinese initiative, begun by Manmohan Singh's government in late 2013. And just as importantly, it demonstrated the Modi government's willingness to air differences with Beijing freely and openly, in contrast to long-established Indian practice.

Since the late 1980s, when bilateral ties were finally normalized after more than twenty years of estrangement after the 1964 border war, India's China policy has been characterized by caution and restraint, reflecting the power differential between the two.[29] During the post-Cold War period, New Delhi has practiced its own version of "congagement"[30]—working to nurture trade and investment ties, within limits, and cooperating to advance shared interests in key areas of global governance, like climate change but also balancing Beijing's military and diplomatic heft through military modernization at home, the acquisition of a nuclear deterrent, the forging of strategic partnerships with old friends (like Vietnam) and new ones (like Australia, Japan, and the United States), and greater involvement in regional institutions, from the East Asia Summit to the Shanghai Cooperation Organization. Throughout, it has also tried to avoid disagreeing with China in public, aiming instead to manage differences them quietly, through conventional diplomatic channels, behind closed doors.

Why, then, did New Delhi issue such a strong statement as it did on the eve of the BRF in May 2017? Part of the answer obviously concerns the CPEC project, since it directly impinges upon territory that India considers its own. But this is not the only reason. The other part of the answer runs deeper, connecting with New Delhi's growing mistrust of Beijing's intentions toward India, and indeed the wider Indo-Pacific region, and its mounting concern about Chinese assertiveness in the wake of the Global Financial Crisis, especially after Xi's elevation to the presidency in late 2012.[31]

India's political elite has of course long harbored worries about the effects that China's rapid economic development might have on its independence, prosperity, and security, and New Delhi has tried to hedge against possible security challenges arising from China in various ways, including acquiring nuclear weapons and new delivery systems after 1998.[32] But during the 2000s, many respected and influential Indian analysts were still cautiously positive about the prospects for building a "wide-ranging and healthy bilateral relationship."[33] This mood began to change toward the end of the decade, however, as a series of Chinese actions undermined New Delhi's confidence. In April 2009, China blocked an ADB loan for a project in Arunachal Pradesh, which Beijing claims as "South Tibet," highlighting both that claim and China's ability to use regional institutions as a stick with which to beat India. In October, China issued a formal diplomatic protest about a prime ministerial visit to that Indian state. At the same time, Beijing also began to issue "stapled" visas, instead of regular ones, to Indian residents of Jammu and Kashmir visiting China, arguing that because that area was in dispute, it should be recognized as such. The PRC also intensified the building of dual-use infrastructure up to and along the disputed Sino-Indian Line of Actual Control (LAC). In parallel, it stymied attempts to put pressure on Pakistan to release those responsible for orchestrating the November 2008 Mumbai terrorist attacks.[34] By the early 2010s, as a result, influential Indian analysts began to talk of China less as a putative partner in the management of the emerging multipolar order, and more of a "challenge" that "impinges directly on India's geopolitical space."[35]

During this period, in Manmohan Singh's second term as leader of the Congress Party-dominated UPA government, China policy also began to divide Left and Right in Indian politics. Criticism of Singh's approach from the Opposition BJP became increasingly vocal, and was taken up by Modi himself when he emerged as that party's candidate for the prime ministership in the long run-up to the 2014 election.[36] Indeed, although many argue—rightly—that core elements of Modi's foreign policy builds upon positions established under the Congress-led coalition,[37] it was clear that even before the election his government was going to adopt a bolder China policy than its predecessor.[38] During the campaign in late 2013 and early 2014, Modi made robust public comments about China, most clearly in calling on Beijing to set aside its "mindset of expansion."[39] He also made a series of moves intended to demonstrate his—and India's—independence, including inviting the leader of the Tibetan government in exile, Lobsang Sangay, to his swearing-in ceremony as Prime Minister.[40] Modi's first three state visits outside of South Asia—to Japan, the United States, and Australia—were also clear signs of intent, signaling that his government was not going to allow Beijing to bully India or circumscribe its ties with like-minded partners in the region.

For the most part, Modi's government has stuck with this more robust approach since 2014, despite mixed views in New Delhi about its effectiveness, especially in countering Chinese influence over India's regional neighbors.[41] Its response to PLA incursions in Ladakh during Xi's visit to Gujarat in September 2014 has been mentioned—Modi sent troops to the LAC and publically called out the transgression. This set the tone for further acts of "defiance," as Bajpai has observed. Some of these have been merely rhetorical, including comments made by Indian officials and ministers about India's sovereignty over Arunachal Pradesh, visas, water sharing, the trade deficit, and Beijing's refusal to allow India into the Nuclear Suppliers' Group and to put accused Pakistani terrorists on UN lists.[42] Modi has also reiterated his earlier statements, made on the campaign trail, about China's supposedly "expansionist" tendencies and its need to change its behavior toward bordering states.[43] Other acts have been more tangible. New Delhi's willingness to see the mid-2017 Doklam standoff—in which the PLA and

Indian troops confronted each other in an area of Bhutan Beijing claims as its own—through to the end, despite dire threats of punishment aired by the Chinese media and foreign ministry, is one example of this changed attitude.[44] Others including India's efforts to deepen and broaden ties with key strategic partners, especially Japan and the United States, and to reconvene the Quadrilateral Security Dialogue (the "Quad"), despite concerns about Australia's wavering China policy, in particular.[45]

DEBATING THE BRI

The evolution of the BRI from late 2013 onward, and its emergence as Xi's "signature policy,"[46] exacerbated existing worries in New Delhi and placed even more pressure on Modi's government and its preferred approach to managing Beijing. In particular, the BRI generated anxiety about China's intentions toward India and the wider Indo-Pacific, especially about its use of "economic statecraft" to achieve its objectives, and about its potential impact on India's political and strategic autonomy and that of neighbors.[47] These concerns tapped into long-standing and deeply rooted beliefs about the causes of India's subjection to British imperial rule and removal of its political autonomy—beliefs which underpin a persistent skepticism in Indian politics about free trade and cross-border flows of investment, and about connectivity, clear in both secular- and Hindu nationalist policy agendas.[48]

In the run-up to the BRF, these latter beliefs came to the fore in India's public debate over the BRI, as critical voices grew louder and more positive Indian assessments of the initiative and the opportunities it might hold for the country were sidelined.[49] The title of Ashok Malik's op-ed in the *Daily Pioneer*, published a few days before the forum and reprinted by the Observer Research Foundation (ORF), a leading Delhi think tank, reflected this new mood: "OBOR: For India it's a road to subjugation." Malik—who on August 1, 2017, became Indian president Ram Nath Kovind's press secretary—argued that

> It is facile to believe the Chinese are seeking to build infrastructure in other countries only because they themselves have excess infrastructure capacities and are looking for ancillary manufacturing locations…and new markets for their products outside China. [. . .] [N]obody makes such ambitious investment decisions at a time when global demand is in a slump. [. . .] Far from being a force for stability, One-Belt-One-Road is disturbing domestic and regional political balance[s] and weakening democratic institutions in the countries it enters. It is already producing a series of client states. Their very existence is dependent on furthering Chinese interests.[50]

These arguments were echoed by a series of other prominent commentators. In the *Economic Times*, for instance, Dhruva Jaishankar of Brookings India also argued that the commercial logic of the BRI is questionable, pointing to the "white elephant" of the Mattala Rajapaksa International Airport, dubbed the world's "most underused,"[51] and the development of "dual use" facilities, especially ports. Connectivity should be achieved in transparent ways through multilateral engagement, he argued, because "drawing lines upon a map in a unilateral fashion" strikes many as "sinister."[52] Writing in *Outlook India*, Rajeswari Pillai Rajagopalan from ORF was even blunter: the BRI was an "imperialistic plan" that would plunge regional states into debt traps from which they would struggle to emerge, if at all.[53]

Other influential analysts drew comparisons with earlier European imperial projects. At a forum hosted by the Institute of South Asian Studies at the National University of Singapore that coincided with the BRF, C. Raja Mohan outlined parallels between the BRI and European colonial infrastructure projects, arguing: "[w]hat China is doing today is exactly what the British were doing in the nineteenth century, of creating new ports, creating new commercial nodes, setting new licensing standards." The ambition of this initiative, however, dwarfed its British equivalent: "unlike in the past, [where] it is said that Britain built an empire in an absent minded fit . . . here it is being done by design…a conscious deliberate program to link the world under the auspices of the Chinese."[54] These views chimed with official perceptions and helped justify India's stand on the BRI on the eve of the Beijing Forum—with Modi's assertion that the present Chinese government is inherently "expansionist" and with the broader argument that the initiative is a Chinese project designed for Chinese ends, insensitive to the concerns and needs of others.[55]

FROM CRITIC TO COMPETITOR

In the past, these kinds of worries about the limits that economic connectivity have in the past imposed on political autonomy, and might impose in the future, have stymied India's engagement in regional infrastructure projects and deeper integration into regional markets.[56] Interestingly, however, since the advent of the BRI New Delhi has also moved to accelerate a number of preexisting infrastructure development projects and to begin new ones. These include projects targeted at building or upgrading domestic infrastructure and those to be delivered in partnership with South Asian states or others beyond the immediate region, notably Japan, and, more recently, the other two Quad states, Australia and the United States. These projects complement or extend past or existing initiatives, including long-standing Africa-India healthcare projects that embed telemedicine and involve the creation of Internet connections in remote areas.[57] And they build on India's developing expertise in the on-time and on-budget completion of major domestic infrastructure projects, such as the ten urban metros in existence or under construction; the solar power plants and rooftop installations slated to deliver 100 GW by 2020, funded in part by the World Bank; the major new airport terminals in Bengaluru, Delhi, Hyderabad, Kolkata, Mumbai, and so on; Gujarat's Gujarat International Finance Tec-City; the US$10bn "Sagar Mala" port upgrade program; the US$15bn Japanese-funded and Japanese-supported Ahmedabad–Mumbai high-speed rail link; and the US$100bn Delhi-Mumbai Industrial Corridor, also progressing with Japanese assistance.

Across South Asia and beyond, into east Africa and South East Asia, India has now engaged in a series of major infrastructure projects that, while dwarfed by the declared scale of the BRI, run in parallel or compete with components of China's initiative. These include road and rail building under the auspices of the South Asian Sub-Regional Economic Cooperation (SASEC), and important measures to improve trade facilitation, which will better connect India to South East Asia; the nascent Asia-Africa Trade Corridor concept New Delhi is beginning to develop with Tokyo; the substantial investments made in Chabahar Port in Iran, and the associated rail link intended to run into Afghanistan that is part of the bigger so-called International North South Transportation Corridor into Russia and onwards into Europe; and the nascent discussions among the Quad states about how they might collaborate on regional connectivity.

CONNECTING WITH SOUTH EAST ASIA

The SASEC grouping, now involving Bangladesh, Bhutan, India, the Maldives, Nepal, Sri Lanka, and Myanmar, was first formed in 2001 to find ways to cooperate on economic issues beyond those being explored in the South Asian Association for Regional Cooperation, long deadlocked by differences between India and Pakistan. Working with the ADB, SASEC works on discrete projects, successfully delivering some forty of these infrastructure and development initiatives up to mid-2016, at a cost of US$7.7bn.[58]

SASEC is now part way into delivering a new set of initiatives detailed in the ten-year operational plan it published in 2016. These include joint projects that align with those of other regional forums, including the Bay of Bengal Initiative for Multisectoral Technical and Economic Cooperation. Together, they aim to upgrade cross-border roads and rail connections, develop better port infrastructure, and improve regional airports but also to address regulatory issues concerning trade facilitation, build better energy infrastructure, and establish cross-border trade corridors. In 2016–2018, SASEC was coordinating the expenditure of another US$16–17bn on new and upgraded roads, enhanced port infrastructure, and improvements to airports in Bhutan and Nepal, and an additional half a billion dollars on trade facilitation.[59] It was also discussing another $58bn in energy projects.[60]

Some of these schemes have great potential for India and for the broader region. The 1,360-kilometer India-Myanmar-Thailand Trilateral Highway between Moreh, in Manipur state, and Mae Sot in Thailand, for example, should open up new opportunities for greater overland trade with South East Asia, which already accounts for almost half of India's trade, especially for businesses in the poor North East of the country. It ought also to lessen India's dependence on shipping routes through the Strait of Malacca and South China Sea, at least for moving goods into mainland South East Asian markets, especially in the Mekong region.[61] Begun in 2012—a decade after it was first proposed—the highway has been part funded by the ADB, which sees it as an integral part of the broader "Asian Highway Network," but the Modi government has given it a new impetus in recent months, partly out of concern about the BRI. In August 2017, it approved more than $250m in additional finance for the scheme, reportedly in response to competing Chinese initiatives, having earlier announced funding for the widening and improvement of the Imphal to Moreh highway linking the capital of Manipur to the border town, also in collaboration with the ADB.[62] While it is unlikely that it will be completed by the promised date of 2020, the Trilateral Highway should be finished by the mid-2020s, at the latest.

Connecting to Africa

Like the various SASEC schemes, the AAGC also predates the BRF, but it is clear too that China's unfolding connectivity plans have injected energy into the initiative. The AAGC was prefigured in the joint statement issued after the November 2016 Tokyo summit between Modi and his Japanese counterpart, Shinzo Abe.[63] Yet it was not until the late May 2017 India-Africa summit and African Development Bank meeting held in Gandhinagar in India that the AAGC was described in any detail. Intended to deliver "development and cooperation projects, quality infrastructure and institutional connectivity, capacity and skill enhancement and people-to-people partnerships," its aims echo at least some of those of the BRI.[64] Its slated geographical coverage, however, is narrower, involving India, Japan, and a number of South East Asian states (notably Myanmar, Singapore, and Thailand), Indian Ocean states (Madagascar, the Maldives, Mauritius, and the Seychelles), and East African littoral states (Kenya, Tanzania, Zanzibar, Zambia, and Zimbabwe), as well as Bangladesh and Mongolia.[65]

Indian analysts like S. D. Pradhan, a former deputy national security advisor, are keen to emphasize that, unlike the BRI, the AAGC is properly multilateral and collaborative, aiming at local employment and following international standards for financing.[66] It is also conceived as an extension of long-established partnerships and projects, including India's pioneering and broad-based International Technical and Economic Cooperation (ITEC) program, launched in 1964, and the Africa-India Framework for Cooperation launched at the first India-Africa Forum Summit in 2008 that also encompassed a wide range of education, health, capacity-building, peace, and governance initiatives.[67] The AAGC is being sold, moreover, as a means of tying these various programs up with India's "Look / Act East" policies directed at South East Asia, and Japan's so-called "Expanded Partnership for Quality Infrastructure", outlined at the G7 meeting in May 2016, and its broader development program, recently repackaged to fit with its Free and Open Indo-Pacific concept. The bulk of the funding, however, will likely come from Japan, which has promised US$200bn to the AAGC, supplemented by loans from India's Exim Bank.[68]

Chabahar

India's interest in Iran's Chabahar Port is also long-standing, dating back to the early 2000s, and deep-rooted, since it potentially gives India access to move goods north to Afghanistan and into Central Asia on the International North South Transportation Corridor, bypassing overland routes through Pakistan. It could also provide New Delhi with a strategically useful temporary or even permanent naval facility close to both Pakistan and the Persian Gulf. However, until a deal was struck with Tehran in July 2016, India was unable to make a substantial investment in the port and related infrastructure because of UN sanctions imposed on Iran as a result of its nuclear weapons program. Under the terms of that deal, New Delhi pledged around US$500bn to upgrade the port, build a rail link, and develop a special economic zone.[69] New Delhi has since struck a transit agreement with Tehran, while India Ports Global Private Limited has acquired short-term rights to operate the port, with others, including the Adani Group, interested in a longer-term deal.[70]

The Quad and Indo-Pacific Infrastructure?

Aside from these various initiatives already under way, India has also reportedly been involved in discussions—albeit tentative—with Australia and the United States about other infrastructure projects in the region.[71] Connectivity was apparently on the agenda for the Manila meeting of Quad country officials on the sidelines of the East Asia Summit in November 2017.[72] Since then, their "consultations" have apparently evolved toward a putative plan for the four countries to help coordinate infrastructure funding,[73] as well as other projects, such as the so-called "ASEAN-Australia Infrastructure Co-operation

Initiative" announced in Sydney in March 2018.[74] Modi has also discussed bilateral cooperation aimed at "bolstering regional economic connectivity" with the Trump administration.[75] Exactly what these would entail, however, individually and collectively, is so far unclear, with few concrete proposals or mechanisms outlined.

CONCLUSION

Despite an attempt to "reset" Sino-Indian relations in the aftermath of Doklam New Delhi remains both outside the BRI and critical of it. Rightly or wrongly, Modi continues to resist Chinese pressure to endorse the BRI in some way, as he did at his "informal summit" with Xi in Wuhan in late April 2018.[76] New Delhi's objections to the initiative, this chapter has argued, are deeply rooted, and go beyond the issue of the CPEC project and Kashmir, arising from growing concern about China's intentions generated by Beijing's attempts to build influence in South Asia, project military power into the Indian Ocean, and coerce its neighbors, especially those with which, like India, it is has territorial disputes.

These concerns are also driving New Delhi to accelerate connectivity initiatives to which it was already committed, like the SASEC road, rail, and facilitation projects, and toward new one, to be delivered in collaboration with multiple partners in varying combination. Whether these succeed is yet to be seen, but it should be observed that India's capacity to develop effective programs in bilateral, minilateral, and multilateral settings is improving, and while its domestic infrastructure remains often dire, its capacity to deliver good-quality results is also getting better. Within India, new airports and metro systems—most notably in Delhi—have been constructed well and within budget, on occasion with Japanese financial and technical support. Outside India, there are also successes, including the ADB-funded rail line between Mazar-e-Sharif and Hairatan, completed in ten months by an Indian-led team.[77] These efforts are, of course, small scale compared to the stated ambition of the BRI, but they indicate a willingness to compete with China, bilaterally or in partnership with others.

NOTES

1. The best short analysis of the BRI and its drivers remains Peter Cai's "Understanding the Belt and Road Initiative," *Lowy Institute for International Policy Analysis*, March 2017, https://www.lowyinstitute.org/publications/understanding-belt-and-road-initiative. For a longer study that puts the BRI into a wider context, see also

Yong Wang, "Offensive for Defensive: The Belt and Road Initiative and China's New Grand Strategy," *The Pacific Review* 29(3) (2016), pp. 455–463.

2. On the CPEC, see especially Andrew Small, "First Movement: Pakistan and the Belt and Road Initiative," *Asia Policy* 24 (2017), pp. 80–87.

3. Ministry of External Affairs, India, "Official Spokesperson's Response to a Query on Participation of India in OBOR/BRI Forum," May 13, 2017, http://www.mea.gov.in/media-briefings.htm?dtl/28463/Official+Spokespersons+response+to+a+query+on+participation+of+India+in+OBORBRI+Forum.

4. Ibid.

5. Suman Bery, "India's Economic Diplomacy in the Belt and Road Era," *East Asia Forum*, July 5, 2017, http://www.eastasiaforum.org/2017/07/05/indian-economic-diplomacy-in-the-belt-and-road-era/.

6. Ashley Tellis, "China and India in Asia," in Francine R. Frankel and Harry Harding (eds.), *The India-China Relationship: What the United States Needs to Know* (Washington, DC: Woodrow Wilson Center and Columbia University Press, 2004), p. 141. See also Manjeet Singh Pardesi, "Modi's China Policy—Change or Continuity?" in Sinderpal Singh (ed.), *Modi and the World: (Re) Constructing Indian Foreign Policy* (Singapore: World Scientific, 2017), p. 4. China and India broke off diplomatic relations in 1962, as a result of their border war. Although they reestablished formal diplomatic ties in 1979, most analysts agree that normalization of relations did not occur until Rajiv Gandhi's visit to Beijing in 1988, which produced a joint statement reaffirming shared principles and promising cooperation in a range of areas.

7. Steven Ciobo, "Belt and Road Forum," May 14, 2017, http://trademinister.gov.au/releases/Pages/2017/sc_mr_170514b.aspx.

8. When comment has been offered on the BRI by Indian spokespeople, it is to reiterate the points made in the May 2017 statement. See, for example, Ministry of External Affairs, India, "Response to Question No. 2735 Belt and Road Initiative of China from Shri A. K. Selvaraj, Rajya Sabha," August 10, 2017, http://www.mea.gov.in/rajya-sabha.htm?dtl/28857/question+no2735+belt+and+road+initiative+of+china.

9. OBOR was outlined in two public speeches made by Xi Jinping—one delivered in Kazakhstan in early September 2013, and the other in Jakarta, a month later. See Ministry of Foreign Affairs, PRC, "President Xi Jinping Delivers Important Speech and Proposes to Build a Silk Road Economic Belt with Central Asian Countries," September 7, 2013, http://www.fmprc.gov.cn/mfa_eng/topics_665678/xjpfwzysiesgjtfhshzzfh_665686/t1076334.shtml and Ministry of Foreign Affairs, PRC, "Xi Jinping: Let the Sense of Community of Common Destiny Take Deep Root in Neighbouring Countries," October 25, 2013, http://www.fmprc.gov.cn/mfa_eng/wjb_663304/wjbz_663308/activities_663312/t1093870.shtml.

10. India's General Election is such a complex exercise that it takes place over several weeks. In 2014, voting occurred from April 9 to May 12.

11. For a useful account, see Rajdeep Sardesai, *2014: The Election That Changed India* (New Delhi: Penguin, 2014).

12. BRICS Post, "China, India Conclude "Very Positive' Talks," February 12, 2013, http://thebricspost.com/china-india-conclude-very-positive-talks/.

13. Abhijit Singh, "China's Maritime Silk Route: Implications for India," *IDSA Comment*, Institute for Defence Studies and Analyses, New Delhi, July 16, 2014, http://www.idsa.in/idsacomments/ChinasMaritimeSilkRoute_AbhijitSingh_160714.

14. Wei Wei, "Reviving the Silk Road: Connecting India, China and Central Asia," *Economic Times*, April 14, 2014, http://www.fmprc.gov.cn/mfa_eng/wjb_663304/zwjg_665342/zwbd_665378/t1146648.shtml.

15. Ankit Panda, "Narendra Modi Gets Tough On China," *The Diplomat*, February 25, 2014, https://thediplomat.com/2014/02/narendra-modi-gets-tough-on-china/.

16. Singh, "China's Maritime Silk Route."

17. Ananth Krishnan, "China Wants India to Play Key Role in 'Silk Road' Plan," *The Hindu*, August 10, 2014, http://www.thehindu.com/news/international/world/china-wants-india-to-play-key-role-in-silk-road-plan/article6301227.ece.

18. Ministry of External Affairs, India, "Joint Statement between the Republic of India and the People's Republic of China on Building a Closer Developmental Partnership," September 19, 2014, http://mea.gov.in/bilateral-documents.htm?dtl/24022.

19. Kanti Bajpai, "Narendra Modi's Pakistan and China Policy: Assertive Bilateral Diplomacy, Active Coalition Diplomacy," *International Affairs* 93(1) (2017), pp. 80–81.

20. Victor Mallet, "China-India Border Stand-off Overshadows Xi Jinping's Deals," *Financial Times*, September 19, 2014, https://www.ft.com/content/28c61aae-3f0f-11e4-a861-00144feabdc0.

21. Salman Siddiqui, "CPEC Investment Pushed from $46b to $62b," *The Express Tribune* (Pakistan), April 12, 2017, https://tribune.com.pk/story/1381733/cpec-investment-pushed-55b-62b/.

22. Katharine Houreld, "China and Pakistan Launch Economic Corridor Plan Worth $46 billion," *Reuters*, April 20, 2015, https://www.reuters.com/article/us-pakistan-china/china-and-pakistan-launch-economic-corridor-plan-worth-46-billion-idUSKBN0NA12T20150420.

23. C. Raja Mohan, *Modi's World: Expanding India's Sphere of Influence* (New Delhi: HarperCollins, 2015), p. 103.

24. Elizabeth Roche, "India Protests China's Plans for $46 billion PoK Investments," *LiveMint*, May 14, 2015, http://www.livemint.com/Politics/NX9251BYbqEXgIBM9Ch55L/India-protests-Chinas-plans-for-PoK-investments.html.

25. Subrahmanyam Jaishankar, "India, the United States and China," International Institute for Strategic Studies Fullerton Lecture, July 19, 2015, https://www.youtube.com/watch?v=et2ihw8jHaY&feature=youtu.be&t=46m27s. In the Indian system, the Foreign Secretary is the chief civil servant in the Ministry of External Affairs (MEA). The External Affairs Minister leads the MEA.

26. See, for example, Jabin T. Jacob, "India and OBOR: It's Not Complicated," *BRICS Post*, October 16, 2016, http://thebricspost.com/india-and-obor-its-not-complicated/, Prem Shankar Jha, "Why India Must Embrace China's One Belt One Road Plan," *The Wire*, August 13, 2016, https://thewire.in/58810/india-must-embrace-chinas-one-belt-one-road-plan/; and Srinath Raghavan, "India Must Involve Itself in the China-Pakistan One Belt, One Road initiative to Stay in the Game," *Hindustan Times*, March 23, 2017, http://www.hindustantimes.com/columns/india-must-involv

e-itself-in-the-china-pakistan-one-belt-one-road-initiative-to-stay-in-the-game/story-uTtxhRzcn8iCnUHsB91haJ.html.

27. Patricia Uberoi, "Problems and Prospects of the BCIM Economic Corridor," *China Report* 52(1) (2016), p. 27.

28. See, for example, Ministry of External Affairs, India, "Speech by Foreign Secretary at Raisina Dialogue in New Delhi," March 2, 2016, http://mea.gov.in/Speeches-Statements.htm?dtl/26433/Speech_by_Foreign_Secretary_at_Raisina_Dialogue_in_New_Delhi_March_2_2015. For a wider assessment of India's position prior to the BRF, see also Tanvi Madan, "What India Thinks about China's One Belt, One Road Initiative (But Does Not Explicitly Say)," *Order from Chaos* blog, Brookings Institution, March 14, 2016, https://www.brookings.edu/blog/order-from-chaos/2016/03/14/whatindia-thinks-about-chinas-one-belt-one-road-initiative-but-doesnt-explicitly-say/.

29. Pardesi, "Modi's China Policy," pp. 11–13. See also Tellis, "China and India in Asia."

30. This concept is central to Aaron Friedberg's *A Contest for Supremacy: China, America, and the Struggle for Mastery in Asia* (New York: Norton, 2011).

31. On Sino-Indian relations in the early twenty first century, see especially Jeff M. Smith, *Cold Peace: China-India Rivalry in the Twenty-First Century* (Lanham, MD: Lexington, 2013); and Frédéric Grare, *India Turns East: International Engagement and US-China Rivalry* (London: Hurst & Co, 2017).

32. On the role played by concerns about China in India's decision-making concerning the acquisition of a nuclear deterrent, see Andrew B. Kennedy, "India's Nuclear Odyssey: Implicit Umbrellas, Diplomatic Disappointments, and the Bomb," *International Security* 36(2) (2011), pp. 120–153.

33. C. Raja Mohan, "The Evolution of Sino-Indian Relations: Implications for the United States," in Alyssa Ayres and C. Raja Mohan (eds.), *Power Realignments in Asia: China, India, and the United States* (New Delhi: Sage, 2009), p. 279. Among Congress Party politicians, indeed, there was considerable enthusiasm for some kind of China-India partnership. See, for example, Jairam Ramesh, *Making Sense of Chindia: Reflections on China and India* (New Delhi: India Research Press, 2005); and Prem Shankar Jha, *Crouching Dragon, Hidden Tiger: Can China and India Dominate the West?* (Berkeley, CA: Soft Skull Press, 2010).

34. Harsh V. Pant, "India Comes to Terms with a Rising China," in Ashley J. Tellis, Travis Tanner, and Jessica Keough (eds.), *Strategic Asia 2011–12: Asia Responds to its Rising Powers* (Seattle and Washington, DC: National Bureau of Asian Research, 2012), p. 108.

35. Sunil Khilnani, Rajiv Kumar, Pratap Bhanu Mehta, Prakash Menon, Nandan Nilekani, Srinath Raghavan, Shyam Saran, and Siddharth Varadarajan, *NonAlignment 2.0: A Foreign and Strategic Policy for India in the Twenty First Century* (New Delhi: Centre for Policy Research, 2012), p. 13. The authors of this report were and remain aligned, for the most part, with the Congress Party.

36. Rup Narayan Das, "Modi Faces Pressing Questions About India's China Policy," Jamestown Foundation, May 23, 2014, https://jamestown.org/program/modi-faces-pressing-questions-about-indias-china-policy/.

37. Ian Hall, "Multialignment and Indian Foreign Policy under Narendra Modi," *The Round Table: The Commonwealth Journal of International Affairs* 105(3) (2016), pp. 271–286. See also Rajesh Basrur, "Modi's Foreign Policy Fundamentals: A Trajectory Unchanged," *International Affairs* 93(1) (2017), pp. 7–26, Sumit Ganguly, "Has Modi Truly Changed India's Foreign Policy?" *The Washington Quarterly* 40(2) (2017), pp. 131–143; and Ian Hall, "Is a 'Modi Doctrine' Emerging in Indian Foreign Policy?" *Australian Journal of International Affairs* 69(3) (2015), pp. 247–252.

38. Hoo Tiang Boon, "The Hedging Prong in India's Evolving China Strategy," *Journal of Contemporary China* 25(101) (2016), pp. 792–804.

39. Quoted in Pardesi, "Modi's China Policy," p. 3.

40. Colonel R. Hariharan, "Unraveling the Direction of India's China Policy," *Indian Defence Review*, June 24, 2014, http://www.indiandefencereview.com/news/unraveling-the-direction-of-indias-china-policy/.

41. For a useful overview by a former diplomat turned analyst, see also Kishan S. Rana, "India and China in Asia," *China Report* 53(2) (2017), pp. 87–106.

42. Bajpai, "Narendra Modi's Pakistan and China Policy," pp. 82–83.

43. Ibid., p. 85.

44. For a useful brief analysis of the standoff and its implications for Indian policy, see Kanti Bajpai, "Modi's China Policy and the Road to Confrontation," *Pacific Affairs* 91(2) (2018).

45. Ian Hall, "Meeting the Challenge: The Case for the Quad," in Andrew Carr (ed.), "Debating the Quad," *Centre of Gravity* 39 (Canberra: Strategic and Defence Studies Centre, ANU, 2018).

46. Tom Miller, *China's Asian Dream: Empire Building along the Silk Road* (London: Zed Books, 2017), p. 12.

47. On economic statecraft in general, and on China's in particular, see *inter alia* Robert D. Harris and Jennifer M. Harris, *War by Other Means: Geoeconomics and Statecraft* (Cambridge, MA. and London: Belknap, 2016); and William J. Norris, *Chinese Economic Statecraft: Commercial Actors, Grand Strategy, and State Control* (Ithaca and London: Cornell University Press, 2016). On the relationship between China's economic statecraft and the BRI, see especially Nadège Rolland, *China's Eurasian Century: The Political and Strategic Implications of the Belt and Road Initiative* (Washington, DC: Bureau of Asian Research, 2017).

48. Surajit Mazumdar, "Big Business and Economic Nationalism in India," in Anthony d'Costa (ed.), *Globalization and Economic Nationalism in Asia* (Oxford: Oxford University Press, 2012), pp. 59–83. For context, see also Aseema Sinha, *Globalizing India: How Global Rules and Markets are Shaping India's Rise to Power* (Cambridge: Cambridge University Press, 2016).

49. For a very useful overview of the debate, focusing on the MSR in particular, see Amitendu Palit, "India's Economic and Strategic Perceptions of China's Maritime Silk Road Initiative," *Geopolitics* 22(2) (2017), pp. 292–309.

50. Ashok Malik, "OBOR: For India it's a Road to Subjugation," *Observer Research Foundation Commentaries*, May 8, 2017, www.orfonline.org/research/obor-for-india-its-a-road-to-subjugation/. For earlier assessments, see Shreya Upadhyay, "'One Belt, One Road' and India's Strategic Autonomy," *APPS Policy Forum*,

August 5, 2015, https://www.policyforum.net/one-belt-one-road-and-indias-strategic-autonomy/; Kabir Taneja, "Why India is Worried about China's Ambitious One Belt One Road Initiative," *Scroll.in*, March 28, 2016, http://scroll.in/article/805632/why-india-is-worried-about-chinas-ambitious-one-belt-one-road-initiative; and Dipankar Banerjee, "China's One Belt and One Road Initiative—An Indian Perspective," *ISEAS Perspective*, Issue 2016, No. 14, March 31, 2016, https://www.iseas.edu.sg/images/pdf/ISEAS_Perspective_2016_14.pdf.

51. On this airport, which India may purchase from the current owners, see also Tara Francis Chan, "India is Buying World's Emptiest Airport in its Battle for Territorial Dominance with China," *Business Insider*, December 13, 2017, http://uk.businessinsider.com/india-and-china-are-fighting-for-control-in-sri-lanka-2017-12?r=US&IR=T.

52. Dhruva Jaishankar, "India Doesn't Have a Lot to Lose by Boycotting OBOR. Read Why," *Economic Times*, May 21, 2017, http://economictimes.indiatimes.com/news/defence/india-doesnt-have-a-lot-to-lose-by-boycotting-obor-read-why/articleshow/58766498.cms. For a similar analysis, see Srikanth Kondapalli, "Why India is not Part of the Belt and Road Initiative Summit," *Indian Express*, May 15, 2017, http://indianexpress.com/article/opinion/why-india-is-not-part-of-the-belt-and-road-initiative-summit-4656150/.

53. Rajeswari Pillai Rajagopalan, "One Belt, One Road A Tool in China's Imperialistic Plan," *Outlook India*, May 14, 2017, https://www.outlookindia.com/website/story/one-belt-one-road-a-tool-in-chinas-imperialistic-plan-how-can-india-wean-away-ot/298889.

54. C. Raja Mohan, "Decoding India's Reservations on China's Belt and Road Initiative," *ISAS Seminar*, May 17, 2017, https://www.youtube.com/watch?v=ToXlt5CtlV8. It should also be noted that C. Raja Mohan has warned against seeing the BRI purely "through the prism of geopolitics"—see his "Silk Road Focus: Chinese Takeaway," *Indian Express*, March 10, 2016, http://indianexpress.com/article/opinion/columns/chinese-takeaway-15/.

55. Harsh V. Pant and Ritika Passi, "India's Response to China's Belt and Road Initiative: A Policy in Motion," *Asia Policy* 24 (2017), p. 88.

56. For a useful brief account, see Rahul Mukherji, *Political Economic of Reforms in India* (New Delhi: Oxford University Press, 2014).

57. Shyam Saran, "India and Africa: Development Partnership," *RIS Discussion Papers* 180 (Research and Information System for Developing Countries), December 2012, http://ris.org.in/images/RIS_images/pdf/dp180_pap.pdf.

58. South Asia Subregional Economic Cooperation, with the Asian Development Bank, *South Asia Sub-Regional Economic Cooperation Operational Plan* (2016), https://www.adb.org/sites/default/files/institutional-document/193351/sasec-operational-plan2016-2025.pdf, p. 2. The completed and ongoing projects are listed in Appendix 1, pp. 24–28.

59. Ibid., Appendix 2, pp. 29–31, and Appendix 4, pp. 33–34.

60. Ibid., Appendix 5, pp. 36–37.

61. Naresh Bana and K. Yhome, "The Road to Mekong: The India-Myanmar-Thailand Trilateral Highway Project," *ORF Issue Brief*, February 7, 2017, https://ww

w.orfonline.org/research/the-road-to-mekong-the-india-myanmar-thailand-trilatera l-highway-project/.

62. "India Revives Highway Plan Amid China's Belt and Road Push," *Straits Times*, August 14, 2017, https://www.straitstimes.com/asia/south-asia/india-revi ves-highway-plan-amid-chinas-belt-and-road-push. See also Archana Chaudhary and Dhwani Pandya, "India Builds Highway to Thailand to Counter China's Silk Road," *Bloomberg*, August 9, 2017, https://www.bloomberg.com/news/articles/ 2017-08-08/china-s-silk-road-lends-urgency-to-india-s-regional-ambitions; Dipak K. Dashi, "Imphal-Moreh Highway Expansion Likely to Get Cabinet Nod," *Times of India*, July 11, 2017, https://timesofindia.indiatimes.com/india/imphal-moreh-highw ay-expansion-likely-to-get-cabinet-nod/articleshow/59550183.cms.

63. Ministry of Foreign Affairs of Japan, "Japan-India Joint Statement," November 11, 2016, http://www.mofa.go.jp/files/000202950.pdf. See also Jagannath Panda, "The Asia-Africa Growth Corridor: An India-Japan Arch in the Making?" *Focus Asia: Perspective and Analysis*, November 21, 2017, http://isdp.eu/content/uploads /2017/08/2017-focus-asia-jagannath-panda.pdf.

64. Research and Information System for Developing Countries, Economic Research Institute for ASEAN and East Asia, and Institute of Developing Economies, *Asia Africa Growth Corridor: Partnership for Sustainable and Innovative Development: A Vision Document*, 2017, http://www.eria.org/Asia-Africa-Growth-Corrid or-Document.pdf, p. 2.

65. Ashis Biswas, "Will More Countries Join Indo-Japanese 'Asia Africa Growth Corridor'," *Dhaka Tribune*, February 22, 2018, https://www.dhakatribune.com/ bangladesh/foreign-affairs/2018/02/21/will-countries-join-indo-japanese-asia-afri ca-growth-corridor/.

66. S. D. Pradhan, "Asia-Africa Growth Corridor: A Positive Initiative," *Times of India*, October 28, 2017, https://blogs.timesofindia.indiatimes.com/ChanakyaCode/ asia-africa-growth-corridor-a-positive-initiative/.

67. Saran, "India and Africa: Development Partnership."

68. Maulik Pathak, "India-Japan Partnership to Play Key Role in Asia-Africa Corridor," *LiveMint*, May 25, 2017, https://www.livemint.com/Politics/gfSbaVJjfHu oUKPTMxrU8L/IndiaJapan-partnership-to-play-key-role-in-AsiaAfrica-corr.html.

69. Lindsay Hughes, "Bypassing Pakistan: Afghanistan, India, Iran and Chabahar," *Future Directions International Strategic Analysis Paper*, April 26, 2016, http:// www.futuredirections.org.au/wp-content/uploads/2016/04/Bypassing-Pakistan-Afgh anistan-India-Iran-and-Chahbahar.pdf.

70. Moushumi Das Gupta, "Indian Set to Begin Operations at Chabahar Port by May-end," *Hindustan Times*, February 22, 2018, https://www.hindustantimes.com /india-news/indian-set-to-begin-operations-at-chabahar-port-by-may-end/story-x7i uqE5jk41hsZZ9Lgfc2M.html.

71. Chidanand Rajghattal, "US 'Quad' Plan with India, Japan and Australia to Offer Options for Asian Countries beyond China," *Times of India*, October 28, 2017, https://timesofindia.indiatimes.com/world/us/us-quad-plan-with-india-japan-and-australia-to-offer-options-for-asian-countries-beyond-china/articleshow/6131 0986.cms.

72. Hall, "Meeting the Challenge," pp. 13–14.

73. Jason Scott, Emi Nobuhiro and Iain Marlow, "U.S.-Led Group Mulls Asia Infrastructure Effort Amid China Push," *Bloomberg*, February 19, 2018, https://www.bloomberg.com/news/articles/2018-02-18/u-s-led-group-mulls-asia-infrastructure-plan-australia-says.

74. Angus Grigg, Lisa Murray, and Andrew Tillett, "Malcolm Turnbull Unveils ASEAN-Australia Infrastructure Cooperative," *Australian Financial Review*, March 18, 2018, http://www.afr.com/news/world/asia/australia-challenges-china-on-infrastructure-20180318-h0xmu1.

75. "United States and India: Prosperity Through Partnership," White House, June 26, 2017, https://www.whitehouse.gov/briefings-statements/united-states-india-prosperity-partnership/.

76. A number of commentators speculated prior to the meeting that Modi would sign up to the BRI. See, for example, Debasish Roy Chawdhury, "Will the Xi-Modi Summit Lead to Deals on Belt and Road, Investments, and the Border?" *South China Morning Post*, April 25, 2017, http://www.scmp.com/week-asia/geopolitics/article/2143161/trump-border-belt-and-road-and-investments-xi-modi-summit.

77. How to Build a Railway in Afghanistan in 10 Months, Case Study, *Development Asia* (ADB), August 2016, https://development.asia/case-study/how-build-railway-afghanistan-10-months.

Chapter 9

Southeast Asia and the BRI

Integrative or Divisive?

Mark Beeson

Trying to assess the implications of "China's rise," or its reemergence as the most important actor in a region it has traditionally dominated, is a challenge for all China's neighbors. It is especially difficult for the Southeast Asian region. Not only are the less powerful states of Southeast Asia increasingly susceptible to China's growing "geoeconomic" influence, but they are at the epicenter of what is generally considered to be one of the world's most potentially combustible strategic flashpoints: the South China Sea.[1]

Trying to decide whether China represents more of a threat or an opportunity in such circumstances is far from straightforward. The remarkable diversity of circumstances and attributes that distinguishes the membership of the Association of Southeast Asian Nations (ASEAN) means that there is no uniform opinion about quite what China's rapid economic and strategic expansion may mean, or about how ASEAN itself should respond.

These tensions have been thrown into sharp relief by the recent inauguration of the One Belt, One Road initiative (OBOR), or the Belt Road Initiative (BRI). Southeast Asia is a potentially key part of this grandiose vision, with the so-called Maritime Silk Road (MSR) poised to play a critical role in extending China's economic influence and potentially integrating East and Southeast Asia through the development of—still much needed—infrastructure. The possible need for such investment and development may seem to make the BRI the proverbial no-brainer for the region's policy elites, who remain preoccupied with domestic economic development. However, some fear it will entrench Chinese influence in Southeast Asia, making regional states even more dependent on China economically, and eroding ASEAN's much-vaunted "centrality" and importance in the process.[2]

To try to make sense of the complex impact of China's rise and the policy challenges it presents for the ASEAN states collectively and individually, it is helpful to provide a little historical context, something I do in the first section of this chapter. Following this, I detail some of the economic connections that already exist between China and the Southeast Asia states, before considering the implications of China's increasingly "assertive" foreign policy and its impact on the region. As I explain, there is evidence to support both a positive and a negative story about China's impact, an usurping conclusion, perhaps, given the scale and unprecedented nature of China's plans. What we can say is that—if realized—the BRI will have a major impact on both the regional states' economic relations *and* on their internal and external relations.

HISTORICAL CONTINGENCY

China is generally regarded as the world's oldest continuing civilization. Indeed, Lucian Pye famously argued that China was a "civilization pretending to be a nation."[3] Whatever the merits of that argument, there is no doubt that China has been a major cultural and economic force in what we now think of as Southeast Asia for hundreds, if not thousands of years.[4] The influence of Confucianism is still visible in Myanmar and especially Vietnam,[5] although in the latter's case this is no guarantee of amicable relations, of course. On the contrary, the People's Republic of China's (PRC) last international conflict was against Vietnam and ended in humiliation for China's communist leadership.[6] It is also important to remember that at that time—1979—the PRC was still regarded as a revolutionary source if political and strategic instability in a part of the world that was preoccupied with—even somewhat paranoid about—security.[7]

The other associated historical legacy that continues to loom large in possible explanations of Southeast Asian attitudes to China, therefore, is the formation of ASEAN itself. Notwithstanding all the noble rhetoric about fraternal cooperation, the promotion of common cultural values and the other familiar ASEAN tropes, the principal reason that ASEAN emerged when it did was as a response to the existentially threatening strategic dynamics of the Cold War, which were being violently played out in Southeast Asia itself.[8] The challenge of managing intra-regional tensions between Indonesia, Malaysia, and the Philippines were made even more compelling by the war in Vietnam and the struggle between the superpowers, in which China was playing an active part. Add to this the challenge of nation-building and economic development and the attractions of strategic cooperation and possible strength in numbers offered by ASEAN became increasingly compelling.[9]

These brief historical observations are merited because there is an important but inconclusive debate about the significance of China's rise that not only draws on history to make different arguments but which is directly relevant to the contemporary relationship between the PRC and the ASEAN states, whether they are considered collectively or in isolation. Most famously in the contemporary period, Graham Allison has argued that China's rise is very likely to prove increasingly destabilizing as a dissatisfied rising power (the PRC) seeks to challenge, if not replace, a declining hegemon (the United States).[10] Exhibit A in support of this thesis is China's increasingly assertive actions in the disputed South China Sea region, about which it makes expansive, supposedly historically informed claims.[11]

Before making any detailed comments about the impact of China's claims on Southeast Asia, it should be noted that this is not the only way of thinking about the implications of China's rise. Even if we discount some of the official and academic commentary that has emerged from China as self-serving, some knowledgeable observers argue that China's rise is generally regarded as more of an opportunity than a threat, and entirely in keeping with long-term historical patterns in the region:

> East Asia's states see considerably more opportunity than danger in China's rise . . . East Asian states prefer China to strong rather than weak because a strong China stabilizes the region while a weak China tempts other states to try to control the region.[12]

Of course, we cannot extrapolate straightforwardly from the past, nor can we assume that former patterns of interstate relations will necessarily help to explain today's very different "global" rather than regional environment. What we can say is that the tribute system over which China formerly presided offers an important alternative example to the standard Westphalian template, and one that displayed a degree socially determined variation.[13] Historically, "Chinese hegemony" looked rather different to the contemporary American version and there is no reason to suppose that if it is restored, it would not have distinctive Chinese characteristics once again. This is why explanations that favor "theoretical parsimony," and which neglect contingent factors, are not terribly useful when trying to account for different historical outcomes and patterns of development.[14]

Having said that, comparisons can be illuminating, even where they highlight similarities. It has become increasingly common to suggest that the BRI represents a "new Marshall Plan" for Asia, for example.[15] Given the BRI's monumental potential scale and ambition, which is detailed elsewhere in this collection, there is clearly something in that idea. There is, of course, one crucial difference: America's postwar grand strategy was conceived and implemented in the context of the Cold War. The principal goal was restoring and defending a discredited capitalist system against—what were then seen as credible attractions of—an alternative Soviet model.[16] While there is no doubt that Chinese-style capitalism is significantly different to America's, Donald Trump's neo-mercantilist rhetoric notwithstanding,[17] this is a difference in variety, not principle. Ideology is nothing like as important as it was during the Cold War, despite all the discussion of the Washington versus the Beijing consensus.[18]

The key question now is whether China's actions generally and the BRI in particular represent a new form of "geoeconomic" power and influence, that is significantly different from the more familiar geopolitical ambitions that characterized America's period of international order building following the Second World War.[19] At one level the answer is clearly yes: the creation of an enduring, highly institutionalized system of economic organizations was unprecedented and helped to entrench America's hegemonic position.[20] China's efforts to create an alternative order via institutions such as the Asian Infrastructure Investment Bank (AIIB), while not insignificant as we shall see, are modest by comparison at this stage. Even more significantly, the operating principles and norms of the AIIB are not radically different to those of the other international financial institutions the US did so much to create and control.[21] In other words, the United States enjoys enduring patterns of institutionalized influence that have not been erased by China's rise, even if it is not clear that this is recognized by the Trump administration.

Yet even if China's influence is—at this stage, at least—not as pervasive or consequential as America's has been, there is no doubt that its ambitions are growing and are being inadvertently assisted by the actions of the Trump regime.[22] Under such circumstances, it has been suggested that China's growing economic stature has enabled it to "shift from a grand strategy that merely sought to enable its economic goals to one that can begin to leverage its growing economic power to achieve foreign policy goals that previously may have been out of reach."[23] Given the nexus of economic and strategic ambitions that has emerged in Southeast Asia, it has rapidly become the quintessential test of China's ability to realize such ambitions.

THE MARITIME SILK ROAD

When Xi Jinping announced the original Silk Road initiative in Astana, Kazakhstan, in September 2013, there was no mention of the MSR. Shortly afterward, while on a visit to Indonesia, however, Xi outlined China's intention to build a "Maritime Silk Road of the 21st Century." The speech was significant not only because it indicated that the original BRI project would be expanded to include the MSR but because Xi's speech included a number of key ideas that have become standard parts of the PRC's rhetoric about regional relations, which were clearly designed to win over a potentially skeptical audience. Xi was at pains to emphasize that China was intent on developing "win-win cooperation," in which the PRC would work collaboratively with ASEAN to create a "community of common destiny." In an implicit criticism of the United States and its occasional prickly relationship with Indonesia, Xi suggested that "there is no one-size-fits-all development model in the world" and that "we should respect each other's right to independently choose social system and development path."[24]

Before considering the specifics of the MSR initiative, it is worth putting Xi's speech in context as it helps to explain the wider objectives of which the MSR is such a potentially significant part. First, the MSR can be seen as a specific response to China's diminished diplomatic position in Southeast Asia. Only a few years before, China had generally defied expectations by launching what was a highly successful regional "charm offensive,"[25] that had built on its growing economic power and importance to clinch attractive bilateral trade deals with the ASEAN states.[26] The rhetoric that accompanied such deals emphasized that China's rise was an opportunity rather than a threat from which both China and Southeast Asia would benefit. This rosy vision was dramatically undercut by China's increasingly assertive pursuit of territorial claims in the South China, however. The MSR was part of an effort to redress the balance and reestablish the idea that China's rise was ultimately beneficial and no threat to ASEAN's centrality in regional affairs.

This latter claim has proved problematic, as we shall see, but it is not hard to see how it might have seemed intuitively attractive to a Southeast Asian region that was being drawn ever more closely into China's expanding economic orbit. By 2016, China had become ASEAN's largest single trade partner (US$368 billion),[27] a position that was continuing on an upward trajectory even before the announcement of the MSR. However, whatever nervousness ASEAN states such as Indonesia might have felt about their increasing economic dependence on China, it must have been offset by the memory of the United States' traumatic, much resented,[28] intervention in regional affairs during the Asian financial crisis of the late 1990s, which caused profound economic and political problems across the region.[29] Xi's none-too-subtle references about the importance of policy autonomy and distinctive indigenous paths to prosperity would not have been lost on his audience.

Xi Jinping would also have been aware of the fact that, despite China's growing importance as a trade partner for ASEAN, it was not a significant source of direct foreign investment (FDI). ASEAN's FDI was dominated by the European Union, followed by intra-ASEAN investment. Although American FDI was in sharp decline and China's modestly rising, as of 2016, the United States was still a larger investor than the PRC.[30] Consequently, the MSR offered a mechanism with which to entrench China's economic importance and reinstate the image it had painstakingly tried to cultivate through its "good neighbor policy."[31]

Unpacking the MSR

It is striking and revealing that much of the commentary generated by both the BRI and the MSR, especially in the United States, has focused on its potential geopolitical significance and the possible threat it poses to the established order.[32] Such concerns culminated in the Obama administration's ill-conceived efforts to persuade close allies such as the UK and Australia not to take part in the AIIB, which was intended to play a major part in actually funding the necessary investment in regional infrastructure. Whatever one may think about China's supposed grand strategic objectives and the possible role of the AIIB, one fact would seem incontrovertible: there *is* a continuing need for infrastructure investment across the broadly conceived Asian region. Despite the so-called East Asian miracle, Southeast Asia was estimated to require an additional US$ 2,759 billion, or 5 percent of GDP, in additional infrastructure spending between 2016 and 2030. The current annual average in Southeast Asia is US$184 billion, meaning that there is a major gap that is significantly holding back economic development across the region. If the possible impact of climate change is added to these already daunting figures, they increase by something like 16 percent.[33]

In such circumstances, China's leaders would seem to be pushing on an open diplomatic door, no matter what suspicions may be harbored about their possible long-term intentions. This is not to suggest that China's motives are entirely altruistic or without an underpinning geopolitical and/or geoeconomic logic, however. On the contrary, the MSR, like the original BRI, is explicitly designed to achieve a number of possible economic and strategic objectives by integrating a number of geographic regions:

> the MSR will incorporate and/or connect with multiple distinct transportation corridors such as the China-Pakistan Economic Corridor, the decades-old United Nations Economic and Social Commission Trans-Asia Railway that connects Kunming to Thailand, China- Bangkok-Laos and Kunming-Vietnam-Cambodia, the Mekong River Development initiative, the China-India-Bangladesh-Myanmar Economic Corridor, and the multilateral Greater Mekong Subregion Economic Cooperation Program . . . indicating that the MSRI is a "living," mutable scheme, China issued new maps of the MSRI in April 2015 that indicate it had been extended to the South Pacific.[34]

Recently, Australia has been invited to consider becoming part of the MSR project, triggering predictably difficult policy discussions on the part of its policymaking elites, which struggle to reconcile their implacably opposed strategic and economic objectives.[35] While Australia's unique history and reliance on "great and powerful friends" such as the United States might make such policy conundrums especially acute, it is far from alone.

The degree to which China's economic rise has transformed regional economic relations and fortunes—even without the MSR—is remarkable. Indeed, one of the more striking features of Southeast Asia's long-term economic development and integration is that—unlike Northeast Asia— it has primarily been driven by external actors and/or the private sector.[36] In this context, China's growing economic interaction with the region is following a well-worn template. Significantly, it was a model of state-led regional engagement that was originally pioneered primarily by China's great regional rival and sometime foe, Japan.[37] Although the overall pattern of engagement as far as Southeast Asia has often been one of economic subordination and dependence, there have undoubtedly been benefits, too: not only has any sort of trade and investment enhanced regional development prospects, but the mutually exclusive regional leadership ambitions of Japan and China opens up the theoretical possibility that the ASEAN's states can play off one rival against the other.

Networking the Region

Like Japan before it, China has become a central part of an increasingly integrated set of regional production networks that have facilitated the transnationalization of the auto, electronics, and clothing industries in particular.[38] The emergence of "factory Asia" has been one of the more noteworthy features of a generalized evolution of a regional division of labor. There are a number of aspects of this phenomenon and the respective roles of China and the ASEAN states that are worth keeping in mind. First, China's rapid economic rise has not decimated ASEAN's manufacturing capacity as some feared.[39] On the contrary, wages in China itself have overtaken even ASEAN states such as Thailand and Malaysia; Indonesia and the Philippines have even lower labor costs.[40] Deeper economic integration with China is not necessarily a bad thing, therefore. Second, China's interest in pursuing regional trade agreements, such as the Regional Comprehensive Economic Partnership, is part of the broader strategy of promoting greater integration and the consolidation of regional production networks with China at their center.[41] Finally, however, there are limits to the extent of such processes precisely because of the infrastructure gaps that the MSR seeks to fill.

Consequently, some of the first projects the MSR seeks to complete are centered on transportation, without which greater integration will be much more difficult. Southeast Asia was originally the principal focus of the MSR but it has subsequently expanded to include South Asia and reflects the famous sea voyages of Ming dynasty admiral and explorer Zheng He in the fifteenth century. Given the attention that is currently paid by Chinese leaders to historical claims and legacies, such factors cannot be entirely dismissed when thinking about the motivations of China's foreign policy elites. A more prosaic explanation of the MSR's expansion, however, is offered by those scholars who draw attention to the projects geostrategic significance as part of the so-called "string of pearls" and China's ambitions to expand its influence and military presence to the Indian Ocean region.[42]

The strategic impact of the MSR on the more narrowly conceived Southeast Asian region is taken up next. The point to emphasize at this stage is that it is not possible to neatly separate the economic and strategic implications of either the BRI or the MSR, however convenient that may be analytically. It is important to recognize that the provision of new infrastructure in Southeast Asia will benefit China, too, facilitating regional economic development, raising productivity, opening up new markets and prospective production platforms. Indeed, some observers argue that "the goal of China's economic diplomacy is to create a modern tribute system, with all roads literally leading to Beijing."[43] While the ultimate goal of China's policies remains contentious, the focus on upgrading Southeast Asia's ports is less so in such circumstances given the importance of maritime trade in Southeast Asia. More ambitious—and more controversial—has been the proposal to link the mainland Southeast Asian states with a series of high-speed rail connections.

As with most aspects of the proposed MSR the scale of the proposed pan-Asian railway network is remarkable. It is envisaged that the network, if completed, will have three major components: the central route will connect Kuming and Singapore, via Vientiane, Bangkok, and Kuala Lumpur. The Western route will also connect Kunming to Singapore but include Dali, Baoshan, Ruili, and Yangon. The Eastern route also terminates in Singapore but goes via Yuxi, Mengzi, Hekou, Hanoi, Ho Chi Minh, and Phnom Penh. Seven of ASEAN's members will consequently have a direct stake and interest in the success of China's project. The nature of China's potential "structural power" over its much "smaller" neighbors has long been a source of concern, however.[44] In the case of Cambodia in particular, there is plentiful evidence that China has been able to use economic leverage to influence the behavior of the notoriously corrupt and brutal regime of Hun Sen. Even here, however, it is argued that China cannot "cultivate devoted client states easily."[45]

Similar arguments are made about the constraints facing China in the rail project, despite the nature of China's integrated to finance and development, which has the potential to increase the dependence debtor states—an issue of growing concern and controversy among the poor Pacific island economies of late.[46] Nevertheless, some observers argue that China's high-speed rail proposals are not a "vehicle of a 'grand strategy' for China to seek leverage and influence in SEA, and consequently alter the status quo."[47] Time will tell whether such claims prove accurate, but what we can say in the meantime is, first, China already has a demonstrated capacity to deliver such developmental projects on an epic scale; second, the MSR generally and the high-speed rail project in particular offer one way of solving China's domestic overcapacity problem in the infrastructure development sector.[48] Indeed, such an approach to public, foreign and strategic policy is entirely compatible with the more "comprehensive" view of security that has been characteristic of East Asia generally and of China in particular.[49] It is the possibility that China's MSR initiative may have more to do with long-term grand strategic ambitions and a wider notion of what makes a country secure that makes the policy so consequential.

THE MSR'S SECURITY DIMENSION

One of the most enduring ideas in international political economy is that greater economic interdependence across national borders reduces the prospects of conflict as states come to realize that they have too much to lose in the vent of conflict. While there is a good deal of evidence that this may, indeed, be the case, history provides some sobering reminders of the limits to this thesis. Norman Angel had the great misfortune of arguing that war had become irrational as a consequence of the pacifying impact of commerce just as the First World War erupted.[50] Nevertheless, such arguments persist and there has been a striking and enduring decline in interstate violence for decades that appears to support claims about the existence of a "capitalist peace."[51]

And yet Southeast Asia is currently host to what many take to be one of the world's most volatile and dangerous sources of strategic tension. For some influential observers, it is China's very success as a rapidly expanding capitalist economy that makes it so dangerous.[52] In a similar vein, prominent realist scholars argue that the only feasible strategy for the United States as a consequence is to put off the inevitable day of reckoning for as long as possible by doing everything it can to inhibit China's economic growth.[53] It is instructive that the Trump administration now considerers China's admission to the World Trade Organization, which did more than anything else to accelerate its development and transform its domestic economy, to have been a mistake.[54] Whatever the historical merits of that argument may be, the reality is that—in the absence of America's traditional liberal leadership role—China has rapidly moved to position itself as a champion of international free trade and continuing international economic integration. The BRI/MSR initiatives are a very tangible manifestation of this ambition.

Geoeconomics in Practice

There is a good deal of debate about the extent of China's ambitions and the degree to which it is able or actually willing to replace the United States as a regional, let alone a global, hegemon.[55] At this stage, despite America's relative decline and China's seemingly unstoppable rise, the debate remains inconclusive. This is hardly surprising: on the one hand, the speed and scale of China's rise are historically unprecedented; on the other, we have only one real example of what hegemonic transition actually looks like.[56] Significantly, when the United States replaced Great Britain as the world's dominant power it was in many ways swapping like for like, as one essentially liberal political and economic power replaced another. While China may no longer be especially "communist," it is certainly authoritarian, and this poses a major potential challenge to the existing international order. Indeed, China's growing influence in East Asia has the potential to entrench illiberal approaches to governance and undermine the strategic balance that has endured for nearly half a century. The states of Southeast Asia may prove to be a key focus and bellwether of potentially competing visions of regional order.

In the absence of outright war—which despite recent developments, remains both the most likely scenario, and the only one about which anything meaningful can be said—geoeconomics assumes an even greater importance. If we consider geoeconomics to be the application of economic instruments to achieve geopolitical ends,[57] then such an approach to foreign and strategic policy plays to China's existing strengths and may help it to transform the *strategic* as well as the economic environment in East and Southeast Asia. While most attention has been given the very visible manifestations of China's regional ambitions, we need to appreciate that the PRC's policies have the ability to change the strategic calculus of states which potentially have the ability to obstruct China's increasingly grandiose and all-encompassing goals.

From a Chinese perspective, convincing Southeast Asians that its continuing rise is beneficial has become more important and more difficult as a direct consequence of its recent actions. Significantly, even in a Southeast Asian region that is showing a widespread potential to relapse into illiberalism and authoritarian rule, public opinion is something political elites take more seriously and cannot easily control. Vietnam is the country in which adverse opinion about relations with China has played the biggest part in shaping domestic and foreign policy,[58] but it is not alone. In this context, China's own actions have been the principal cause of undermining the previously beneficial impact of its "charm offensive" and "peaceful rise" discourse. The essentially confrontational nature of China's territorial claims in the South China Sea is the principal factor causing anxiety. China's active militarization of disputed maritime areas and its willingness to ignore international law have sent an unambiguous message about the lengths to which it is prepared to go in pursuit of what it sees as its rightful territorial claims.[59]

The PRC is willing to take such provocative actions and even risk outright conflict with the United States because it is also subject to domestic pressures and a rising tide of nationalist sentiment that China's current leadership has been instrumental in stoking.[60] Consequently, Xi Jinping "cannot risk being perceived as a leader who allows China to be humiliated by foreigners, in particular by Japan or by Western countries."[61] The consequences of China's seemingly nonnegotiable attitude toward the South China Sea dispute is amplified by the fact that it is a part of the region in a way that the United States is not; this has given the PRC's actions an immediacy and importance that the Southeast Asian states have been unable to ignore.[62] Whether they are capable of effectively responding to this challenge either individually or especially collectively is quite another question, however. The dominant response among the smaller Southeast Asian states has been to adopt a "hedging" strategy.[63]

All other things being equal, one might have expected that the ASEAN states would collectively have sought to "balance" against China's rise, as much mainstream international relations theory would lead us to expect. And yet rather than trying to counter Chinese power and influence, most Southeast Asian states have preferred neither to balance nor to bandwagon, for that matter. According to some observers, this marks the development of a sophisticated strategy on the part of the ASEAN states as they seek to maintain the existing "preponderance of power in favor of the United States."[64] More prosaically—and accurately, in my view—ASEAN's much-discussed hedging strategy amounts to little more than "secur[ing] as many benefits as possible from as many states as possible."[65] And yet the reality is that even this relatively modest goal, which ought to be facilitated by the growing rivalry between China and Japan on the one hand, and China and the United States on the other, is proving difficult for the ASEAN states to realize, especially as a collective entity.

It is in this context that China's comprehensive approach to pursuing national interests and its evolving geoeconomic strategy becomes consequential. As we have seen, Cambodia and, to a lesser extent, Laos have become increasingly reliant on Chinese trade, aid, and investment.[66] In the case of Cambodia in particular, this has meant that the prospects of ASEAN reaching a collective position on what is potentially the greatest single long-term challenge to regional security since its formation in 1967 is well-nigh impossible, despite the fact that China's actions directly threaten the sovereignty and security of some of its members. In part, this reflects a fundamental difference in orientation between ASEAN's maritime and mainland states; the latter being less directly affected by China's territorial claims. And yet things are not quite so straightforward. Despite the nationalistic bluster of Philippines' leader Rodrigo Duterte in the run-up to his election as president, of late he has been notably less critical of and hostile to China, despite the Philippines winning a favorable judgment regarding China's territorial claims in the United Nations.[67] This abrupt transformation in the foreign policy of the Philippines, which includes a significant cooling toward the United States, has come about because Duterte calculates that "the Philippines stands to gain a lot, particularly in terms of infrastructure investments and development aid, if it desists from continuing the confrontational strategy of the Aquino administration."[68] However, given the powerful domestic lobby in the Philippines that remains supportive of the alliance with the United States, it is far from certain that China's geoeconomic influence will prevail in the growing strategic context with the United States.

Yet China's impact on other ASEAN states suggests that it shouldn't be discounted either. Myanmar is an example of both the effectiveness of, and obstacles to, China's grand strategic objectives. One the one hand, China has expended significant political and economic capital cultivating Myanmar's political and military elites, especially at times when they were international pariahs.[69] Myanmar occupies a unique place in China's overall plans as it has the capacity to physically link the BRI and MSR, at the same time as providing China access to the Indian Ocean. One might have expected that Myanmar would have been a major recipient of Chinese investment as a result. Significantly, however, it has not materialized. Not only do Chinese leaders feel that they have been marginalized by the political changes in Myanmar, but there has been widespread popular anxiety about its growing influence. This growing anti-China sentiment has been inflamed by concerns about a potential mega-development in the Kyaukpyu special economic zone, which is expected to include a deep-sea port, an industrial zone, and a major housing project. However, as Yun Sun points out, "many Burmese wonder why Myanmar should borrow money from China to support an ambitious Chinese project designed to serve China's political and economic agenda."[70]

There are similar questions being asked about the environmental impacts of China's BRI initiative in particular and its attitude to its neighbors concerns about water security in particular. Even the supposed benefits that the BRI is expected to bring in terms of infrastructure are not an unalloyed benefit along the Mekong River, and may be an extension of China's established approach to development and water security in the region. As Fawthorp observes, "Any idea of environmental protection for the wonders of the Mekong has been marginalized by China's grand Belt and Road Initiative (BRI) with its focus firmly fixed on trade, infrastructure development, and, along the Mekong, dam construction."[71] China already has a record on ignoring the wishes of other states along the Mekong, as it takes an uncompromising, "China first" approach to water utilization and security.[72] There is also growing and successful local resistance to further possible dam building along the Mekong from communities concerned about the impact on the environment.[73] Given ASEAN's limited ability to resolve complex environmental challenges,[74] it will only add to its diminished reputation.

Significantly, ASEAN's influence was already in question as a consequence of its limited influence over Myanmar's domestic politics and its relationship with China, despite the popular fiction that it played a decisive "socialization" role in what may yet prove to be Myanmar's abortive democratization process.[75] In this regard, Myanmar is emblematic of ASEAN's wider failings. The ASEAN grouping's distinctive operating principles makes it potentially vulnerable to the actions of states that fail to subscribe to its informally negotiated consensus positions. Whatever the merits of the so-called "ASEAN Way" of face-saving diplomacy and voluntarism that distinguishes ASEAN,[76] it means the grouping has no capacity to compel member compliance on contentious issues. Where individual states remain recalcitrant it may be impossible for the ASEAN states to arrive at a collective position. This is precisely what happened at the ASEAN Summit in 2012 hosted by Cambodia, where collective agreement on a joint position on China's territorial claims proved impossible; the first time the ASEAN states had been unable to produce the sort of anodyne statement that normally accompanies such meetings. The reason was clear: Cambodia did not want to upset China, upon which it had become increasingly dependent for economic assistance.[77] Cambodia's divisive support of China at the expense of fellow ASEAN members has been repeated recently, when if intervened to block any reference to The Hague-based Permanent Court of Arbitration ruling against Beijing's territorial claims or routine descriptions about the "militarization" of the South China.[78]

China's ability to divide the ASEAN grouping on what is arguably the single most important strategic challenge to have emerged since its inception is testimony to the effectiveness of the PRC's geoeconomic diplomacy. By effectively buying off potential swing states, China has skillfully exploited the inherent vulnerability of the ASEAN grouping: its purported ability to use moral suasion to achieve consensus. In retrospect, this may be an indictment of ASEAN's "widening" process, which saw the organization rapidly expand to include new members such as Cambodia, Laos, Myanmar, and Vietnam. The politics of widening have proved problematic for even the more powerful and influential EU, however. It was a challenge that ASEAN was struggling to meet even before China's actions exposed the organization's internal divisions. The successful implementation of the MSR looks likely to quite literally cement China's place as an economic force in the region, a force which some of ASEAN's weaker states will find difficult to resist.[79]

CONCLUSION

China's influence over the region that it has dominated for hundreds, if not thousands, of years is once again becoming profoundly significant. Indeed, the very tangible basis of China's contemporary engagement with its neighbors may make this iteration of a modern-day tribute system even more consequential than the one that European imperialism swept away. The BRI generally and the MSR in particular mean that the potential attractions of Chinese investment, and the potential costs of being excluded from regional production networks that revolve around China, may be too great to ignore. Even a country like Singapore, traditionally a close ally of the United States, now seeks to position itself as "a steadfast, reliable and sincere friend of China"—not to mention China's largest source of inward investment.[80] Tacit statements about the long-term development of bilateral ties could hardly be given more concrete expression.

Other Southeast Asian states become even more closely tied to, and reflective of, the PRC's regional strategies. Cambodia is perhaps an extreme example of this possibility, largely as a consequence of the brutal and corrupt nature of its domestic politics, but it plays an outsize role in facilitating China's strategic goals, nevertheless. While there is a continuing debate about the effectiveness of ASEAN as a regional institution, there is less doubt about its difficulties in dealing with China and maintaining any semblance of a unified position. As a result, Southeast Asia's hedging strategies look rather more like making the best of an unpalatable set of potentially incompatible policy choices, rather than a sophisticated, far-sighted response to changing geopolitical and geoeconomic circumstances, as some have claimed.[81] More pointedly, perhaps, ASEAN's ineffectual response to China's growing power and influence may have long-term consequences for both its own reputation and "centrality," and for the wider geopolitical context of which it is a diminished part.

It is difficult to imagine that East Asia generally and Southeast Asia in particular will not be part of some sort of Chinese "sphere of influence" in the future—and possibly the near future at that. The advent of the transactionally minded Trump administration may have accelerated a number of long-term trends in the region, but the direction of travel seems unambiguous: the United States was in relative decline compared to China even before Trump appeared.[82] Even when he's gone it is difficult to see how the major trend lines will be turned around given some of America's formidable domestic political and even economic problems. The fact that China lends the United States the money to underwrite its hegemonic position looks unsustainable in the long term. As they say, when something looks like it can't go on forever, it generally doesn't. True, extrapolation may be dangerous, and there are many things that could go wrong in China, too, but many of Southeast Asia's political elites appear to be jumping on the Chinese bandwagon, albeit with different degrees of enthusiasm. Many in the West may not like China's geo-economic practices, but they may have to get used to them. They are already doing so in Southeast Asia.

NOTES

1. Robert D. Kaplan, *Asia's Cauldron: The South China Sea and the End of a Stable Pacific* (New York: Random House, 2014).
2. M. Majumdar, "The ASEAN way of conflict management in the South China Sea," *Strategic Analysis* 39 (1) (2015), 73–87.
3. Lucian Pye, "China: Erratic state, frustrated society," *Foreign Affairs* 69 (4) (1990), 58.
4. A. Reid, *Charting the Shape of Early Modern Southeast Asia* (Washington: University of Washington Press, 1999).
5. Gilbert Rozman, *The East Asian Region: Confucian Heritage and Its Modern Adaptation* (Princeton: Princeton University Press, 1991).
6. Zhang, "China's 1979 war with Vietnam: A reassessment," *The China Quarterly* 184 (2005), 851–874.
7. Peter Van Ness, *Revolution and Chinese Foreign Policy: Peking's Support for Wars of National Liberation* (Berkley: University of California Press, 1970).
8. Mark Beeson, "Living with giants: ASEAN and the evolution of Asian regionalism," *TRaNS: Trans-Regional and -National Studies of Southeast Asia* 1 (2) (2013), 303–322.
9. Mark Beeson, "Sovereignty under siege: Globalisation and the state in Southeast Asia," *Third World Quarterly* 24 (2) (2003), 357–374.
10. Graham Allison, *Destined for War: Can America and China Escape Thucydides's Trap?* (Boston: Houghton Mifflin Harcourt, 2017).
11. M. Taylor Fravel, "China's strategy in the South China Sea," *Contemporary Southeast Asia* 33 (3) (2013), 292–319.
12. David C. Kang, *China Rising: Peace, Power, and Order in East Asia* (New York: Columbia University, 2007), 4.
13. See David C. Kang, *East Asia before the West: Five Centuries of Trade and Tribute* (New York: Columbia University Press, 2010); and Andrew Phillips, "Contesting the confucian peace: Civilization, barbarism and international hierarchy in East Asia," *European Journal of International Relations* 24 (4) (2018), 740–764.

14. Chalmers Johnson and Edward Barry Keehn, "A disaster in the making: Rational choice theory and Asian studies," *The National Interest* 36 (1994), 14–22.

15. Andrew Browne, "China builds bridges and highways while the U.S. mouths slogans," *Wall Street Journal*, 30 January 2018, https://www.wsj.com/articles/china-builds-bridges-and-highways-while-the-u-s-mouths-slogans-1517308205.

16. John Lewis Gaddis, *Strategies of Containment: A Critical Appraisal of Post-war American Security Policy* (Oxford: Oxford University Press, 1982).

17. Greg Ip, "On trade, world wonders whose rules U.S. plays by," *Wall Street Journal*, 28 January 2018, https://www.wsj.com/articles/u-s-move-to-change-the-global-rules-at-davos-falls-flat-1517175222.

18. Mark Beeson and Fujian Li, "What consensus? Geopolitics and policy paradigms in China and the US," *International Affairs* 91 (1) (2015), 93–109.

19. Robert D. Blackwill and Jennifer M. Harris, *War by Other Means: Geoeconomics and Statecraft* (Harvard: Harvard University Press, 2016).

20. Jonathan Agnew, *Hegemony: The New Shape of Global Power* (Philadelphia: Temple University Press, 2005).

21. Mark Beeson and Fujian Li, "China's place in regional and global governance: A new world comes into view," *Global Policy* 7 (4) (2016), 491–499.

22. Andrew Browne, "China gloats as Trump squanders U.S. soft power," *Wall Street Journal*, 28 February 2017, https://www.wsj.com/articles/china-gloats-as-trump-squanders-u-s-soft-power-1488278788.

23. William J. Norris, *Chinese Economic Statecraft: Commercial Actors, Grand Strategy, and State Control* (Ithaca: Cornell University Press, 2016), 61.

24. Xi Jinping, "Regulations," Speech by Chinese President Xi Jinping to Indonesian Parliament, Jakarta, October 3 2013, http://www.asean-china-center.org/english/2013-10/03/c_133062675.htm.

25. Joshua Kurlantzick, *Charm Offensive: How China's Soft Power Is Transforming the World* (New Haven: Yale University Press, 2007); and Mark Beeson and Fujian Li, "Charmed or alarmed? Reading China's regional relations," *Journal of Contemporary China* 21 (73) (2012), 35–51.

26. Gregory Chin and Richard Stubbs, "China, regional institution-building and the China-ASEAN free trade area," *Review of International Political Economy* 18 (3) (2011), 277–298.

27. The ASEAN Secretariat, *ASEAN Economic Community Chartbook* (Jakarta: ASEAN, 2017), 22.

28. Richard A. Higgott, "The Asian economic crisis: A study in the politics of resentment," *New Political Economy* 3 (3) (1998), 333–356.

29. Mark Beeson, Kanishka Jayasuriya, Hyuk-Rae Kim, and Richard Robison (eds.), *Politics and Markets in the Wake of the Asian Crisis* (London: Routledge, 2000).

30. Ibid., 44.

31. Chien-peng Chung, "The 'good neighbour policy' in the context of China's foreign relations," *China: An International Journal* 7 (1) (2009), 107–123.

32. G. John Ikenberry and Darren Lim, *China's Emerging Institutional Statecraft: The Asian Infrastructure Investment Bank and the Prospects for Counter-hegemony* (Washington: Brookings Institute, 2017).

33. ASEAN Development Bank, *Meeting Asia's Infrastructure Needs* (Manilla: ADB, 2017).

34. Jean Marc Blanchard and Colin Flint, "The geopolitics of China's maritime silk road initiative," *Geopolitics* 22 (2) (2017), 227.

35. Geoff Raby, "Xi Jinping's one belt, one road triumph and Australia's Sino confusion," *Australian Financial Review*, 17 May 2017, https://www.afr.com/news/economy/xis-one-belt-one-road-triumph-and-australias-sino-confusion-20170517-gw6qef.

36. Joe Studwell, *How Asia Works: Success and Failure in the World's Most Dynamic Region* (London: Profile Books, 2013).

37. Mark Beeson, *Regionalism and Globalization in East Asia: Politics, Security and Economic Development*, 2nd Edition (Basingstoke: Palgrave, 2014).

38. See Jeffrey Henderson and Khalid Nadvi, "Greater China, the challenges of global production networks and the dynamics of transformation," *Global Networks* 11 (3) (2011), 285–297; and Henry Wai-chung Yeung, *Strategic Coupling: East Asian Industrial Transformation in the New Global Economy* (Ithaca: Cornell University Press, 2016).

39. Anne Booth, "China's economic relations with Indonesia: Threats and opportunities," *Journal of Current Southeast Asian Affairs* (2) (2011), 141–160; Kenta Goto, Kaoru Natsuda, and John Thoburn, "Meeting the challenge of China: The Vietnamese garment industry in the post MFA era," *Global Networks* 11 (3) (2011), 355–379.

40. "A tightening grip," *The Economist*, 12 March 2015, https://www.economist.com/briefing/2015/03/12/a-tightening-grip.

41. Richard Baldwin, "21st century regionalism: Filling the gap between 21st century trade and 20th century trade rules," *Centre for Economic Policy Research* 56 (2011), 1–24; and Prema–Chandra Athukorala, "Production networks and trade patterns in East Asia: Regionalization or globalization?" *Asian Economic Papers* 10 (1) (2011), 65–95.

42. David Brewster, "Silk roads and strings of pearls: The strategic geography of China's new pathways in the Indian Ocean," *Geopolitics* 22 (2) (2017), 269–291.

43. Tom Miller, *China's Asian Dream: Empire Building along the New Silk Road* (London: Zed Books, 2017), 18.

44. Jeffrey Reeves, "Structural power, the Copenhagen school and threats to Chinese security," *The China Quarterly* 217 (2014), 140–161.

45. John D. Ciorciari, "A Chinese model for patron—client relations? The Sino-Cambodian partnership," *International Relations of the Asia-Pacific* 15 (2) (2015), 249.

46. Amanda Hodge, "China's debt-trap diplomacy snares our Asian neighbours," *The Australian*, 13 January 2018, https://www.theaustralian.com.au/nation/world/chinas-debttrap-diplomacy-snares-our-asian-neighbours/news-story/7c6b04ac4e473f96d9ff3b7ec5abe102.

47. Dragan Pavlićević and Agatha Kratz, "Testing the China threat paradigm: China's high-speed railway diplomacy in Southeast Asia," *Pacific Review* 31 (2) (2017), 157.

48. Barry Naughton, "China and the two crises," in T. J. Pempel and K. Tsunekawa (eds.), *Two Crises, Different Outcomes: East Asia and Global Finance* (Ithaca: Cornell University Press, 2015), 110–134; and "Making sense of capacity cuts in China," *The Economist*, 9 September 2017, https://www.economist.com/leaders/2017/09/09/making-sense-of-capacity-cuts-in-china.

49. Wang Jisi, "China's search for a grand strategy," *Foreign Affairs* 90 (2) (2010), 68–79; Xi Jinping, "New Asian security concept for new progress in security cooperation," Ministry of Foreign Affairs of the People's Republic of China, 28 May 2014, http://www.fmprc.gov.cn/mfa_eng/zxxx_662805/t1159951.shtml; and Mark Beeson, "Security in Asia what's different, what's not?" *Journal of Asian Security and International Affairs* 1 (1) (2014), 1–23.

50. Norman Angell, *The Great Illusion* (New York: Cosimo Classics, 2007).

51. Eric Gartzke, "The capitalist peace," *American Journal of Political Science* 51 (1) (2007), 166–191.

52. Allison, *Destined for War.*

53. John Mearsheimer, *The Tragedy of Great Power Politics* (New York: W.W. Norton, 2001), 402.

54. Shawn Donnan, "US says China WTO membership was a mistake," *Financial Times*, 20 January 2018, https://www.ft.com/content/edb346ec-fd3a-11e7-9b32-d7d59aace167.

55. Richard Saull, "Rethinking hegemony: Uneven development, historical blocs, and the world economic crisis," *International Studies Quarterly* 56 (2) (2012), 323–338; Charles Kupchan, "The normative foundations of hegemony and the coming challenge to Pax Americana," *Security Studies* 23 (4) (2014), 219–257; Aaron L. Friedberg, *A Contest for Supremacy: China, America, and the Struggle for Mastery in Asia* (New York: W.W. Norton, 2011); and Mark Beeson, "Hegemonic transition in East Asia? The dynamics of Chinese and American power," *Review of International Studies* 35 (1) (2009), 95–112.

56. Joseph S. Nye, "The changing nature of power," *Political Science Quarterly* 105 (2) (1990), 177–192.

57. Blackwill and Harris, *War by Other Means*, 8.

58. Carl Thayer, "Vietnam's foreign policy in an era of rising Sino-US competition and increasing domestic political influence," *Asian Security* 13 (3) (2017), 1–17.

59. Bill Hayton, *The South China Sea: The Struggle for Power in Asia* (New Haven: Yale University Press, 2014).

60. Jessica Chen Weiss, *Powerful Patriots: Nationalist Protest in China's Foreign Relations* (Oxford: Oxford University Press, 2014). But also see, Alistair Ian Johnston, "Is Chinese nationalism rising? Evidence from Beijing," *International Security* 41 (3) (2017), 7–43.

61. Linda Jakobson, *China's Foreign Policy Dilemma* (Sydney: Lowy Institute, 2013), 5. But also see Kai Quek and Alistair Ian Johnston, "Can China back down? Crisis de-escalation in the shadow of popular opposition," *International Security* 42 (3) (2018), 27.

62. Kaplan, *Asia's Cauldron.*

63. Cheng-Chwee Kuik, "How do weaker states hedge? Unpacking ASEAN states' alignment behavior towards China," *Journal of Contemporary China* 25 (100) (2016), 1–15.

64. Evelyn Goh, "Great powers and hierarchical order in Southeast Asia: Analyzing regional security strategies," *International Security* 32 (3) (2008), 132.

65. Anne-Marie Murphy, "Great power rivalries, domestic politics and Southeast Asian foreign policy: Exploring the linkages," *Asian Security* 13 (3) (2017), 174.

66. David Hutt, "Laos is a key link for China's OBOR ambitions," *Asia Times*, 15 July 2017.

67. Andrew Browne, "China throws out South China sea rule book," *Wall Street Journal*, 20 December 2016, https://www.wsj.com/articles/china-throws-out-south-china-sea-rule-book-1482226667.

68. Richard J. Heydarian, "Tragedy of small power politics: Duterte and the shifting sands of Philippine foreign policy," *Asian Security* 13 (3) (2017), 232.

69. J. Haacke, "China's role in the pursuit of security by Myanmar's State Peace and Development Council: Boon *and* bane?" *The Pacific Review* 23 (1) (2010), 113–137.

70. Yun Sun, "China's belt and road in Myanmar," *The Diplomat*, 26 December 2017, https://thediplomat.com/2017/12/chinas-belt-and-road-in-myanmar/.

71. Tom Fawthrop, "The unfolding Mekong development disaster," *The Diplomat*, 1 April 2018, https://thediplomat.com/2018/03/the-unfolding-mekong-development-disaster/.

72. Jim Glassman, *Bounding the Mekong: The Asian Development Bank, China, and Thailand* (Hawaii: University of Hawaii Press, 2010).

73. Maarwan Macan-Markar, "Greens take on China's infrastructure projects in Southeast Asia," *Nikkei Asian Review*, 26 March 2018, https://asia.nikkei.com/Economy/Greens-take-on-China-s-infrastructure-projects-in-Southeast-Asia.

74. Adam Simpson, "The environment in Southeast Asia: Injustice, conflict and activism," in Alice Ba and Mark Beeson (eds.), *Contemporary Southeast Asia*, 3rd Edition (Basingstoke: Palgrave, 2018), 164–180.

75. Matthew Davies, *Realising Rights: How Regional Organisations Socialise Human Rights* (London: Routledge, 2014).

76. Amitav Acharya, *Constructing a Security Community in Southeast Asia: ASEAN and the Problem of Regional Order* (London: Routledge, 2001).

77. Ian Storey, *ASEAN and the Rise of China* (London: Routledge, 2013).

78. Alex Willemynas, "Cambodia blocks Asean statement on South China Sea," *The Cambodia Daily*, 25 July 2016, https://www.cambodiadaily.com/news/cambodia-blocks-asean-statement-on-south-china-sea-115834/.

79. Mark Beeson, "Can ASEAN Cope with China?" *Journal of Current Southeast Asian Affairs* 35 (1) (2015), 5–28.

80. Tommy Koh, "Singapore's friendship with China," *The Straits Times*, 2 May 2017, https://www.straitstimes.com/opinion/singapores-friendship-with-china.

81. Goh, "Great powers and hierarchical order in Southeast Asia," 113–157.

82. Christopher Layne, "This time it's real: The end of unipolarity and the Pax Americana," *International Studies Quarterly* 56 (1) (2012), 203–213.

Chapter 10

Keeping the "China Dream" at Arm's Length

Australia's Response to the Belt and Road Initiative

Andrew O'Neil

INTRODUCTION

In the first half of 2018, tensions swirled around Sino-Australian relations. A bid by the Chinese telecommunications giant, Huawei, to be part of Australia's new 5G mobile network was met with suspicion in senior ranks of the Turnbull government, which had received blunt warnings from national and allied intelligence agencies that Huawei's entry into the network would pose unacceptable risks to the integrity of a strategic sector of Australia's critical infrastructure.[1]

At the same time, China's provision of concessional loans to South Pacific countries, including Australia's former dependency Papua New Guinea, triggered warnings from Canberra that its regional neighbors were at risk of falling into a debt trap with the implication they would be vulnerable to future Chinese pressure.[2] Australia's public expression of concern over China's creeping militarization of the South China Sea, which saw the landing of H-6K nuclear-capable bombers on Woody Island in May, was dismissed by Beijing as "irresponsible."[3] An attempt by the Turnbull government in June to reset Australia's relationship with Beijing fell flat, with China's ambassador to Australia noting that Canberra had to work harder to avoid a "Cold War mentality."[4]

All of this was overlaid by rising concerns in Australia about the conduct of the Trump administration toward US allies in Asia. Despite the best efforts of the Pentagon and US diplomats to reassure regional allies, the Trump administration's determination to underscore the costs of alliances, its retreat to an

"America First" protectionist trade posture, and the president's penchant for praising authoritarian leaders unnerved Australian policy makers. This was brought into stark relief in June following the summit between Trump and North Korean leader Kim Jong-un that witnessed the US president pouring praise on Kim while publicly excoriating US NATO allies after the G7 summit just days earlier. Citing financial costs as a major consideration, Trump announced following the US-DPRK summit that the United States would be terminating "provocative" annual joint military exercises with South Korea.[5] Reportedly, the decision was not discussed with Seoul or Tokyo, although it appeared Beijing was aware of the impending announcement.[6] While US officials were quick to note that withdrawing American forces from the Korean Peninsula was not being considered, significantly they did not rule out discussing this option in future negotiations with North Korea.[7]

Against this background, Australia's management of relations with China remains a delicate balancing act. Governments in Canberra are acutely aware of the acute export dependence of key sectors of the Australian economy on gaining unfettered access to the China market. Influential sectors of the business community are especially active in lobbying Canberra to temper its public rhetoric on China to maintain smooth trading and investment relations. At the same time, security agencies and strategic policy specialists highlight the growing ability of China to exert coercive influence in Australia's region and within Australia itself through operations sanctioned by the Communist Party of China (CPC). Australian governments continue to pursue a "bracketing" approach to bilateral relations with Beijing whereby it is assumed that Australia can compartmentalize its highly successful economic relationship with China from any fallout in the edgier political and strategic domains. However, this approach is becoming trickier to maintain as Beijing becomes more assertive in the strategic and political domains and as Australian policy makers are increasingly attuned to the risks of accommodating China's preferences as its power expands.

In many respects, the Belt and Road Initiative (BRI) promulgated by Xi Jinping in 2013 provides a critical test case for how Australia is seeking to manage its complex relationship with China. While the BRI is typically conceived of as a mega-infrastructure project designed to drive greater connectivity between Chinese provinces and Central Asia, Southeast Asia, West Asia, and Europe, it also springs from the so-called China Dream that envisages "the PRC to be an authoritarian capitalist civilisation-state that has international influence backed up by a strong military."[8] Put another way, the BRI synthesizes a bold economic plan with an equally bold vision of China as the dominant Asian and global power. For Australia, therefore, the BRI captures a significant strategic dilemma: how to capitalize on the unprecedented opportunities provided by the scale of China's economic growth while at the same time avoiding becoming part of China's sphere of strategic influence. This dilemma is accentuated by the Trump administration's decision to retreat from US economic leadership in the Indo-Pacific and Washington's evident inclination to do the same in the strategic domain.

This chapter analyses Australia's reaction to the BRI and argues that it can only be understood fully by seeing it within the broader context of Australia's well-established strategy of hedging toward China. Using Evelyn Goh's formulation of hedging as "a set of strategies aimed at avoiding (or planning for contingencies in) a situation in which states cannot decide upon more straightforward alternatives such as balancing, bandwagoning or neutrality,"[9] I argue that contrary to those who claim Australia's approach to the BRI lacks direction, Canberra's response aligns with Australia's policy settings with respect to China overall. The chapter begins with a brief overview of the BRI and emphasizes its sweeping scope that goes well beyond specific "Silk Road" initiatives. In the next section, I examine the main drivers of Australia's China policy and explain how these have ineluctably shaped Australia's response to the BRI since it was promulgated in 2013. The final section of the chapter outlines three factors that will be crucial in influencing Australia's future approach to BRI, including under a prospective Labor government.

UNPACKING THE BELT AND ROAD INITIATIVE

The BRI is closely associated with a package of substantial political and economic measures—sometimes referred to as "the Silk Road" initiatives—designed to drive greater trade and investment connectivity between key areas in China and Central Asia, Southeast Asia, West Asia, and Europe. The BRI vision has at its heart an unprecedented series of large-scale infrastructure projects designed to establish "an economic corridor including about 65 countries and areas along the ancient Silk Road or the Belt and Road lines."[10] Since 2013, the BRI has been formally embedded in Chinese government planning documents, most notably the 2015 vision document authorized by the State Council and jointly released by the National Development and Reform Commission, the Ministry of Foreign Affairs, and Ministry of Commerce. It is also a feature of China's thirteenth five-year plan, which covers the period from 2016 to 2020.[11] The BRI has a conspicuous profile in Chinese interactions with neighboring Asian states in particular, many of which are lack developed infrastructure to cater to expanding populations and increasing economic aspirations.

In material terms, the BRI is powered by several institutions that provide significant lending capacity to countries looking for accessible capital to build large-scale infrastructure projects. The most prominent of these is the

Asian Infrastructure Investment Bank (AIIB) which, along with the New Development Bank and the New Silk Road Fund, is designed to compete internationally with the World Bank, International Monetary Fund, and Asian Development Bank for the financing and cofinancing of development projects.[12] Created in 2016 as a multilateral financing institution, the AIIB has achieved significant capitalization based on membership of more than eighty countries—including a number that are openly wary of BRI—although China remains overwhelmingly the single largest shareholder. While the AIIB is the most salient institution supporting the BRI, as one study recently points out, in terms of BRI-related lending thus far, it is China's established banks that have led the way.[13] In addition to the prospective lending by Chinese banks, at the time of writing (July 2018) Beijing is estimated to have spent at least US$34 billion on BRI-related projects, "focussed primarily on connectivity projects such as railways, ports, and energy pipelines and grids."[14] China's lack of insistence on financing preconditions, particularly in relation to governance and regime-type, has strong appeal among a number of countries that resent the relatively strict terms and conditions stipulated by Western-led institutions such as the World Bank.

In terms of sheer scope, BRI is the most ambitious initiative of its type since the US Marshall Plan of the 1940s. Its origins can be traced to a recalibration of Chinese grand strategy in the wake of the US "pivot" to Asia announced by the Obama administration in 2011. Outlined by the influential Peking University academic Wang Jisi, the conceptual framework of BRI hinged on China avoiding a direct contest with the United States in maritime Asia and instead "marching West" to exert influence in China's "inner Asian frontiers." Rather than seek to match the United States in an area (i.e., the maritime sphere) where it remained dominant, China would attempt to expand its strategic footprint in key geographical areas by exploiting its accelerating economic influence and its status as a major continental power.[15] As it has evolved, the BRI has in many respects become the signature enterprise for Chinese grand strategy. Although it is presented internationally by Chinese leaders as "open, inclusive, and win-win for balanced economic cooperation," within China many "have a more robust view of BRI as a cultural and moral alternative to what is seen as the US-led world order."[16]

While significant attention has focused on the geopolitical dimensions of BRI and what it means for the scale of Beijing's great power ambitions, as Peter Cai has argued, economic motives figure just as prominently in China's BRI strategy. Powerful domestic economic considerations, including the need to divert excess industrial capacity and build up the development of poorer regions in China, are key in Beijing's thinking.[17] An important element of BRI appears to be the platform it provides for Chinese companies to be more ambitious in their export strategies and to drive increasing external engagement in key markets.[18] Domestically, the economic development of China's western interior looms large in Beijing's BRI calculations. At the provincial level, the idea of networking, to a far greater extent, China's western provinces with neighboring economies has been an objective of the CPC since at least the 1980s.[19] This is especially prominent in the case of Xinjiang, where "Beijing believes poverty and underdevelopment is at the heart of rising militancy in the restive province and that the best strategy to address the root cause is integrating Xinjiang with the neighbouring region."[20]

International reactions to BRI have, predictably, tended to mirror existing views about the merits or otherwise of China's rise, its increasingly muscular economic influence, and perceptions of Beijing's expanding presence globally. Unsurprisingly, those countries that are balancing against China's rise, the United States and Japan, have refused to join the AIIB to avoid being under the umbrella of a Chinese-led institution. While China's arch-rival India remains exercised about the reach of BRI projects into Pakistan and Sri Lanka (including into the disputed territory of Kashmir), New Delhi has nevertheless joined the AIIB.[21] Some European countries, including Germany, have expressed concern that the BRI will further promote China's strategic influence and pose a potential threat to liberal democracy within the European Union because of Chinese sympathy for counterpart authoritarian governments.[22] In the Indo-Pacific, a range of countries have signed up to BRI including Indonesia, Malaysia, Thailand, Sri Lanka, Singapore, Timor-Leste, and, most recently, Papua New Guinea.[23] India, Vietnam, and Japan have publicly expressed reservations about BRI and linked the initiative with what they portray as a geopolitical threat from China.[24] In the middle, there are a significant minority of countries that, although welcoming the BRI in generic terms, have exhibited reluctance to become directly involved in helping Beijing operationalize its vision. Australia is part of this group.

AUSTRALIA'S RELATIONSHIP WITH CHINA AND THE BRI

In response to a question in 2014 from German chancellor Angela Merkel on what drives Australia's contemporary China policy, then Australian prime minister Tony Abbott is reported to have replied, "fear and greed."[25] The binary nature of Abbott's response struck a chord among some analysts, but the reality is that Australia has always had a complex and complicated relationship with China that defies easy characterization. Historically, the two countries' different systems of governance have stoked tensions over human rights, and Australia's alliance with the United States has meant that Canberra and Beijing have periodically been at odds over strategic and political issues. Yet, as Ann Kent observed in the mid-1990s, "the Australia-China relationship has been linked by one constant: commercial ties, which have been historically viewed as central to Australia's economic prosperity."[26] Today, China accounts for just under one-quarter of all of Australia's two-way trade and inward FDI from China is growing rapidly. Australian businesses still regard China as the "go-to" market for scale and trajectory of opportunities and there are few signs this perspective is changing in the face of relatively more modest Chinese economic growth. People-to-people links remain strong, in large part due to the significant Chinese diaspora in Australia and the buoyant market for tourism and Chinese students attending Australian universities.

However, evidence of interference by Beijing in Australia's domestic system and China's assertive build up in the South China Sea have provoked deep unease among senior Australian policy makers. This is despite polling indicating that more than 80 percent of Australian respondents regard China as more of an economic partner than a military threat.[27] The Turnbull government's introduction in 2017 of new counter-espionage and foreign interference legislation (enacted in 2018) followed the commissioning in 2016 of a top-secret investigation of Chinese infiltration of Australian political life. The investigation reportedly revealed that the CPC was targeting high levels of the Australian government with a view to exercising direct influence over policy.[28] These revelations emerged after an extended series of disclosures surrounding Beijing's influence operations in Australia that have encompassed attempts to bribe officials, pressure local Chinese language media outlets to reflect the CPC's line on key issues, the monitoring of Chinese studying in Australian universities, and recruiting sympathetic advocates to articulate the CPC's position in high-level fora, including media outlets.[29]

The Turnbull government emphasized publicly its concern over Chinese activities in Australia while underscoring its commitment to a "rules-based international order" when referring to China's militarization activities in the South China Sea. Although criticized in some quarters for endorsing a posture of "strategic mistrust" toward China, the Turnbull government's basic policy approach is supported by the Labor Opposition, which has historically claimed the mantle of pioneering the constructive relations with China since Gough Whitlam's groundbreaking visit to the PRC in 1971. Despite arguing that Australia's policy approach can be articulated in "more sophisticated" language, senior Labor figures have made it clear they support the Turnbull government's legislative initiatives to counter Chinese influence domestically in Australia and challenging Beijing's selective disregard of international law and norms of behavior concerning territorial claims in the region.[30]

Conflicting perspectives in Australia over how to manage relations with China have been evident for some time, but they are increasingly manifested in entrenched, and at times zero-sum, debates. On one side are those who argue that Australia should distance itself from US policies that cast China in adversarial terms and instead seek to build on Australia's existing strategic partnership with Beijing concluded under the Gillard government. Australia must define its own strategy toward China based on its unique national interests that are different to those of the United States, particularly under the Trump administration, which has embraced a nationalistic and confrontational approach in dealing with Beijing.[31] From this perspective, it is counterproductive to Australia's long-term national interests for it to drift into an adversarial relationship with China as Beijing seeks to expand its footprint in the Indo-Pacific and globally. Operating within this framework, it makes more sense for Australia to work to accommodate Beijing's expanding strategic ambitions with an eye on strengthening economic and political ties with China over coming decades. This both reflects and extends Hugh White's "China choice" thesis that Australia is best served by persuading the United States to accommodate China's widening strategic footprint as it transitions to great power status.[32]

The contra position is that Australia is best served in the long run by pushing back against Chinese attempts to expand its strategic influence internationally, including ambit territorial claims made by Beijing in the South China Sea. From this perspective, the US alliance and an active American presence in the Indo-Pacific provides a necessary block against China's temptation to exert pressure against countries that choose not to opt in to its strategic vision as the world's newest great power. More specifically, Australia needs to avoid bandwagoning—or giving the impression it is bandwagoning—with Beijing in response to the US-China power transition in the Asia-Pacific. The US alliance is important in constraining China's tendency to pressure countries that do not share Beijing's vision, as is building coalitions with like-minded states, including Japan and India. As distinct from the "accommodationist" school in Australian thinking, the "constrainment" school endorses an active policy of limiting Chinese influence and ensuring that Australia retains the ability to exercise autonomy in determining its own policy preferences on matters of national importance. For those in this camp, evidence of Chinese attempts to influence domestic affairs in Australia merely reinforces the importance of asserting autonomy in strategic policy.

These lines of debate, however, obscure a more complicated picture for Australian policy makers. Growing economic interdependence with China and Beijing's rising influence in the Indo-Pacific has inevitably cast a shadow over Australian decision-making. Yet, there is no evidence that policy makers have decided to pursue a consistent strategy that endorses either accommodation or constrainment as a *single* preferred option. This is in contrast to Japan and the United States, both of which have embraced an active balancing strategy against China. Australia has on several occasions accommodated China in the sense that it has acceded to Beijing's policy preferences when, all things being equal, Australia would have maintained its existing position. In 2008, confronting sharp criticism from Beijing, the Rudd Government terminated Australia's involvement in the Quadrilateral Security Dialogue with the United States, Japan, and India.[33] And Australia's 2013 Defence White Paper (DWP) conspicuously omitted any reference to the lack of transparency in China's military modernization that had appeared in the 2009 DWP, which had provoked strong public condemnation from Beijing.[34]

Yet, for every instance of accommodation, there are examples of constrainment in Australia's approach to China. Australia was one of only a handful of countries that publicly condemned China's declaration in 2013 of an Air Defence Identification Zone in the East China Sea. While resisting calls to join with the United States in undertaking joint Freedom of Navigation Operations in the South China Sea, the Turnbull government has maintained the tempo of Australian air and naval patrols through the region despite direct warnings from Beijing that this risks confrontation with Chinese forces.[35] Moreover, the Turnbull government has demonstrated renewed vigor in criticizing China's conduct in the South Pacific, an area traditionally designated as Australia's "patch." Sensitive to indications that Beijing is widening its influence in the region, Canberra has expressed public concern over the prospect of China being granted military basing rights in the South Pacific as a quid pro quo for large-scale investment in individual countries.[36] This concern over an expanding Chinese strategic footprint in the region extended to the Turnbull government providing the Solomon Islands and Papua New Guinea with a commitment to fund the construction of underwater Internet cables and the creation of a cybersecurity center based in Honiara. This commitment was aimed expressly at pushing out Chinese firm Huawei, which had signed a deal with the Solomon Islands government to provide high-speed telecommunications cables.[37] The deal was reportedly assessed by Australian security agencies as providing potential "backdoor" access for Huawei to Australia's telecommunications due to the Australian mainland being identified as the "landing point" for the undersea cables.[38]

Australia's strategy toward China therefore exhibits classic features of hedging, and while there are periods where active constrainment measures may appear more prominent in the approach of individual governments, policy makers are careful to maintain a degree of equilibrium to avoid the impression that Australia is pursuing either balancing or bandwagoning. This is evident in Australia's approach to the BRI.

Since Xi Jinping's formal invitation to Australia to sign on to the BRI in his 2014 speech to the Australian Parliament, Canberra has exhibited mixed signals regarding its position.[39] As Nick Bisley points out, this has tended to mirror the initial reluctance exhibited by Australia in response to China's establishment of the AIIB in 2014.[40] Seen as a rival to the World Bank and the Asian Development Bank, the AIIB was closely tied to the BRI because it was identified as the primary institutional funding mechanism for infrastructure projects approved under the aegis of the BRI. During its initial development, Australia welcomed the AIIB but avoided any commitment to join, emphasizing instead the need for as wider membership as possible and coordinating its position with those of its allies.[41] Australia eventually signed on to the AIIB in 2015 to become a founding member of the board of governors but only after a major debate in Cabinet that was reportedly split between the prime minister and the foreign minister expressing initial skepticism and the Treasurer and Trade Minister strongly in support.[42] Overlaying the debate was intense pressure from the Obama administration on Australia not to join; it seems the Abbott government became more open to joining the AIIB once it was clear there a bandwagon effect was occurring among US allies including the United Kingdom, South Korea, and Germany.[43]

As Allan Gyngell writes, the debate over the AIIB "was just one of the challenges facing all Australian governments of the period as they tried to find ways of integrating and balancing the complex economic, strategic and political interests with China that were now in play."[44] Notwithstanding its decision in 2015 to resist US pressure and join the AIIB, Australia remains wary of fully committing itself to the BRI. Discussions between Canberra and Beijing over how Australia might cooperate on the BRI did not emerge until after the signing of the China-Australia Free Trade Agreement in June 2015 and Australia's accession to the AIIB as a founding member later the same month.[45] Public attention focused on how investment from BRI could contribute to the development of northern Australia, a major theme in the Abbott government's domestic infrastructure strategy that would be maintained under the Turnbull government. Following the Commonwealth's release in 2016 of the White Paper on Developing Northern Australia, official Chinese statements began linking the BRI with infrastructure development in northern Australia.[46]

Attending the landmark Belt and Road Forum in Beijing in May 2017, Trade Minister Steven Ciobo noted there were "clearly complementarities between the Northern Australia Initiative and the Belt and Road Initiative."[47] However, this statement followed the Turnbull government's rejection earlier in the year of a proposal from Beijing that a formal link be made between the Northern Australia Infrastructure Facility (NAIF)[48] and the BRI.[49] This was despite strong support from major Australian businesses and high-level endorsement by the Chinese leadership. In September 2017, Australia and China signed a formal Memorandum of Understanding (MoU) that committed to Australian companies cooperating with Beijing on BRI-related infrastructure projects *in third-party countries*.[50] Yet, there remain divisions within the Australian government over the BRI that reportedly revolve around concerns that Australia will be locked in to supporting China's future strategic vision, the lack of quality assurance underpinning Chinese–led infrastructure projects, and that backing will further promote emerging Chinese dominance in the trade sphere.[51] National security agencies continue to express the sharpest concerns, with economic agencies and sections of DFAT reportedly more supportive of Australia joining the BRI.[52] Influential Australian business groups are essentially unanimous in their enthusiasm for BRI and have lobbied the Turnbull governed to sign up to what they portray as "the project of the century."[53]

While the Turnbull and now Morrison governments continue to resist proposals for BRI projects in Australia, some State and Local governments have ignored Canberra and announced they would welcome large-scale infrastructure investment as part of the BRI. There have even been cases of Chinese developers operating in Australia who have badged their projects as "One Belt, One Road," which in turn have been endorsed as such by the Chinese government.[54] Yet, what concerns the Turnbull government more is the apparent BRI bandwagon effect among Australia's neighbors. Australia's closest regional neighbors, PNG and Timor-Leste, have committed themselves formally to the BRI, and in the case of PNG have contrasted favorably the "flexibility" of Chinese lending with what they argue is the "paternalistic" approach of Australia's aid program.[55] As a proportion of PNG's total debt repayment obligations, China accounts for one-quarter and Beijing's has emerged as PNG's single largest bilateral creditor.[56] The Turnbull government's response has been to explore an alternative multilateral infrastructure development scheme with Japan and the United States, but there is little evidence of tangible progress toward agreement.[57] More concretely, Canberra has signaled it will fund major infrastructure projects in the South Pacific unilaterally, with Foreign Minister Julie Bishop stating that "the consequences of regional countries entering into some of these [BRI] financing arrangements will be detrimental to their long-term sovereignty."[58]

For Australia, the challenges resulting from BRI serve to crystallize competing agendas in the domestic discourse over China; the positions individuals have taken on BRI have almost always reflected their broader position on how Australia should engage with China. Those in the strategic community have seen it through the lens of security while those in the business world have constructed BRI through the lens of economic opportunity. In this respect, the binary nature of the Australian "debate" over BRI has been predictable, and is unlikely to change.

Because Australia has not formally committed itself to the BRI in a comprehensive way, some critics have argued that the country lacks a coherent strategy for dealing with Beijing's grand vision.[59] Former Australian ambassador to China, Geoff Raby, has written that "Canberra continues to tie itself in knots over how to respond [to the BRI], just as it did with the AIIB."[60] But this overlooks the deliberate nature of Australia's approach toward the BRI that reflects the classic traits of the hedging strategy that Australia has embraced in its broader China policy. Since China's ascent to great power status became apparent in the 2000s, successive Australian governments have adopted a blend of strategies designed to capitalize on economic opportunities while limiting China's capacity to challenge core elements of Australian strategic policy, including the alliance with the United States.[61] Policy makers have determined that the optimal strategy for Australia should be to constrain Chinese influence domestically and in the region while accommodating Beijing when the costs to sovereignty and broader policy goals are low. In the case of the BRI, Australian policy makers see it as both expressing and exemplifying China's intent to become the dominant power in Asia, and for this reason they are cautious in their engagement.

The Turnbull government's endorsement of bilateral consultations with Beijing over how Australian companies can slot into Chinese funded infrastructure projects in third countries undermines the claim that Australia has either rejected or ignored the BRI. At the same time, Canberra's evident reluctance at being locked into the BRI through the NAIF mirrors a classic hedging approach. Notwithstanding the Labor Opposition's decision to remain "open-minded" about the BRI, it too has stopped short of committing unreservedly to China's vision.[62] Unsurprisingly, positions staked out in Australia regarding the merits or otherwise of the BRI strongly reflect broader positions on how Australia should be engaging China. The hedging posture adopted by policy elites toward the BRI and engagement with China generally is not simply the result of competing perspectives within government and civil society over how best to manage relations with Beijing; it is a deliberate strategy aimed at avoiding becoming part of China's expanding sphere of influence while at the same time ensuring that Australia capitalizes on the unprecedented economic opportunities presented by China's continuing rise.

AUSTRALIA AND THE FUTURE OF THE BRI

It is by no means assured that the vision articulated by China's leaders for the BRI will come to fruition. As many have pointed out, the BRI lacks detail and there remain numerous obstacles to the vision being achieved, not the least of which is the degree of "buy in" from states. Like Australia, some major economies have placed significant conditions on their commitment to the BRI. Singapore has concluded an MoU with Beijing at the head of government level but this only endorses joint project collaboration between Singaporean and Chinese firms in third countries.[63] Others that initially signed comprehensive MoUs with Beijing to collaborate on the BRI are attempting to impose greater constraints on specific project agreements with China; indeed, changes of government can lead to a reassessment of the value of prior BRI commitments. In Malaysia, where the previous Najib Razak administration had signed up to the BRI with very few conditions, the *Pakatan Harapan* government in office since June 2018 has insisted on more rigorous conditions for Chinese companies operating on infrastructure projects inside Malaysia.[64]

Questions also remain about the extent to which the BRI is simply a repackaging of existing projects under a catchall banner and whether high profile Chinese-led infrastructure projects will provoke more blowback of the kind that already exists regarding Chinese investment in the Indo-Pacific. Still, as Nadege Rolland has observed:

> If it unfolds as Beijing envisions, the implications [of the BRI] would certainly be far reaching: an integrated and interconnected Eurasian continent with enduring authoritarian political systems, where China's influence has grown to the point it has muted any opposition and gained acquiescence and deference; a new regional order with its own political and economic institutions, whose rules and norms reflect China's values and serve its interests; and a continental stronghold insulated to some degree from American seapower.[65]

Even in the face of resistance from the United States, the BRI promises to broaden China's strategic footprint and increase the radius of its influence not just in the Indo-Pacific but globally. For small and medium-sized powers aligned with the United States, this will pose significant challenges that will be accentuated in the event the Trump administration's contraction of America's worldwide commitments becomes embedded in US global strategy.[66]

What factors will shape Australia's future position on the BRI? The first and most obvious is how the BRI itself evolves. Thus far, as a number of analysts have pointed out, while the BRI has been clarified in grand strategic terms, how it will be implemented and delivered "on the ground" remains elusive.[67] In terms of a purely transactional cost-benefit analysis, future Australian governments will remain wary of formally committing to an initiative that lacks operational detail. As Ian Hall notes, "Australia's approach to BRI—which amounts to 'wait and see' while also asking politely for more transparency—is not unreasonable."[68] Moreover, the potential moral hazards associated with smaller countries signing up to financing arrangements that expose them to significant, and in some cases unserviceable, debt repayments concerns Canberra. This is particularly salient in the South Pacific, which is hungry for investment in infrastructure to power economic growth and where China has a growing presence. Noting that Australia is "thinking constructively yet clearly about the principles, rules and institutions that underpin an initiative such as Belt and Road given its scale ambition and complexity," the Secretary of the Department of Foreign Affairs and Trade has disclosed that "in our discussions [with China] we have emphasised the importance of projects embracing international standards, accountability and best practice, including social and environmental impact."[69]

The second major factor shaping Australia's position with respect to BRI will be the domestic political climate, including how China is perceived across other areas of policy. While, as noted earlier, there is a gap between elite and public opinion in Australia regarding the extent to which China is seen as a potential security threat, revelations concerning Chinese espionage activities targeted at Australia have undoubtedly dented the case of those advocating a comprehensive commitment to the BRI. The Labor Opposition has shown more general enthusiasm for the BRI than the Coalition government, but it has also supported strong countermeasures against Chinese espionage activities within Australia. A high degree of bipartisanship characterized the passage of tough new legislation through the Commonwealth Parliament in June 2018 aimed at blunting foreign influence and foreign interference in Australia's political system.[70] Although the Labor Party by inclination remains more open-minded than the Coalition about comprehensive engagement with China—and therefore engaging with the BRI—it is also conscious that there is strong linkage between domestic debate in Australia over Chinese influence and foreign policy.

Finally, China's conduct in other areas of international policy will influence how Australian governments view the pros and cons of committing to the BRI. Given that the BRI is regarded as a major expression of China's global strategic ambitions, Beijing's approach to territorial issues in the Indo-Pacific will inevitably shape Australian perceptions of the merits of committing more fully to the BRI. China's militarization of the South China Sea and how Beijing seeks to deal with other states regarding territorial conflicts will loom especially large in Australian calculations. Policy makers have been focused on articulating concerns publicly over China's regional conduct, as well as its domestic conduct within the Australian polity, in an attempt to assert national sovereignty. But these public statements have also been intended to convey a broader signal to like-minded states in the Indo-Pacific that Canberra intends to actively resist Beijing's attempts to shift the regional order in its favor at the expense of other countries. It would be inaccurate here to assume that Australia is merely emulating the position of its principal security ally, the United States. Over an extended period, Australian governments have repeatedly demonstrated a willingness to carve out a position toward China that reflects Australia's unique national interests. Indeed, under the Trump administration the United States has become more critical of allies and less inclined to defend their interests. Notably, however, there is no sign Australia's propensity to challenge Beijing publicly has become any less assertive during the Trump administration; if anything, Canberra's willingness to challenge China has become more conspicuous since January 2017.

CONCLUSION

Like other states in its region, Australia pursues a blend of strategies in its approach to China. Taken together, these amount to an overall strategy of hedging whose guiding objective is to exploit the economic rewards flowing from China's rise while protecting against a worst-case scenario of Chinese hegemony. As one analyst has put it, hedging aims "to offset risks by pursuing multiple policy options that are intended to produce mutually counteracting effects, under the situation of high uncertainty and high stakes."[71] Australia's response to the BRI can only be fully appreciated when viewed in this context. The BRI is rightly seen as both an unprecedented economic opportunity and an expression of China's intent to exercise great power influence globally. Those who argue that Australia should comprehensively endorse the BRI overlook the latter dimension while those who criticize Australia's BRI engagement discount the reality of the former.

Whether Australia's hedging strategy remains viable in future will be acutely dependent on the type of pressure Beijing may bring to bear on Australia's interests. During downturns in the bilateral relationship, Beijing has been willing to make life harder for Australian businesses operating in China, it has imposed a freeze on ministerial visits, and it has excoriated Australia's policy stance through formal channels as well as popular domestic media outlets, including *The Global Times*. But pressure from Beijing will not be the only variable impacting on the sustainability of Australia's hedging strategy. Much will also hinge on the fundamental question of whether Australian policy elites are willing to bear the potential economic costs of challenging China on political and strategic issues. Building informal coalitions with like-minded countries that are similarly pursuing hedging strategies toward China, reinforcing multi- and minilateral security architecture in the Indo-Pacific, and strengthening the security alliance with the United States will be important ingredients in promoting confidence among Australian policy makers that a long-term hedging strategy toward China is a realistic policy goal.

More generally, the time has come for serious conversation in Australia about the assumption on the part of policy makers that Australia can necessarily compartmentalize its highly successful economic relationship with China from fallout in the edgier political and strategic domains. Beijing's increasing impatience with what it sees as dissent in the Indo-Pacific fundamentally challenges the view that small and medium-sized countries can have their cake and eat it too when it comes to interacting with China. Indeed, in many important respects, the BRI lies at the intersection of this discussion. How Australia crafts its policy approach to the BRI in the future will be a key pointer to whether policy makers genuinely believe they can continue to reap the benefits of China's growing economic ascendancy without bending to the seemingly inexorable geopolitical winds of the twenty-first century.

NOTES

1. Andrew Probyn, "Huawei's History in Britain May Help Explain Why Australia is so Nervous," *ABC News Online*, 16 June 2018, http://www.abc.net.au/news/2018-06-16/huawei-britain-history-helps-explain-australia-anxiety/9875582.
2. David Wroe, "Looking North: PNG Signs On to China's Belt and Road Initiative," *The Sydney Morning Herald*, 21 June 2018, https://www.smh.com.au/world/asia/looking-north-png-signs-on-to-china-s-belt-and-road-initiative-20180621-p4zmyv.html.
3. "China Rebukes Australia, US for "Irresponsible Comments" on South China Sea," *SBS News Online*, 3 June 2018, https://www.sbs.com.au/news/china-rebukes-australia-us-for-irresponsible-comments-on-south-china-sea.
4. Andrew Tillett, "Less Bias and Bigotry Needed to Save Australia-China Relationship, Envoy Warns," *The Australian Financial Review*, 19 June 2018, https://www.afr.com/news/less-bias-and-bigotry-needed-to-save-australiachina-relationship-envoy-warns-20180618-h11jtv.
5. Eric Schmitt, "Pentagon and Seoul Surprised by Trump Pledge to Halt Military Exercises," *The New York Times*, 12 June 2018, https://www.nytimes.com/2018/06/12/world/asia/trump-military-exercises-north-south-korea.html.
6. See the tweet dated June 12 by BBC China correspondent Stephen McDonnell who attended a media conference (before Trump's announcement) where the Chinese Foreign Ministry noted that "our suspension for suspension process is right and has been realised." See: https://twitter.com/stephenmcdonell/status/1006595784148582400?lang=en.
7. Joe Gould and Leo Shane, "Trump's Proposed Troop Moves in South Korea Raise Concern for Lawmakers," *Defense News*, 12 June 2018, https://www.defensenews.com/news/pentagon-congress/2018/06/12/trumps-proposed-troop-moves-in-south-korea-raise-concerns-for-lawmakers/.
8. William Callahan, "China's "Asian Dream": The Belt Road Initiative and the New Regional Order," *Asian Journal of Comparative Politics*, 1(3), 2015, p. 235.
9. Evelyn Goh, *Meeting the China Challenge: The US in Southeast Asian Security Strategies*, East-West Center Policy Studies, no. 16, Washington, DC, 2005, p. viii.
10. Yong Wang, "Offensive for Defensive: The Belt and Road Initiative and China's New Grand Strategy," *The Pacific Review*, 29(3), 2016, p. 456.

11. Astrid Nordin and Mikael Weissmann, "Will Trump Make China Great Again? The Belt and Road Initiative and International Order," *International Affairs*, 94(2), 2018, pp. 239–240.

12. Nina Trentmann, "China-led Infrastructure Bank Secures AAA Rating from Fitch," *The Wall Street Journal*, 14 July 2017, https://www.wsj.com/articles/china-led-infrastructure-bank-secures-aaa-rating-from-fitch-1500054398.

13. Shahar Hameiri and Lee Jones, "China Challenges Global Governance? Chinese International Development Finance and the AIIB," *International Affairs*, 94(3), 2018, pp. 575–579.

14. "China's Belt and Road Initiative, Five Years in," *Stratfor Assessments*, 22 June 2018, https://worldview.stratfor.com/article/chinas-belt-and-road-initiative-five-years.

15. Zorawar Daulet Singh, "Locating the Belt and Road in China's Broader Policy Shifts," *Strategic Affairs*, 24 June 2017, p. 11.

16. Callahan, "China's 'Asian Dream,'" p. 237.

17. Peter Cai, "Understanding China's Belt and Road Initiative," *Lowy Institute Analysis*, March 2017, https://www.lowyinstitute.org/publications/understanding-belt-and-road-initiative

18. Tom Hancock, "China Encircles the World with One Belt, One Road Strategy," *The Financial Times*, 4 May 2017, https://www.ft.com/content/0714074a-0334-11e7-aa5b-6bb07f5c8e12

19. Tim Summers, "China's "New Silk Roads": Sub-national Regions and Networks of Global Political Economy," *Third World Quarterly*, 37(9), 2016, p. 1633.

20. Cai, "Understanding China's Belt and Road Initiative," p. 7.

21. Asian Infrastructure Investment Bank, "Members and Prospective Members of the Bank," https://www.aiib.org/en/about-aiib/governance/members-of-bank/index.html.

22. Laura Tingle, "Europe Signals Alarm at Assertive China's Belt and Road Initiative," *The Australian Financial Review*, 18 February 2018, http://www.afr.com/news/world/europe/europe-signals-alarm-at-assertive-chinas-belt-and-road-initiative-20180217-h0w95z.

23. "PNG Prime Minister Peter O'Neill Meets with Xi Jinping, Signs up to China's Belt and Road Initiative," *ABC News Online*, 22 June 2018, http://www.abc.net.au/news/2018-06-22/png-prime-minister-peter-oneill-meets-with-xi-jinping-in-beijing/9897248.

24. Andrew Small, "The Backlash to Belt and Road," *Foreign Affairs*, 16 February 2018, https://www.foreignaffairs.com/articles/china/2018-02-16/backlash-belt-and-road.

25. John Garnaut, "'Fear and Greed' Drive Australia's China Policy, Tony Abbott Tells Angela Merkel," *The Sydney Morning Herald*, 16 April 2015, https://www.smh.com.au/politics/federal/fear-and-greed-drive-australias-china-policy-tony-abbott-tells-angela-merkel-20150416-1mmdty.html.

26. Ann Kent, "Australia-China Relations, 1966–1996: A Critical Overview," *The Australian Journal of Politics and History*, 42(3), 1996, p. 379.

27. Lowy Institute for International Policy, *Lowy Institute Poll 2018: Understanding Australian Attitudes to the World*, June 2018, p. 27.

28. Chris Uhlmann, "Top Secret Report Uncovers High Level Chinese Interference in Australian Politics," *Nine News Online*, 28 May 2018, https://www.9news.com.au/national/2018/05/28/17/38/chinese-communist-party-interference-australian-politics.

29. For background analysis, see Clive Hamilton, *Silent Invasion: China's Influence in Australia*, Hardie Grant Books, Sydney, 2018; and John Fitzgerald, "Australia: Special Forum on Chinese Interference in the Internal Affairs of Democratic States," *The Asan Forum*, 24 April 2018, http://www.theasanforum.org/australia-2/.

30. See the speech by Opposition Foreign Affairs spokesperson Penny Wong to the Australia-China Business event on 19 June at Parliament House: https://www.pennywong.com.au/speeches/australia-china-business-council-parliament-house-canberra/.

31. Bob Carr, "Obsessions with Foes Could Make the US a Perilous Friend," *The Australian*, 23 June 2018, https://www.theaustralian.com.au/news/inquirer/obsession-with-foes-could-make-us-a-perilous-friend/news-story/c0f37786ef2cc71a1929f22f3ccd7d67.

32. Hugh White, *The China Choice: Why We Should Share Power*, Oxford University Press, Oxford, 2013.

33. Tanvi Madan, "The Rise Fall and Rebirth of the Quad," *War on the Rocks*, 16 November 2017, https://warontherocks.com/2017/11/rise-fall-rebirth-quad/.

34. Brendan Nicholson, "Defence White Paper Pivots Over China Threat," *The Australian*, 4 May 2013, https://www.theaustralian.com.au/national-affairs/defence/defence-white-paper-pivots-over-china-threat/news-story/d31a6a528a105f963e5f83986cc596a4?sv=3036c36b6a1e637bce5b24ab0305c2e.

35. For discussion, see Andrew O'Neil, "Middle Powers and the South China Sea: Stepping Up, or Stepping Out?" in Tetsuo Kotani, Christopher Roberts, and Tran Truong Thuy (eds.), *The South China Sea: Transitions in Maritime Security and the Rules-Based Order*, Palgrave Macmillan, Basingstoke, 2020.

36. Ben Smee and Dan McGarry, "'Impossible'": China Denies Planning Military Base in Vanuatu," *The Guardian*, 10 April 2018, https://www.theguardian.com/world/2018/apr/10/concerns-china-in-talks-with-vanuatu-about-south-pacific-military-base.

37. Matthew Doran and Stephen Dziedzic, "Deal to be Inked for Solomon Islands Undersea Internet Cable Australia Stopped China Building," *ABC News Online*, 13 June 2018, http://www.abc.net.au/news/2018-06-13/solomon-islands-undersea-cable-internet-china/9861592.

38. "Australia Keeps China Out of Internet Cabling for Pacific Neighbor," *Reuters*, 13 June 2018, https://www.reuters.com/article/us-australia-solomonislands-internet/australia-keeps-china-out-of-internet-cabling-for-pacific-neighbor-idUSKBN1J90JY.

39. "Address by the President of the People's Republic of China, Monday 17 November 2014, Parliament of Australia," http://parlinfo.aph.gov.au/parlInfo/search/display/display.w3p;query=Id:%22chamber/hansardr/35c9c2cf-9347-4a82-be89-20df5f76529b/0005%22.

40. Nick Bisley, "Australia's Oddly Absent Belt and Road Strategy," *Lowy Interpreter*, 12 October 2017, https://www.lowyinstitute.org/the-interpreter/australia-s-oddly-absent-belt-and-road-strategy.

41. Mike Callaghan and Paul Hubbard, "The Asian Infrastructure and Investment Bank: Multilateralism on the Silk Road," *China Economic Journal*, 9(2), 2016, pp. 126–127.

42. Phillip Coorey, "Australia to Join Asian Infrastructure Investment Bank, Says Joe Hockey," *The Australian Financial Review*, 24 June 2015, http://www.afr.com/news/politics/australia-to-join-asian-infrastructure-investment-bank-says-joe-hockey-20150624-ghwevx.

43. Sabrina Snell, "US Allies Split with Washington, Bank with China," *US-China Economic and Security Review Commission Issue Brief*, 31 March 2015, https://www.uscc.gov/sites/default/files/Research/Asian%20Infrastructure%20Investment%20Bank_Issue%20Brief.pdf.

44. Allan Gyngell, *Fear of Abandonment: Australia in the World Since 1942*, La Trobe University Press in conjunction with Black Inc., Melbourne, 2017, p. 354.

45. Elena Collinson, "Australia and the Belt and Road Initiative: An Overview," *UTS ACRI Facts*, 5 November 2017, http://www.australiachinarelations.org/sites/default/files/20171205%20ACRI%20Facts_Australia%20and%20the%20Belt%20and%20Road%20Initiative_An%20overview.pdf.

46. Commonwealth of Australia, *Our North, Our Future: White Paper on Developing Northern Australia*, Commonwealth of Australia, Canberra, 2016; and Elena Collinson, "Australia and the Belt and Road Initiative."

47. "Minister for Trade, Tourism and Investment: Belt and Road Forum Doorstop, Beijing, 14 May 2017," http://trademinister.gov.au/transcripts/Pages/2017/sc_tr_170514.aspx?w=tb1CaGpkPX% 2FlS0K%2Bg9ZKEg%3D%3D.

48. Established under an Act of the Commonwealth Parliament in 2016, the NAIF's defined mission is to provide "up to $5 billion over 5 years in concessional finance to encourage and complement private sector investment in infrastructure that benefits Northern Australia. This may include developments in airports, communications, energy, ports, rail and water." See Department of Industry, Innovation and Science, "Northern Infrastructure Facility," https://industry.gov.au/industry/Northern-Australia-Infrastructure-Facility/Pages/default.aspx.

49. Primrose Riordan, "China Snubbed on Belt and Road Push," *The Australian*, 20 March 2017, https://www.theaustralian.com.au/national-affairs/foreign-affairs/china-snubbed-on-road-and-port-push/news-story/1534e4f7de0ab0031818854d24ae0a91.

50. James Laurenceson, Simone van Nieuwenhuizen, and Elena Collinson, "Decision Time: Australia's Engagement with China's Belt and Road Initiative," *Australia-China Relations Institute Report*, UTS, November 2017, p. 3.

51. Conversations with Australian government officials, Canberra, March 2018.

52. Andrew Greene and Andrew Probyn, "One Belt, One Road: Australian "Strategic" Concerns Over Beijing's Bid for Global Trade Dominance," *ABC News Online*, 23 October 2017, http://www.abc.net.au/news/2017-10-22/australian-concerns-over-beijing-one-belt-one-road-trade-bid/9074602.

53. See Arnoud Balhuizen, "How the Belt and Road Initiative is Fuelling a Global Commodity Upswing," *The Australian Financial Review*, 27 February 2018, https://www.afr.com/brand/business-summit/how-the-belt-and-road-initiative-is-fuellin

g-a-global-commodity-upswing-20180225-h0wn51; and Dan Wilkie, "Call to Business—Get on Board China's Belt and Road," *Australia-China Business Review*, 18 May 2018, https://www.acbr.com.au/call-business-get-board-chinas-belt-and-road.

54. Michael Walsh and Bang Xiao, "One Belt, One Road: China Lists $400m Gold Coast Theme Park as "Key Project" of Global Initiative," *ABC News Online*, 5 March 2018, http://www.abc.net.au/news/2018-03-05/china-lists-planned-gold-coast-theme-park-as-a-key-project/9508904.

55. Ben Packham, "China's More Flexible Support Better than Australia's, Says PNG," *The Australian*, 12 June 2018, https://www.theaustralian.com.au/national-affairs/foreign-affairs/chinas-more-flexible-support-better-than-australias-says-png/news-story/c5c0ad5f5a0dead450f595ce84886b5d.

56. Bill Bainbridge, Bethanie Harriman, and Jack Kilbride, "PNG Prime Minister Peter O'Neill Visits Beijing to Sign One Belt, One Road Trade Deal," *ABC News Online*, 20 June 2018, http://www.abc.net.au/news/2018-06-20/png-pm-to-visit-china-to-sign-one-belt-one-road-deal/9888054.

57. Phillip Coorey, "Australia Mulls Rival to China's "Belt and Road" with US, Japan, India," *The Australian Financial Review*, 18 February 2018, https://www.afr.com/news/australia-mulls-rival-to-chinas-belt-and-road-with-us-japan-india-20180216-h0w7k5.

58. David Wroe, "Australia Will Compete with China to Save Pacific Sovereignty, Says Bishop," *The Sydney Morning Herald*, 18 June 2018, https://www.smh.com.au/politics/federal/australia-will-compete-with-china-to-save-pacific-sovereignty-says-bishop-20180617-p4zm1h.html.

59. See for example, James Laurenceson, Simone van Nieuwenhuizen, and Elena Collinson, "Australia's Misplaced fear Over China's Belt and Road," *The Diplomat*, 16 November 2017, https://thediplomat.com/2017/11/australias-misplaced-fear-over-chinas-belt-and-road/; and Shahar Hamieri, "What's Driving Chinese Infrastructure Investment Overseas and How Can We Make the Most of It?" *The Conversation*, 26 June 2018, https://theconversation.com/whats-driving-chinese-infrastructure-investment-overseas-and-how-can-we-make-the-most-of-it-98697.

60. Geoff Raby, "Xi Jinping's One Belt, One Road Triumph and Australia's Sino Confusion," *The Australian Financial Review*, 17 May 2017, https://www.afr.com/opinion/columnists/xis-one-belt-one-road-triumph-and-australias-sino-confusion-20170517-gw6qef.

61. For discussion, see James Manicom and Andrew O'Neil, "Accommodation, Realignment, or Business as Usual? Australia's Response to a Rising China," *The Pacific Review*, 23(1), 2010, pp. 23–44; James Reilly, "Counting on China? Australia's Strategic Response to Economic Interdependence," *The Chinese Journal of International Politics*, 5, 2012, pp. 369–394; and Thomas Wilkins, "Australia: A Traditional Middle Power Faces the Asian Century," in Bruce Gilley and Andrew O'Neil (eds.), *Middle Powers and the Rise of China*, Georgetown University Press, Washington, DC, 2014, pp. 149–170.

62. Using textbook hedging rhetoric, Labor's Foreign Affairs spokesperson Penny Wong characterizes the BRI as a "game changer" and observes that "my point is not whether the BRI is good or bad, or whether it's beneficial or destabilising. My point

is that it is different, and that is a fundamental change in the way strategic business is done." Senator the Hon. Penny Wong, "Peace and Prosperity in a Time of Disruption: Speech to the Lee Kuan Yew School of Public Policy, Singapore, January 24, 2018," https://www.pennywong.com.au/speeches/peace-and-prosperity-in-a-time-of-disruption-lee-kuan-yew-school-of-public-policy-singapore/.

63. Akane Okatsu, "Singapore Signs Deal with China on Belt and Road," *Nikkei Asian Review*, 9 April 2018, https://asia.nikkei.com/Politics/International-Relations/Singapore-signs-deal-with-China-on-Belt-and-Road.

64. Ben Bland, "Malaysian Backlash Tests China's Belt and Road Ambitions," *The Financial Times*, 24 June 2018, https://www.ft.com/content/056ae1ec-7634-11e8-b326-75a27d27ea5f.

65. Nadege Rolland, "China's 'Belt and Road' Initiative: Underwhelming or Game Changer?" *The Washington Quarterly*, 40(1), 2017, p. 137.

66. For a sceptical take on the pliability of US grand strategy, see Patrick Porter, "Why America's Grand Strategy Has Not Changed: Power, Habit, and the US Foreign Policy Establishment," *International Security*, 42(4), 2018, pp. 9–46.

67. For an excellent analysis on this point, see Hong Yu, "Motivation Behind China's 'One Belt, One Road' Initiatives and Establishment of the Asian Infrastructure Investment Bank," *Journal of Contemporary China*, 26(105), 2017, pp. 353–368.

68. Ian Hall, "Belt and Road: The Case for 'Wait and See,'" *Lowy Interpreter*, 16 October 2017, https://www.lowyinstitute.org/the-interpreter/belt-and-road-case-wait-and-see.

69. "Secretary of the Department of Foreign Affairs and Trade, Frances Adamson, Speech to Asialink Business and Macquarie University Thought Leadership Dinner, 1 November 2017," http://dfat.gov.au/news/speeches/Pages/asialink-business-and-macquarie-university-thought-leadership-dinner.aspx.

70. Greg Sheridan, "We've Put Some Bite in Our National Security Bark," *The Australian*, 28 June 2018, https://www.theaustralian.com.au/opinion/columnists/greg-sheridan/weve-put-some-bite-in-our-national-security-bark/news-story/23e275dfce7c8013beffb4724e6e30c4.

71. Kuik Cheng-Chwee, "The Essence of Hedging: Malaysia and Singapore's Response to a Rising China," *Contemporary Southeast Asia*, 30(2), 2008, p. 163.

Conclusions

Assessing BRI's Implications for Regional Order

Michael Clarke and Matthew Sussex

The second BRI Forum, held in Beijing during April 2019, was supposed to represent an important step in the PRC's consolidation of its ambitious order-building project. At the forum, Xi Jinping heralded the participation of 126 nations in BRI projects by quoting a Chinese proverb: "A tower is built when soil on earth accumulates, and a river is formed when streams come together."[1] And yet despite much fanfare about its ability to generate "win-win" cooperation, the initial widespread enthusiasm for the initiative had by this time become somewhat more muted. The forum also took place amid concerns about "debt-trap diplomacy,"[2] heightened by US-PRC strategic and trade tensions, boycotts by leaders from India and Turkey (among others),[3] and a seeming lack of interest from Middle Eastern states. Hence by mid-2019 it seemed that the most important questions about Xi's capacity to translate China's still-growing latent power into a new center of gravity for the global trading order remained as yet unanswered.

In fairness the BRI's initial outcomes were always going to be patchy. It is also axiomatic that the midpoint of any new trading regime's development is typically its most problematic,[4] and where teething issues tend to be magnified into broader concerns. The same was true, for instance, during the consolidation of European economic cooperation under the auspices of the EEC following the Cold War, just as significant concerns about the nature of US commitments to Asia were raised in the aftermath of the Second World War.

Yet at a time of heightening strategic rivalry between major powers, a generational shift in wealth and power to Asia, and a much more globalized economy in which the PRC's leadership is being viewed with skepticism over its geopolitical intentions,[5] the litmus test for BRI will likely come over the next decade rather than in the establishment phase that is presently concluding.

What will this look like in terms of the policy positions of regional actors? Will the BRI enable China to offer a sustained footprint that rivals US power, as it simultaneously seeks to manage an ever-expanding suite of security dilemmas—encompassing both rising and hostile powers—and a host of trans-border social and economic issues? And as China's own view of its "periphery" is reshaped further outwards, will its internal economic and political stability be underpinned by BRI, or hindered by it?

In this volume we have sought to answer these questions by offering our assessments of the conceptual foundations of BRI, its domestic and external rationales, and its initial effects on regional order. And while no collection of views on the topic will ever be definitive, and acknowledging that BRI remains prey to a variety of internal and exogenous shocks, we nonetheless believe that three useful conclusions can be made. These are related to BRI's overall *scope*; its emerging regional economic and geopolitical *impacts* on existing multilateral and bilateral power relations; and the potential for BRI to *shape* the future of regional order in Asia.

Our first conclusion, on the BRI's scope, is that a Sino-centric economic order—if not a security order—is beginning to coalesce in two separate subregions: Central Asia and Southeast Asia. Of the two, China's consolidation of its position as the framework partner for cooperation in Central Asia has been clearest. As Michael Clarke and Matthew Sussex demonstrate in their chapter, Russia now has few options but to accept a default of its interests to the PRC given that an opt-out to BRI is unworkable. Likewise, Beijing has accepted that partnership with Moscow will also result in negative optics, and has quietly been transforming its investment and trade edge over the Eurasian Union into strategic advantage.[6] At the same time it has generated significant leverage over Russia itself in the aftermath of the GFC and Western sanctions over Ukraine and Crimea, and Vladimir Putin seems to have largely conceded that Russia will occupy the status of junior partner in the relationship.[7]

In Southeast Asia it is notable that although this subregion is home to some of the most significant resistance to China's geopolitical moves—especially in the maritime domain of the South China Sea—most ASEAN nations remain strongly supportive of BRI.[8] While this has yet to amount to a fundamental reshaping of the US-led security order, the Trump administration's failure to articulate a coherent Indo-Pacific strategy has compounded its decision to abrogate the United States' leading role as a hub for trade liberalization. As a result, concerns about US commitments to the regional security order have begun to prompt regional actors to seek second-tier balancing solutions, either through coalitions of like-minded middle powers or loose mechanisms like the Quadrilateral Security Dialogue.[9] But clearly neither of these can substitute for US deep engagement, and we can expect the PRC to focus heavily on this region in the future, in a bid to entice ASEAN nations closer to Beijing's orbit. A mixture of perceived coercion and consent has seen Singapore, Malaysia, Cambodia, and Vietnam taking part in the initiative, and Indonesia, the Philippines, and Thailand have also gravitated East.[10]

Within that security sphere only Australia—reflecting its inability to consider any other security arrangement than the US alliance—remains fundamentally opposed to BRI membership, and where "analysis of the BRI tells us more about what the observer thinks about China than it tells us about BRI."[11] Likewise in the South Pacific the PRC has been highly active, launching a host of infrastructure and investment projects, which both Washington and Canberra have been unable to match. And despite strident warnings about debt traps and connectivity concerns over 5G networks, US and Australian diplomacy has largely failed to sway nations such as Fiji, Vanuatu, and New Zealand (the latter of which is now performing an important role in setting transparency standards among BRI members).[12]

Elsewhere the BRI's scope has been more mixed. A number of EU states have become wary about engaging too deeply in BRI, although Italy has been an outlier in this respect. And as Lai-Ha Chan argued, the BRI has served to markedly deepen Sino-Indian strategic rivalry in South Asia. Here, the developing PRC footprint via the China-Pakistan Economic Corridor, as well as a sustained investment push into the Maldives and Sri Lanka, was offset by India's bailout and debt-for-equity swap over Mattala Rajapaksa International Airport,[13] which prompted renewed fears about entrapment dilemmas posed by participation in BRI projects. As Ian Hall points out in his own chapter, India's resistance to BRI has also been reflected in the amplification of its own series of ventures—such as SASEC and the AAGC—designed to extend New Delhi's influence into Southeast Asia and Africa respectively.

Turning to the *impacts* of BRI on existing trading and security alignments, it is clear that—as Mark Beeson correctly notes—both a positive and a negative story is possible. On the one hand, the geoeconomic benefits of both the Maritime Silk Road and continental BRI investment corridors promise to significantly improve connectivity and cement the PRC as the primary hub for economic activity in Asia. In turn, this is providing a centrifugal pull that smaller actors will arguably find very difficult to resist. This is also a key theme of Jane Golley and Michael Wesley's contribution, which stresses the multifaceted nature of the BRI: not a monolithic whole but rather an attempt to stitch together and resolve many of the contradictions of China's rise that have seen it an attractive economic partner at the same time as its expansion has promoted friction with its neighbors, and also with the United States. As Golley and Wesley argue, this should be seen in the context of China's own internal transformations, in which the decision to cast the BRI as Xi Jinping's main legacy project means that a great deal of internal political capital has been staked on its success.[14] And while this will make it harder for Beijing to sell BRI as a liberalizing trade venture (since the BRI is tied to the fortunes of the CCP), in many respects the PRC has been aided by an external environment in which the SCO, ASEAN, and other integrative economic organizations are not fundamentally dependent on a "liberal" rules-based order. Coupled to the erratic Presidency of Donald Trump, a significant space has therefore been opened for BRI to fill, in terms of establishing a regional geoeconomic center of gravity.

But on the other hand, Hall and Beeson both agree that BRI has served to deepen existing territorial disputes and potentially exposed Beijing to push back from rising powers like India, as well as coalitions of middle powers in Southeast and Northeast Asia. Andrew O'Neil takes this further, arguing that great power politics will increase the pressure on hedging states like Australia to make concrete strategic choices in respect to their security and economic ties. Indeed, given its position as a firm ally of the United States but also with China as its main trading partner, Australia represents an excellent test case for how BRI will play out in internal debates.[15] For O'Neil, two factors are important here. The first concerns the extent to which Australian policy elites will be able to bear the costs of challenging China; and the second pertains to the extent to which Canberra can continue to decouple its trade relationship with Beijing from the geostrategic impacts of its rise on regional order. Hence O'Neil highlights an important paradox for middle powers: that while they can influence agendas to an extent, they are nonetheless highly vulnerable to the pressures that can be brought to bear on their foreign and security policy choices by more powerful actors.

Stefanie Kam's exploration of China's security diplomacy in Central Asia, South Asia, and the Middle East demonstrates the manner in which BRI has served to amplify and embed preexisting concerns with the "three evils" of "separatism, terrorism and extremism" (i.e., Uyghur militancy and terrorism). In particular, she details how Beijing has increasingly externalized this primarily domestic concern through a greater focus on counterterrorism cooperation throughout these regions both in key bilateral relationships and within the confines of multilateral groupings such as the SCO. In this manner Beijing is attempting to utilize counterterrorism as a tool to not only ensure its domestic interest in stifling Uyghur militancy in Xinjiang but also as a means of enhancing its power and influence in key BRI regions.

The impact of BRI on the Middle East, as Moderchai Chaziza's chapter demonstrates, has also not been straightforward. Through a detailed case study of Chinese diplomacy toward, and investment in, Egypt and Oman under the rubric of the "Maritime Silk Road Initiative" (MSRI), Chaziza shows that while Beijing's engagement with both of these states has increased significantly it has not replaced the United States as their traditional strategic and economic partner. The dynamics of Egypt and Oman's engagement with the MSRI are suggestive of a wider dynamic in which states across Eurasia perceive BRI as but *one* potential source of investment in strategically and economically vital infrastructure. This serves as much needed reminder of the agency of individual states and that engagement in BRI does not necessarily entail alignment with Beijing's broader strategic and economic goals.

In addition to the impacts of BRI on existing trade and security orders, it is important to recognize that there is particular cause for concern for BRI participants with respect to the internal effects of investment strategies that are often one-sided and loosely regulated. In this context Brooke Wilmsen et al. have provided a unique contribution in this volume that comprehensively assesses the social and environmental risks that have arisen from Chinese investment. In Central Asia, Nigeria, and Ghana there have been repeated negative impacts from BRI investment projects. In the Ghanian case, particularly, projects like the Bui Dam were improperly implemented, failed to meet World Bank standards, and resulted in the loss of access for numerous local residents to their livelihoods. The danger of a "hands-off" approach by the PRC—effectively deferring to local laws and regulations that are often poorly defined and enforced in developing nations[16]—is an important sign that while BRI may have been created to give the PRC maximum room to maneuver, a lack of proper processes will deepen criticism of the BRI as a mechanism for exploitation rather than mutual benefit.

Finally, then, we turn to the question of how BRI might affect the future shape of regional order in Asia. Here Nick Bisley's contribution points out that in order to understand what BRI might do, we must first understand what it is intended for. And whereas there are multiple motives, from physical connectivity to promoting economic growth in China's regions, the military-strategic dimension should not be overlooked. Put simply, BRI represents a way to overcome China's dependence on continental trade links that are vulnerable to regional political turmoil, and maritime conduits that are vulnerable to predation or quarantine.[17] Hence the main negative implications for the region from a failed BRI—including indebtedness, the construction of "bridges to nowhere," and the risk that investment drives growth down rather than pump-priming—are also China's risks. In his assessment, Bisley argues against the most optimistic scenario (a maximally successful BRI), in favor of a hybrid result, between an unevenly implemented BRI and a minimally successful one.

The implications for regional order are thus that at the very least BRI will continue to disrupt the alignments of economic and strategic interests in Asia, and that even if it is able to weaken the old order, it will therefore be judged by China to have been successful. For regional actors, the BRI both enhances choice while simultaneously presenting a concern: how much control would Beijing seek over an order centered upon itself?[18] Importantly, Bisley highlights the central paradox of the BRI—which is a point on which all the authors of chapters in this volume are in rare agreement—in that it forges ties that bind, while at the same time being itself a subject of contestation. This in itself is perhaps not surprising, because such dualism can be found in reactions to the rise of other major powers throughout history, reflecting both enthusiasms about opportunities, alongside concerns about risks.[19] But BRI—as both a geoeconomic and geopolitical strategy, and in economic, normative, and military-security terms—represents perhaps the greatest litmus test the US-centric order has yet faced.[20]

While we can assess the domestic and local impacts of BRI with some degree of agreement, and even some confidence based on various scenarios of success and failure, the great unknown remains the ability of the United States itself to react and adapt to China's challenge. In many respects this should be more surprising and worrisome to analysts of regional security dynamics, since an open regionalist trade agenda coupled to institutional rules and norms, underpinned by military primacy and alliances, can no longer be assumed to be the unchanging foundations of American national security policy in Asia. Even in spite of the disruptive effects of the Trump administration on regional confidence and assurance—which has been perhaps even more impactful over a shorter period time than the BRI—internal debates in the United States about the desirability of primacy and deep Asian engagement will continue after the Trump presidency concludes. If this coincides also with its continued relative decline, then in the next decade we may find ourselves writing a very different book: not on the implications of the BRI for regional order but on the nature of regional order under its umbrella.

NOTES

1. Xi Jinping, "Working Together to Deliver a Brighter Future for Belt and Road Cooperation," Keynote Speech at the Opening Ceremony of the Second Belt and Road Summit for International Cooperation, Beijing, July 26, 2019. https://www.fmprc.gov.cn/mfa_eng/zxxx_662805/t1658424.shtml. Accessed June 3, 2019.

2. Patrick Mendis and Joey Wang, "China's Debt-Trap Diplomacy may pave the way for something sinister," *National Interest*, February 3, 2019. https://nationalinterest.org/feature/chinas-era-debt-trap-diplomacy-may-pave-way-something-sinister-42927. Accessed June 3, 2019.

3. "Belt and Road Forum: China's 'project of the century' hits tough times," *Guardian*, April 25, 2019. https://www.theguardian.com/world/2019/apr/25/belt-and-road-forum-chinas-project-of-the-century-hits-tough-times. Accessed June 3, 2019.

4. John Gerard Ruggie, "International regimes, transactions and change: embedded liberalism in the postwar economic order," *International Organisation* 32 (2), 1982, pp. 379-415.

5. See for instance Richard Ghiasy, "China's Belt and Road Initiative: security implications and the way forward for the European Union," *SIPRI Policy Brief* (SIPRI: Stockholm), November 2018; Richard Heydarian, "Chinese Chimera: the real concern with the BRI," *Lowy Institute Interpreter*, June 24, 2018; and James Bowen, "Strategic implications of China's Belt and Road Initiative too big to ignore," *ASPI Strategist*, August 31, 2018.

6. On this point see Andrea Kendall-Taylor and David Shullman, "A Russian-Chinese partnership is a threat to US interests," *Foreign Affairs*, May 14, 2019. https://www.foreignaffairs.com/articles/china/2019-05-14/russian-chinese-partnership-threat-us-interests. Accessed June 3, 2019.

7. For a much rosier (and arguably more naïve) view of the relationship, see Nadege Rolland, "A China-Russia condominium over Eurasia," *Survival*, January 29, 2019. Available at https://www.tandfonline.com/doi/full/10.1080/00396338.2019.1568043?af=R. Accessed June 2, 2019.

8. Shannon Tiezzi, "Who Is (and Who Isn't) Attending China's 2nd Belt and Road Forum?," *The Diplomat*, April 27, 2019. https://thediplomat.com/2019/04/who-is-and-who-isnt-attending-chinas-2nd-belt-and-road-forum/. Accessed June 3, 2019.

9. Andrew Tillett, "India dashes hopes for military role for Quadrilateral Security Dialogue," *Australian Financial Review*, March 11, 2019. https://www.afr.com/news/politics/india-dashes-hopes-for-military-role-for-quadrilateral-security-dialogue-20190311-h1c8ak. Accessed June 2, 2019.

10. *China's Belt and Road Initiative (BRI) and Southeast Asia*, IDEAS (London: London School of Economics), October 2018. http://www.lse.ac.uk/ideas/Assets/Documents/reports/LSE-IDEAS-China-SEA-BRI.pdf. Accessed June 1, 2019.

11. For an insightful analysis on this topic see Nick Bisley, "Seeing what you want in Belt and Road," *Lowy Institute Interpreter*, April 18, 2019. https://www.lowyinstitute.org/the-interpreter/seeing-what-you-want-belt-and-road. Accessed May 18, 2019.

12. Fergus Hanson, "Are we being played in the Pacific?" *ASPI Strategist*, September 10, 2018. https://www.aspistrategist.org.au/are-we-being-played-in-the-pacific/. Accessed June 3, 2019.

13. Bharath Gopalaswamy, "Sri Lanka's political shake-up is a win for China," *Foreign Policy*, October 29, 2018. https://foreignpolicy.com/2018/10/29/sri-lankas-political-shake-up-is-a-win-for-china/. Accessed May 27, 2019.

14. Huong Le Thu, "Xi Jinping's legacy is not bridges and pipelines; it's his Thought," *Georgetown Journal of International Affairs*, June 28, 2018. https://www.georgetownjournalofinternationalaffairs.org/online-edition/2018/6/28/xi-jinpings-legacy-is-not-bridges-and-pipelines-its-his-thought. Accessed June 1, 2019.

15. Matthew Sussex and Michael Clarke, "One belt, one road, multiple rules-based orders," *NSC Policy Options Papers*, November 2019. https://nsc.crawford.anu.edu.au/sites/default/files/publication/nsc_crawford_anu_edu_au/2017-11/pop7_one_belt_many_orders.pdf. Accessed March 2, 2019.

16. See also Angela Tritto and Alvin Camba, "The Belt and Road: the good, the bad and the mixed," *Diplomat*, April 15, 2019. https://thediplomat.com/2019/04/the-belt-and-road-the-good-the-bad-and-the-mixed/. Accessed June 1, 2019.

17. Also on this point, see for instance Frank Umbach, "China's Belt and Road Initiative and its energy-security dimensions," *RSIS Working Papers* 320, January 3, 2019; and Peter Cai, "Understanding China's Belt and Road Initiative" (Sydney: Lowy Institute for International Policy), 2017.

18. See Jonathan E. Hillman, "China's Belt and Road Initiative: five years later," testimony to the US-China Economic and Security Review Commission, *Centre for Strategic and International Studies (CSIS)*, January 25, 2018. https://www.csis.org/analysis/chinas-belt-and-road-initiative-five-years-later-0. Accessed June 1, 2019.

19. See for instance the landmark text by Paul Kennedy, *The Rise and Fall of Great Powers* (New York: Random House, 1987).

20. Robert Kaplan, "'Belt and Road' review: a Chinese world order," *Wall Street Journal*, June 2, 2019. https://www.wsj.com/articles/belt-and-road-review-a-chinese-world-order-11559507481. Accessed June 4, 2019.

Index

About the Editors and Contributors

Michael Clarke is associate professor at the National Security College, ANU, and director of the ANU-Indiana University Pan-Asia Institute. He is an internationally recognized expert on the history and politics of the Xinjiang Uyghur Autonomous Region, People's Republic of China, Chinese foreign policy in Central Asia, Central Asian geopolitics, and nuclear proliferation and nonproliferation. He is the author of *Xinjiang and China's Rise in Central Asia – A History* (2011), (with Andrew O'Neil and Stephan Fruhling), *Australian Nuclear Policy: Reconciling Strategic, Economic and Normative Interests* (2015), editor of *China's Frontier Regions: Ethnicity, Economic Integration and Foreign Relations* (2016), editor (with Anna Hayes) of *Inside Xinjiang: Analysing Space, Place and Power in China's Muslim North-West*, (2016), and editor of *Terrorism and Counterterrorism in China: Domestic and Foreign Policy Dimensions* (2018). His commentary on these areas of expertise has also been published by *Foreign Policy*, *The Wall Street Journal*, *CNN*, *South China Morning Post*, *BBC News*, *The Diplomat*, *The National Interest*, and *War on the Rocks* among others.

Matthew Sussex is associate professor and academic director at the National Security College, ANU; and a non-resident fellow at the Lowy Institute for International Policy. His research specializations are centered around security studies with a particular focus on Russia and Eurasia, and incorporate Australian foreign and security policy and great power competition in Asia and Europe. His recently completed solo and collaborative book projects include *Conflict in the Former USSR* (2012); *Violence and the State* (2015); *Power, Politics and Confrontation in Eurasia* (2015); and *Russia, Eurasia and the New Geopolitics of Energy* (2015). He is the lead editor (2017) of a special issue of the *Australian Journal of International Affairs* on the topic of national security.

Nick Bisley is professor of International Relations at La Trobe University. His research and teaching expertise is in Asia's international relations, great power politics, and Australian foreign and defense policy. Nick is currently the editor-in-chief of the *Australian Journal of International Affairs.* He has been a senior research associate of the International Institute of Strategic Studies and a visiting fellow at the East West-Center in Washington DC. He is the author of many works on international relations, including *Issues in 21st Century World Politics*, 3rd Edition (2017), *Great Powers in the Changing International Order* (2012), and *Building Asia's Security* (2009).

Mark Beeson is professor of International Politics at the University of Western Australia. Before joining UWA, he has held appointments at Murdoch University, Griffith University, University of Queensland, York University, and University of Birmingham, where he was also head of department. He is the founding editor of *Critical Studies of the Asia Pacific.* He is the author of *China's Regional Relations: Evolving Foreign Policy Dynamics* (2014); and *Regionalism and Globalization in East Asia* (2007 and 2014).

Lai-Ha Chan is a senior lecturer at the China Research Centre, University of Technology Sydney. Lai-Ha was educated in Macau, Hong Kong, New Zealand, and Australia. Before going to Australia for a PhD research program, she worked for the Hong Kong SAR Government. Her research focuses on China's engagement with global governance, including global health, peacekeeping, environmental protection, and development. From September 2016 to June 2017 she was a Fung Global fellow at the Princeton Institute for International and Regional Studies. She has had articles published on these issues in a range of academic peer review journals including *Contemporary Politics, Global Governance, Third World Quarterly*, and *Australian Journal of International Affairs* and is the author of *China Engages Global Health Governance: Responsible Stakeholder or System Transformer?* (2011) and (with Gerald Chan and Pak K. Lee) *China Engages Global Governance: A New World Order in the Making?* (2012).

Mordechai Chaziza is currently a lecturer in the Department of Politics and Governance, Ashkelon Academic College, Israel. He holds a PhD from Bar-Ilan University, Israel. His doctoral dissertation focused on China's post-Cold War foreign policy in the Middle East, Iraq, Iran, and the Arab-Israeli Peace Process. His academic publications on these issues have appeared in *Middle*

East Policy, *Middle East Review of International Affairs*, *China Report*, *Contemporary Review of the Middle East*, *Israel Journal of Foreign Affairs*, *Asian Journal of Political Science*, and *Chinese Journal of International Politics*.

Jane Golley is an economist focused on a range of Chinese transition and development issues. She is an associate professor and the director of the Australian Centre on China in the World, ANU, and head of the China Numbers research stream. Her career has taken her from the Asia Section of the Australian Commonwealth Treasury to the World Bank in Washington DC, and the UNU's World Institute for Development Economics Research in Helsinki. Jane spent eight years studying and teaching at the University of Oxford, where her thesis was on "The Dynamics of Chinese Regional Development." Returning to ANU, she worked in the School of Economics and then the Crawford School of Economics and Government, where she developed a graduate course on "China in the World." Jane was the president of the Chinese Economic Society Australia in 2010–2012, and continues to be an active member of that society. Her work has been published in *The China Journal*, *China Economic Review*, and *Asian Economic Papers*. She is also editor (with Ligang Song) of *Rising China: Global Challenges and Opportunities* (2011).

Ian Hall is professor in the School of Government and International Relations, Griffith University, Brisbane, Australia. He is currently working on an Australian Research Council–funded Discovery project (2015–2017) on the evolution of Indian thinking about world politics since 1964. Prior to his current appointment, Hall has held positions at the University of St. Andrews, the University of Adelaide, and the Australian National University. He is the author of *The Engagement of India: Strategies and Responses* (2014).

Stefanie Kam Li Yee is a doctoral student at the National Security College, ANU. Prior to commencing her doctoral research Stefanie was a Research Associate with the International Centre for Political Violence and Terrorism Research at the S. Rajaratnam School of International Studies (RSIS), Nanyang Technological University. Her primary research focus lies in the history of terrorism in the Asia-Pacific region, particularly in Southeast Asia. Li Yee graduated from Reed College, Portland Oregon, with a BA in English Literature (2009). She graduated from The University of Chicago (2010) with an MA in English Literature, and has an MSc in International Relations from RSIS (2014). She is coeditor (with Rohan Gunaratna) of the *Handbook of Terrorism in the Asia-Pacific* (2016).

Andrew O'Neil is dean (Research) and professor of Political Science in the Griffith Business School. Prior to this he was head of the School of Government and International Relations (2014–2016) and director of the Griffith Asia Institute (2010–2014). Before coming to Griffith in 2010, Andrew was associate head (Research) in the Faculty of Social Sciences at Flinders University, and prior to entering academia he worked as a Commonwealth public servant with Australia's Department of Defence. Andrew's research expertise focuses on the intersection of strategic, political, and economic change in the Asia-Pacific with particular emphasis on the security dimension of international relations, and he is a frequent media commentator on these topics. Andrew is the recipient of Australian Research Council (Discovery and Linkage Project) funding, and he has also received competitive industry funding from the Department of Foreign Affairs and Trade, the Japan Foundation, and the Department of Defence. He is a former member of the Australian Foreign Minister's National Consultative Committee on National Security Issues and former advisory board member of the Lowy Institute's G20 Studies Centre. Andrew is the former editor-in-chief of the *Australian Journal of International Affairs* and is currently an editorial board member of the *Korean Journal of International Studies*, the *North Korean Review*, the *Journal of Intelligence History*, and *Security Challenges*. He is the author of *Asia, the United States, and Extended Deterrence: Atomic Umbrellas in the 21st Century* (2013) and editor (with Bruce Gilley) of *Middle Powers and the Rise of China* (2014).

Brooke Wilmsen is senior lecturer and convenor of the Sustainability and Development Major in the Department of Social Inquiry at La Trobe University. Wilmsen has a background in Development Studies with a PhD in Geography. She has worked as a resettlement consultant for several international institutions, government affiliates, and private consultancies. She has several years of qualitative and quantitative research experience working on issues of development-forced displacement and resettlement with a focus on the Three Gorges Dam in the People's Republic of China. Brooke has also conducted research on refugee resettlement in Australia. Her scholarship on these issues has been published in *Asian Studies Review*, *Urban Geography*, *Journal of Contemporary China*, *International Journal of Environmental Studies*, and *World Development*.

Michael Wesley is professor of International Affairs and dean of the College of Asia and the Pacific at the Australian National University. He has published on Australian foreign policy, Asia's international relations and strategic affairs, and the politics of state-building interventions. His book *There Goes the Neighbourhood: Australia and the Rise of Asia* (2011) was awarded the John Button Prize for the best writing on Australian politics and public policy. Previously, Wesley was the director of the Coral Bell School of Asia Pacific Affairs at ANU from 2014 to 2016, the executive director of the Lowy Institute for International Policy from 2009 to 2012, director of the Griffith Asia Institute at Griffith University from 2004 to 2009, and assistant director-general for Transnational Issues at the Office of National Assessments (Australia's peak intelligence agency, from 2003 to 2004. He gained his PhD from the University of St. Andrews and his BA (Honors) from the University of Queensland.

Xiao Han is a Research Fellow at the Centre for Contemporary Chinese Studies, University of Melbourne. Her research interests include the transformation of rural China, the Chinese 'go-out' strategy, the techno-politics of (water) infrastructure and the political economy of development. She is working on agrarian change in China as part of the Centre's ARC Discovery Project (DP180100519), which aims to examine (re)configurations of, and the relations between land, labour, and capital, in China's agricultural sector, as well as the environmental practices of different kinds of farms. Xiao completed her PhD in economic geography at the University of Melbourne. Informed by fieldwork in China and Ghana, and data collected from open sources, her doctoral thesis nvestigated the goals, practices and consequences of Chinese governments and corporations when building dams overseas. Xiao's co-authored works has been published in the *Annals of the American Association of Geographers, Journal of Cleaner Production, and Land Use Policy.*

Andrew van Hulten received his PhD in economic geography from the University of Melbourne. His research interests include international capital mobility, gentrification, financial discrimination and involuntary resettlement. He is currently working as a private consultant.

David Adjartey studied for his PhD in anthropology from Latrobe University, Melbourne, in Australia. He also obtained both his Bachelor of Arts and Master of Philosophy degrees in archaeology in 2007 and 2011 respectively from the University of Ghana. He was part of the team that undertook the Bui Dam salvage archaeological work and has since been studying how the Bui Dam forced resettlement has influenced socio-cultural change in the resettlement township through participatory ethnographic filmmaking methods. David also worked as a teaching assistant and visual resource person with the Department of Archaeology and Heritage Studies, University of Ghana, between 2008 and 2015.

www.ingramcontent.com/pod-product-compliance
Lightning Source LLC
Chambersburg PA
CBHW022307280326
41932CB00010B/1013
* 9 7 8 1 4 9 8 5 8 2 7 7 3 *